FOR THE PEOPLE'S CAUSE

From the Writings of
John Murdoch
Highland and Irish Land Reformer

Edited and Introduced
by
James Hunter

Published for the Crofters Commission to commemorate
the Centenary of the Crofters Act of 1886

Edinburgh
Her Majesty's Stationery Office

Photo acknowledgements

p. 4   *John Murdoch* by courtesy of Dr R A F Murdoch

p. 8   *Crofter family, Poolewe 1890* by courtesy of Edinburgh City Libraries

p. 42   *Islay. Ruins of Finlaggan* by courtesy of the National Museums of Scotland

p. 60   *Police and Hussars charging the proclaimed meeting at Ennis: Scene in the courtyard* by courtesy of the Trustees of the National Library of Scotland

p. 78   *Islay. Head of Garvinard Bay* by courtesy of the National Museums of Scotland

p. 94   *A real 'Scottish grievance'* by courtesy of the Trustees of the National Library of Scotland

p. 106   *Islay. The head of Loch Indaal* by courtesy of the National Museums of Scotland

p. 118   *Foula, Shetland c.1902* by courtesy of the National Museums of Scotland

p. 138   *Women watching a crofters' meeting* by courtesy of the Trustees of the National Library of Scotland

p. 166   *After the annual market, cattle are loaded on boats at Castlebay, Barra* by courtesy of Dr. Margaret Fay Shaw, Isle of Carra

p. 186   *Athletic sports in Tiree. 'The tug of war' between the natives, sailors, and marines* by courtesy of the Trustees of the National Library of Scotland

Cover illustrations by courtesy of the Scottish Tourist Board

HMSO publications are available from:

HMSO Bookshops
13a Castle Street, Edinburgh, EH2 3AR   (031) 225 6333
49 High Holborn, London, WC1V 6HB   (01) 211 5656 (Counter service only)
258 Broad Street, Birmingham, B1 2HE   (021) 643 3757
Southey House, 33 Wine Street, Bristol, BS1 2BQ   (0272) 24306/24307
9–21 Princess Street, Manchester, M60 8AS   (061) 834 7201
80 Chichester Street, Belfast, BT1 4JY   (0232) 234488

HMSO Publications Centre
(Mail and telephone orders only)
PO Box 276, London, SW8 5DT
Telephone orders (01) 622 3316
General enquiries (01) 211 5656

HMSO's Accredited Agents
(see Yellow Pages)

And through good booksellers

Contents

Preface

I have tried hard, during the past seven years at the Crofters Commission, to concentrate on crofting present and crofting future. This in the crofting context has proved difficult at all times, and in the particular context of 1986 downright impossible. The past refuses to be denied, and it is therefore fitting that its claim be recognised emphatically once more, this on the occasion of the centenary of the passing of the Crofters Holdings (Scotland) Act 1886.

In pondering the period of the Battle of the Braes and of 'gunboat diplomacy' throughout the Hebridean seaboard, I have obviously read many works. Not least amongst these was Dr James Hunter's authoritative volume 'The Making of the Crofting Community.' I lingered over one fleeting reference to an unpublished autobiographical sketch by John Murdoch said to be on permanent loan to Glasgow's Mitchell Library. The significance of this unpublished work did not occur to me until, some time later, I read a biographical study of Michael Davitt. Here again appeared the fleeting shadow of John Murdoch. Suddenly all became obvious, John Murdoch was the catalyst who had introduced the philosophy of the Irish Land League from his place of employment in the South of Ireland to his ancestral quarter in Inverness. In forsaking the civil service and setting up The Highlander Newspaper, John Murdoch became the forerunner of crofting reform. His was a major contribution to bringing security of tenure to the oppressed population. It seemed that here was an individual with a major claim to being the person who had, *primus inter pares,* 'set the heather on fire'.

The decision was taken that the Mitchell sketch should be brought to light and that the kilted figure of John Murdoch should walk at our side throughout this centenary year.

I am aware that much of which follows was controversial in its day and generation. I do not, however, feel that the activities of Gladstone's third ministry and the legislation which it enacted can be other than a cause for rejoicing today. Had John Murdoch not agitated, and had Gladstone not legislated, it is exceedingly doubtful if there would have been a crofting population in 1986. A population which is the custodian of not one but two cultures. The Celtic and the Viking strands which still happily colour the fabric of Scottish contemporary life.

I appreciate that Her Majesty's Stationery Office does not normally spawn publications with nationalist, with radical, and even with revolutionary overtones. It is, however, important to grasp that Murdoch advocated peaceful revolution. He did not merely advocate it. He helped bring it about. In asking that this particular book should mark the centenary of the crofters' charter, I take personal responsibility for whatever message John Murdoch transmits across the generations, and I want it clearly understood that HMSO is the agent of the Crofters Commission, and more particularly of its chairman, in reinstating John Murdoch to the public eye. In my so doing, I hope that readers of this work will understand the standpoint of an unrepentant twentieth century Highlander! John Murdoch's adversaries are always referred to teasingly as Saxons (ie Sassenach) that is South Britons, or perhaps in the Dublin ambience West Britons, a breed who are always open to a gentle process of re-education where minority indigenous cultures are seen to survive!

I am conscious that much of what is written above is written in the first person. This is not how things really should be. Many people have contributed to this work and it is right that they should be accorded recognition.

First, of course, is Dr James Hunter who has written the following introduction and edited the whole sketch. He tells me that he has written 20 per cent of the work and that John Murdoch himself wrote the remainder. It is, however, important to remember that much of what Murdoch wrote was the reiterative recollection of a very old man. It has therefore cost Dr Hunter several months of diligent research, and not simply in the Mitchell Library, to restore, and then to pare down scientifically, the whole Murdoch for a twentieth century readership. Nor do I believe that many people could have performed the task so successfully. I trust that, when you, like me, have read the following pages, you will agree that we have here a whole man in John Murdoch, rescued from oblivion by the sheer quality of Dr Hunter's researches and labour.

Many other people have played lesser parts in restoring Murdoch to us. I have noted many names and I apologise if I have omitted several more.

I would, however, record the following:—

Dr R A F Murdoch, who has generously foregone any claim to family copyright;

Mr Gillespie and his colleagues at the Mitchell Library;

Dr Ann Matheson of the National Library of Scotland;

Mr John S Gibson formerly of the Department of Agriculture who confirmed to his Department that the work merited publication;

The Department of Agriculture who accepted my request to publish and even, save their blushes, were persuaded to assist a little financially;

Mr Donald MacCormick, antiquarian book dealer, Edinburgh, but for whose vigilance a whole chapter on the Islay clearances would have been lost;

Mrs Gwen Macleod, Edinburgh, for genealogical researches;

Mr Hugh Barron of the Gaelic Society of Inverness (a Society still happily thriving in 1986);

Mrs Catriona Bell and Katy Ferguson, two kind ladies in Islay, the latter at Port Charlotte Museum;

Mr Gilbert Clark, Port Charlotte, Islay;

Messrs Gill and MacMillan, Publishers, Dublin, for kindly releasing Dr Hunter from certain obligations to them;

Dr John MacInnes and Dr Owen Dudley Edwards both of Edinburgh University;

All the members of staff of the Crofters Commission who assisted beyond the call of duty;

and HMSO Edinburgh for great patience in adversity!

And so, for those of you who have borne with me thus far, can I now simply commend to you what will I trust on winter nights in 1986, and indeed for many winters to come, prove a most absorbing and rewarding read.

J F M Macleod

14 November 1985

Introduction

One morning, in the early months of 1882, there walked into the small school at Braes in Skye a big, broad-shouldered and bearded man in Highland dress. 'I remember him vividly,' one of the boys in the single classroom was to write long afterwards, 'because he was the first man I ever saw wearing a kilt.' Asked by their teacher if he would say a word to the pupils, almost all of them the children of local crofters, the stranger asked 'Gaelic or English?' Of the two languages, Gaelic would have been the more readily understood. But the schoolmaster, no doubt aware that he was risking official retribution by permitting his visitor to say anything, was taking no further risks. 'English,' he replied, 'for it is not allowed to speak a word of Gaelic in school hours.' Then the man in the kilt—for it was thus his audience would remember him—addressed the Braes children. On them, as on so many of those to whom he spoke, he made an indelible impression. 'He radiated goodwill,' in the opinion of the lad who was to set down his recollections of the occasion. 'I only saw John Murdoch once, but I never forgot him.'[1]

That John Murdoch had come to Braes at that time was no accident. Nor was it simply fortuitous that, within a week or two of his visit, the name of that straggling crofting settlement was appearing daily in practically every newspaper in the land. When, in April 1882, the Braes people fought a pitched battle with the fifty or so policemen sent to arrest their leaders, they propelled the crofting community's grievances and aspirations into the forefront of British politics. And though Murdoch, a lifelong pacifist, had not sought such a violent means to that end, it nevertheless represented the attainment of an objective towards which he had worked with self-denying single-mindedness since the launch of his weekly newspaper, *The Highlander*, some nine years before.

The Braes crofters, when Murdoch met them shortly before their bloody encounter with the police contingent despatched to crush their rebellion, had dared to demand the restoration of hill pastures of which their townships had been deprived in the course of the mass evictions known as the Highland Clearances. Until they were again given the use of these pastures, the Braes men had informed their landlord, Lord Macdonald, they would pay no rent. To this unprecedented challenge to one of Scotland's more eminent landed proprietors, Lord Macdonald's estate managers responded by resorting to the harsh and intimidating tactics which they had traditionally employed in their dealings with crofting tenants. They decided to evict several Braes crofters. And it was as a result of their decision that there was initiated the series of increasingly ill-tempered incidents which culminated in outright conflict between the Braes people, on the one side, and the forces of law and order, on the other.

That particular skirmish was won by the police. But what had begun at Braes was not destined to end there. Soon other crofting districts entered the fray. Rent strikes became widespread. The large sheep farms created by the men who had organised the clearances were re-occupied forcibly by crofters. Lawlessness became endemic. Whole localities passed out of the jurisdiction of the courts and the police. Public administration came close to collapse. In a vain attempt to restore some semblance of normality, troops and gunboats were sent to Skye, Tiree and Lewis. And eventually the crofting struggle erupted into the House of Commons following the electoral victories of the

Highland Land Law Reform Association—afterwards renamed the Highland Land League. Unable to do otherwise, the government then gave way. In 1886 there was passed the Crofters Act. Crofters were granted security of tenure and a judicial tribunal, the Crofters Commission, was established to determine the rents they should pay. Thus ended a long, sad era of eviction and oppression, persecution and exploitation. The continuance of crofting was assured.[2]

Because of the Crofters Act there are still crofters living in Braes and hundreds of other similar settlements in northern Scotland. Few of them are full-time agriculturalists. Their holdings consist, for the most part, of little more than five or ten hectares of generally indifferent arable land—together with a share in a common pasture of the type at the centre of the troubles in Braes in 1882. But these holdings provide their occupants with houses and with basic incomes which can be supplemented from a wide variety of other sources. And it is this which distinguishes a crofting area from the many other parts of the Highlands and Islands which have been given over to sheep, deer, grouse and intensive forestry. These alternative land uses have had a depopulating effect. Where they are dominant, people are few. In localities where successive generations of crofters have enjoyed the protection of the Crofters Act, in contrast, there is to be found a comparatively dense population. And if the retention of such a population in a rural setting is to be accounted a virtue, then the Crofters Act has to be considered a success.

That is today's general judgment. It is not one which would have been shared by most of those involved in the tumultous events of the 1880s. Last century's landowners disliked the Crofters Act because it curtailed their rights and privileges. Their radical critics, foremost of whom was John Murdoch, condemned the same measure as inadequate. The Crofters Act did not go far enough, in Murdoch's opinion, because it left landlordism intact and because it did little or nothing to restore to the crofters of the 1880s the extensive tracts of land from which their fathers and grandfathers had been removed to make way for sheep. Subsequent legislation, it should be stressed, was to do a good deal to remedy this deficiency—especially in Skye, Tiree and the Western Isles where most of the big farms established at the time of the clearances were eventually bought by the state and resettled by crofters. It has to be acknowledged, however, that many of the Highland land reforms advocated by John Murdoch have still to be brought about—and are unlikely to be achieved without the abolition of the large private estates which still exercise a major influence on land use matters in almost all of northern Scotland. John Murdoch, then, would most certainly not have wished to be associated with the notion that the Crofters Act was in any way a final settlement of the Highland land question. And while the attribution to him of posthumous opinions is necessarily risky, his immediate reaction to the Highlands and Islands of the 1980s, I am convinced, would be one of surprise—not at what has been achieved but at what remains to be accomplished.

And yet I am equally convinced that the centenary of the Crofters Act constitutes an appropriate occasion to commemorate this remarkable Highlander. The Crofters Act was passed in response to a protest movement initiated largely by John Murdoch. And whatever its inadequacies, the Act has served, as already indicated, to maintain much that would otherwise have been lost. Whole communities survive because of the Crofters Act. And because these communities contain the last strongholds of Scots Gaelic, the Act has also had important cultural consequences. That would not have surprised John Murdoch who always believed that land reform, Gaelic revivalism and social advancement were inextricably linked. Only when Highlanders took a proper pride in their language, their history and their background, Murdoch insisted, would they acquire the self-respect and self-confidence without which they would neither win control of the land nor develop the initiative and enterprise which he thought to be the keys to progress of every kind. Today our Highland heritage is still neglected by ourselves. And not the least important aspect of that heritage, as seen from the standpoint of the centenary of the Crofters Act, is the achievement of John Murdoch. To him, more than any other individual, the modern crofting community owes its existence. And what he said and did and wrote remain worthy of our respect.

Not everyone who encountered John Murdoch during his many visits to Skye in the 1880s was as enthralled by his performance as the schoolboy he met in Braes. One sympathiser with the island's landlords remarked, with understandable rancour, that this 'Gaelic-speaking, kilted Highlander', who was generally thought to be provoking much of the unrest among crofters, would have done well to have 'attended more to his own affairs and less to other people's'. This opinion would certainly have been endorsed warmly by the long list of individuals and organisations whom Murdoch had harrassed so persistently and effectively over the years. And even his supporters would have conceded that his relentless advocacy of justice had done nothing to advance his own interests.[3]

Murdoch's career as an excise officer was blighted by the influential enemies he made while campaigning for improved pay and conditions for civil servants. His unwavering commitment to the cause of Highland land reform offended men of power and came close to making him penniless. His publicly proclaimed friendship with leading Irish nationalists and his longstanding identification with their demand for self-government for Ireland resulted in his being viewed with suspicion by the many people who regarded such attitudes as little better than treasonable. Here was a man, it is clear, whose behaviour was seldom determined by a concern for his own welfare.

What, then, were Murdoch's motivations? He himself believed them to be primarily religious. 'I had no right to hoard up money,' he wrote of the convictions which guided his life, 'no right to think of myself as anything better than an instrument in the hand of God to do whatever good came my way?' That may sound more than a little self-satisfied. But Murdoch's spiritual beliefs were not of the kind that induce only complacency. They impelled him to action on behalf of the oppressed. And in his profound, if idiosyncratic, Christian faith there is to be found the source of his certainty that, no matter the strength of the opposition, right lay on the side he had chosen to champion—the side of the ordinary Highland and Irish people whose plight so infuriated him, whose Gaelic culture he thought so precious and whose prospects he did so much to improve. In John Murdoch, then, there was more than a hint of the idealist. But idealism can be deployed constructively. And so it was in Murdoch's case. He was, according to the inscription on the Celtic cross which his friends placed on his grave, "a man of noble ideas, pure and unselfish public spirit, who devoted his life to the uplifting of his downtrodden countrymen'. This book is intended to sustain that assessment.

John Murdoch's writings, one of his acquaintances remarked, were 'voluminous but sporadic'. They amount, in fact, to many millions of words written over a 50-year period and dealing with an almost endless array of subjects. They include a number of pamphlets which survive only in specialised collections. They include innumerable articles contributed to magazines and newspapers in widely-separated parts of Scotland, Ireland and England. They include, too, a number of manuscripts which, for a variety of reasons, remained unpublished during Murdoch's lifetime and which, in at least one instance, have been preserved only by the merest chance.[4]

This book contains only a small selection of that huge output. One chapter is an abbreviated version of a single pamphlet. A second is based on just one series of articles in an Irish nationalist periodical. A third features snippets from the editorial columns of Murdoch's own newspaper, *The Highlander*. But the core of what follows is Murdoch's account of his life. This unfinished autobiography, on which Murdoch worked intermittently in his old age, fills five bulky notebooks. Their hundreds of closely-written pages, penned between 1889 and 1898, were neither revised nor corrected before Murdoch's death. Their contents, therefore, are both discursive and repetitive. And for present purposes these contents have had to be compressed and, on one or two occasions, re-arranged. Murdoch, a first-rate newspaperman, would not, I think have objected too strongly to such sub-editing. And in carrying it out, I have tried to be mindful of this comment made by one of John Murdoch's closest friends at the time of his death in 1903: 'He has left, we believe, a series of reminiscences of his varied and interesting story; and it is to be earnestly desired that these should be placed in kindly and competent hands to present, as far as is now possible, an adequate record of his lifelong, self-denying and public-spirited career.'[5]

John Murdoch was born in the farmhouse of Lynemore in the Nairnshire parish of Ardclach on January 15, 1818. He was the second child and eldest son in the family of nine children born to John Murdoch and Mary Mac-Pherson, three years married at the time of John's birth. John Murdoch senior combined the management of a series of small farms or crofts with employment on a number of Highland estates. His wife, whose own father was considered a "gentleman" and whose mother was the daughter of a family of some substance in the eastern part of Inverness-shire, was of more socially elevated stock than her husband. The boy did not inherit his mother's aspirations to gentility. But he was to comment upon them. And in her son's recollection, at any rate, Mary Murdoch, was decidedly ill at ease in the comparatively lowly position in which she found herself.[6]

Ardclach, where the eastern Highland moors merge with the more fertile and well-wooded lowlands bordering the Moray Firth, was then a Gaelic-speaking locality—as was the Atholl district of Perthshire to which the Murdochs moved in 1821. And both places, John wrote later, 'were very favourable to the growth of Highland sentiment'. But it was the island of Islay, where the family settled in 1827, that John was always to regard as home. 'I feel myself as if I were an Islay man', he told the royal commission set up to inquire into crofting grievances in the wake of the 1882 troubles in Skye. And it was his years in Islay, between the ages of nine and 20, which did much to determine the nature of his later interests and enthusiasms.[7]

The young John Murdoch's formal education, begun in Perthshire and concluded in Islay, was little more than elementary—although, thanks to his parents' determination that their children should receive as much schooling as possible, it was probably less limited than that available to most boys in his position. More important than his classroom experiences, however, was the fact that, even as a teenager, John Murdoch was an avid reader. And more important still was his exposure to, and early interest in, the traditional Gaelic culture which then flourished among Islay's older residents. Among the many people who frequented the Murdoch home in the 1830s were men and women who were steeped in the music, songs, sagas and tales which John Murdoch was to celebrate in his later writings and which, to him at least, demonstrated the enduring worth of Gaelic civilisation.

At that time, too, Murdoch met two individuals whom he was always to admire and whose friendship he was to cherish. One, from a farming background similar to his own, was Archibald Sinclair, later a publisher in Glasgow and, like Murdoch, a Gaelic revivalist, temperance campaigner and land reformer. The other was John Francis Campbell whose father, Walter Frederick, then owned all of Islay.

The elder John Murdoch was one of Walter Frederick Campbell's game-keepers—as well as one of his tenants. And in the normal course of events there would have been no question of there being any but the most restricted contact between the sons of laird and employee, landlord and crofter—a feature of Highland society which Murdoch was always to deplore. 'The landlord,' he wrote in 1853, 'if born at all among his people, is carefully removed from the reach of their Celtic influences and educated so as to have a language and a mode of thinking quite foreign to the sphere in which he is destined to act the most important parts in the serious drama of life. One consequence is that not one landlord in a hundred is capable of communicating directly with the great bulk of the people. There is thus an impenetrable barrier raised between him and them.' Islay's proprietor, however, was that single exception in a hundred. He insisted that his son should be brought up a Gaelic-speaker.[8]

'As soon as I was out of the hands of nursemaids,' John Francis Campbell afterwards recalled, 'I was handed over to the care of a piper. His name was the same as mine, John Campbell, and from him I learned a good many useful arts. I learned to be hardy and healthy and I learned Gaelic. I learned to swim and take care of myself, and to talk to everyone who chose to talk to me. My kilted nurse and I were always walking about in foul weather or fair, and every man, woman and child in the place had something to say to us . . . I worked with the carpenters; I played shinty with all the boys about the farm; and so I got to know a good deal about the ways of Highlanders by growing up a Highlander myself.'[9]

Among the boys with whom John Francis Campbell played shinty was John Murdoch, three years older than the heir to the Islay Estate and already showing every sign of that athletic prowess which the adult exciseman was to turn to good account in his dealings with working men who, as he noted, were frequently more impressed by a show of physical strength than they would have been by 'a diploma in science'. Nor was shinty just a casual pursuit, in John Murdoch's opinion. Like a later generation of Irish nationalists and revolutionaries who were nurtured in the Gaelic Athletic Association and who saw in hurling, Ireland's version of shinty, an explicit assertion of their country's claim to separateness, Murdoch always believed that Highland sports were an integral part of that sense of Highland identity which he strove continually to reinforce. Shinty matches were reported in *The Highlander* for reasons identical to those which lay behind the paper's coverage of efforts to rescue Gaelic tradition from oblivion. Everything which contributed to Highland distinctiveness, John Murdoch considered, deserved to be promoted and encouraged.

It was this shared conviction which brought Murdoch and John Francis Campbell into renewed contact in later life. The latter left Islay for Eton, Edinburgh University and the English bar. But he lost neither his Gaelic nor his interest in the culture to which that language gave him access. Inspired by the work of folklore collectors elsewhere in Europe, Campbell, with the help of a team of assistants, set out to record the ancient stories which both he and Murdoch had heard as boys. The resulting publications, *Popular Tales of the West Highlands* and *Leabhar na Feinne*, contributed enormously to the upsurge of interest in Gaelic tradition which occurred in both Scotland and Ireland in the later nineteenth century. And though his father's bankruptcy meant that John Francis Campbell never inherited Islay, John Murdoch was to declare in 1883 that Campbell's books constituted a 'more glorious and lasting inheritance' than any piece of landed property. 'They would be remembered,' he insisted, 'when estates as such are no more and when the world will have forgotten that the Campbells ever held a clod of land in Islay.'[10]

Campbell, for his part, did not agree with Murdoch's more radical views. 'John Murdoch is preaching socialism openly,' he noted disapprovingly in the early 1880s. But he contributed financially to *The Highlander* and clearly sympathised with Murdoch's frequent attacks on the men who had bought Islay from his father's creditors. The father's record, Murdoch believed, was not entirely blameless. Walter Frederick Campbell, he pointed out, had been guilty of dispossessing a number of tenants whose lands had then been let to incoming southern farmers. But he also 'showed so much regard for the people and so much respect for their ideas that he had his son taught to speak their language'. That made the senior Campbell, in Murdoch's opinion, a better man than almost any other Highland landowner. And in Walter Frederick Campbell's regard for Gaelic is to be found a good deal of the explanation for Murdoch's consistent portrayal of the Islay of his boyhood as a place whose traditional ties between chief and clansmen had not yet been severed completely by eviction, enforced emigration and other manifestations of proprietorial oppression.[11]

Throughout the 1830s, John Murdoch's father was tenant of the little farm of Claggan, a mile or so to the south of Islay House, the Campbell mansion at the head of Lochindaal. The farmhouse has since been rebuilt more than once. The nearby woods are both thicker and higher than they were 150 years ago. But the outlook from Claggan remains much as John Murdoch described it and, standing in what was once the farmyard, it is easy to appreciate his lifelong attachment to this spot and his lingering regret that he had not himself become a farmer. But in the Islay of the 1830s as in so many similar localities ever since, 'it was accepted as a matter of course,' as Murdoch himself observed, 'that any lad of intelligence and proper ambition should look beyond the island for his sphere'. At the age of 20, John Murdoch left home. And within a month or two, he had entered the government's excise department in which he was to serve for 35 years.

This was long before the introduction of competitive examinations as the sole means of entry to the civil service and Murdoch owed his position to the Islay gentlemen who undertook his advancement as a favour to his father. Before him stretched a long and potentially rewarding progression through the excise service's almost endless ranks and grades—as expectant, assistant, supernumary, ride officer, officer, examiner and supervisor. And at first Murdoch seemed set on little more than a conventional career. He expressed few opinions. He worked hard. He collected the innumerable duties then levied on goods and commodities as diverse as bricks, tiles, carriages and candles. And in the exciseman's long familiar role of 'guager', he measured, for taxation purposes, the output of officially recognised distilleries—while pursuing and apprehending some of the many 'smugglers' who were then in the habit of defying the law by making and selling whisky on their own account.

In 1839, however, Murdoch's view of his future role began to change significantly. That May he was posted to Kilsyth in Stirlingshire and, a couple of months after his arrival, was caught up in one of those fervent and impassioned religious revivals which were a recurring feature of Scottish society at that time. To the evangelically-minded divines who were soon to be responsible for the fragmentation of Scotland's ecclesiastical establishment and the formation of the Free Church—which was to become, incidentally, the dominant denomination in the Highlands—the events of 1839 in Kilsyth marked the commencement of a 'great spiritual movement'. All through the summer, they reported, 'the whole community flocked to hear the word with the deepest earnestness'. Murdoch took a much more sceptical view of these proceedings—and especially of the activities of Kilsyth's fundamentalist preachers. But the young exciseman was nevertheless affected profoundly by the spiritual upheaval going on around him. And it was in response to the Kilsyth revival that he first defined his own attitude to Christianity—acquiring, in the process, the peculiarly personal faith which he was to retain for the rest of his life.[12]

At Kilsyth, Murdoch wrote later, 'I confessed that my first interest and duty was in seeking the kingdom of God'. But that kingdom, he became more and more convinced, was not to be found in 'the confused and uncertain preaching which was passed off as the gospel in the pulpits'. Religious truth was to be discovered only in the Bible. And it was up to each and every individual to make the effort needed to obtain it. 'From that time,' Murdoch affirmed, 'I determined to let no human opinion or authority come between me and God's word.' And the opinions and authorities which he thus rejected included both the churches and the clergy.

Organised religion, Murdoch came to believe, spread discord and strife. It divided people. It obscured, rather than elucidated, the central truths of Christianity. 'Churches have become like shops competing for customers for themselves instead of being agents of Christ,' Murdoch argued in the 1870s. It was time for them to 'come out of their sectarian shells', time for them to recognise that their common beliefs were more important than their theological differences. The clergy were interested enough in 'the machinery' of Christianity, Murdoch admitted—in 'the pulpits, the funds, the orthodoxy and so forth'. But they had lost sight of the spiritual essentials of the religion they professed. 'Where is the faith in the God they preach? Where is the fervour which nothing can quench? Where is the self-sacrifice which characterised the early saints?' In their place, and especially in Scotland's Gaelic-speaking communities, there was to be found only 'a gloomy theology which misinformed people take to be distinctively Highland'.[13]

Also obscured by the emanations from the pulpits, in Murdoch's opinion, was Christianity's social message. 'The gospel,' he maintained, 'went direct to the chief evils of the day and pulled them up by the roots.' The churches in contrast, had both failed and betrayed their adherents—not least those Highlanders who supplied them with some of their staunchest congregations. 'It is notorious how little the voice of the Scotch clergy, Established or Free, has been raised against the high-handed work of depopulation which has desolated the land.' Of course it was simpler for the clergy to befriend the powerful rather than the poor. But that had not been Christ's way. 'It was not by ascending into the society of the rich and learned that He of Nazareth and His followers showed their superiority and cultivated the power of doing spiritual good. They were in the markets, in the workshops, in the fishing boats and, no doubt, in the vineyards and farms of the humble workers for daily bread; and their lives stand out today simple and picturesque—so different from the lifeless formalities and stiffened attitudes which are now observable between priests and people.'[14]

Murdoch's newfound spiritual convictions did not lead to any immediate involvement in secular concerns. His first publications, in the shape of two pamphlets issued in the north of England in the early 1840s, were on purely religious topics. And it was on religious issues that he first spoke in public. As can be seen from the tenor of his later criticisms of the churches, however, Murdoch's understanding of Christianity was such as to impel him increasingly into the political arena. To devote himself to the service of God, he said, meant doing his best for his fellows. And that meant, in turn, that injustice had to be condemned and oppression denounced.[15]

Murdoch's resulting sense of solidarity with the victims of exploitation was extraordinarily unlimited. Although he concerned himself primarily with the Highlands and with Ireland, he sympathised strongly with all the other peoples whom he believed to have suffered, like the Celtic populations of the British Isles, from 'Anglo-Saxon' expansionism. 'The dying wail of the cheated redman of the woods rings in our ears across the Atlantic,' he wrote in 1851, castigating Britain's expropriation of lands traditionally occupied by North America's native peoples. Similar confiscations, he foresaw correctly, would soon be underway in Africa. And this anti-imperialism—which set him apart from the increasingly frenetic jingoism and racialism of Victorian society— was to remain central to Murdoch's outlook. 'Our Indian conquests were a series of crimes,' he declared in 1876. 'And what glory is to be had, he demanded on the occasion of Britain's invasion of Afghanistan, 'from fighting semi-civilised but brave and patriotic highlanders. Noble Afghan highlanders, our sympathies are with you!' '[16]

The Highlander was principally interested in advancing the reform cause in northern Scotland, John Murdoch explained to his readers. But that could not be achieved in isolation. 'Thus the cause of the Highland people is not dealt with in an exclusive and narrow spirit, far less in any antagonism to other people.' His paper's purpose, he continued, was to draw Highlanders into the wider world, not to shield them from it. 'Their sympathies are widened, their views are elevated, and they learn to stand erect, not only as Highlanders, shoulder to shoulder, but as a battalion in the great array of the peoples to whom it is given to fight the battles incident to the moral and social progress of mankind.'[17]

This was a consciously warlike metaphor. But Murdoch, because of the interpretation he placed on Christ's teachings, was a steadfast pacifist. And the extent to which both the Irish and the Highlanders had permitted themselves to be employed as soldiers in Britain's wars was one feature of the Celtic character which he always deplored. Politicians were all too fond of romanticising military conflict, Murdoch wrote on the outbreak of hostilities between Russia and Turkey in the 1870s. 'They speak of the mustering squadron and the clattering car, of the neighing of the warhorse and the far-sounding notes of the bugle horn, of the streaming banners, the exciting charge and the ringing shouts of victory.' But the reality was sadly different. 'There is little poetry in the toil of the march, the discomforts of the camp and the miseries of the bivouac; there is but little poetry in becoming ill on the open plain or in dying a miserable death in a wretched hospital. . . . And far worse still is the absence of poetry in the appalling crimes committed. . . . And yet we here see thousands of working men from Russia and thousands of working men from Turkey going into cruel battle to slay one another because the rulers of the one country have thought it right to have a difference with those of the other. We do not, by any means, say that this is the only reason why the present war rages. But we do venture to say that, so far as a large number of those fighting are concerned, the other reasons are nil.'[18]

Capital punishment, in Murdoch's opinion, was a 'barbarity'. Bloodsports were little better. International disputes should be settled by arbitration. And there could be no justification for promoting domestic political change by violent means. 'We have sometimes spoken strongly on the iniquitous laws at present in force in the country and on the inhumane manner in which they have been carried out against our own people. But we have done two things just as clearly and strongly: we have inculcated obedience to these laws whilst they remain in force; and we have advised and urged our people . . . to put forth their strength, not against individual cases of oppression, but towards creating an enlightened and patriotic public opinion in the country which would have the effect of altering, or entirely removing, the laws of which they complain.'[19].

The murder of English landlords by Irish tenants was perfectly understandable, Murdoch observed in the 1860s. But it was nevertheless both criminal and immoral. The same abhorrence of physical force governed his personal conduct. In Skye in the 1880s his persistent championing of rent-striking crofters so infuriated Lord Macdonald's factor, or estate manager, that the latter threatened to knock him down. 'I told him he need not be afraid to strike me,' said Murdoch, 'for I never struck back. I had been a strict peace man for forty years and never, even in putting down smuggling, resorted to offensive, or even defensive, weapons.'[20]

Murdoch's detestation of alcohol was as longstanding as his dislike of violence—and was similarly bound up with his religion. For 60 of his 85 years he was a total abstainer and an advocate of the legally enforced prohibition of strong drink of every kind. One of the Irishmen whom he most admired was Father Theobald Mathew, the priest who did so much to promote teetotalism in Ireland in the 1840s. And though Murdoch regarded alcoholism as a 'physical disease', he was also convinced, like many other nineteenth century radicals and socialists, that the drink trade served to impede the advancement of working people by making it more difficult for them to realise their full potential as human beings. 'The vicious habits induced in the people by this traffic,' he wrote in Ireland in 1857, 'form another pillar by which the usurpers of the people's rights are kept in their oppressive position.'[21]

Smoking too, attracted Murdoch's disapprobation. He believed it to be unhealthy—just as he deplored, a century in advance of modern dietary theory, the fact that 'pithless loaf bread' was taking the place of 'the more solid and nutritious oatcake'. But despite these and other strictures to which it gave rise, Murdoch's faith was not the joyless creed of the Free Church ministers whom he so scorned. Not the least of the Scottish clergy's crimes, in his view, was their deliberate undermining of the Gaelic culture of the Highlands. He lamented the banning of the bagpipe, the fiddle and the strathspey by men whom he described as ignorant zealots. And, unlike them, he never turned to his beloved Bible simply in search of new sins to denounce. When John Murdoch tired of writing, one of his friends remembered, he would rise from his chair, stretch and say: 'I must read one of the psalms of David. There is nothing better for clearing the brain and giving one fresh inspiration.'[22]

From Kilsyth, towards the end of 1839, Murdoch was sent to Middletown in County Armagh. There he saw something of Ireland's countryside just before it was so cruelly changed by the great famine of the 1840s. There he dabbled, inevitably, in Ulster's ecclesiastical conflicts. And there, too, he began to develop that identification with Ireland and its people which is reflected in his reaction to being posted next to Lancashire. 'I was Scotch enough and even Irish enough,' he wrote, 'to dislike my new surroundings very much.' Northern England's miners and millhands seemed both brutalised and ignorant when compared with the Irish and Highland smallholders and farmers whose rich oral culture Murdoch was then coming to appreciate. And though he sympathised with industrial workers and particularly with the unemployed, he saw little prospect of humanising and civilising the factory system and the new economic order with which it was associated. Only by re-establishing their connection with the land, Murdoch thought, could industrial labourers regain both freedom and self-respect.

This also was the opinion of a number of the more influential leaders of the Chartist movement—that epoch-making working-class campaign for parliamentary reform. And in Lancashire, a principal centre of Chartist agitation, Murdoch was necessarily exposed to Chartist ideas. In this respect, as in so many others, Murdoch had much in common with Michael Davitt who, as founder of the Irish Land League and champion of Ireland's smallholders, was subsequently to befriend both Murdoch and the Highland crofters with whose cause Murdoch was so closely associated. Following their eviction from Mayo in 1850, the Davitt family settled in the Lancashire town of Haslingden which Murdoch had visited regularly in the course of his excise work. And it was as a result of his Lancashire experience that Davitt wrote: 'The first man after my father whom I ever heard denouncing landlordism, not only in Ireland but in England, was Ernest Jones.' To Jones, Bronterre O'Brien, Feargus O'Connor and other Chartists, John Murdoch, too, would pay repeated tributes. The 'great truth' which they advocated, he commented, was that 'the people are not free as long as the land is tied up in the hands of the few'.[23]

To Feargus O'Connor, indeed, Murdoch owed the concept which lay behind his novel response to the crisis which overtook Islay in the wake of Walter Frederick Campbell's bankruptcy in 1847. O'Connor's National Land Company had been formed in England the year before. Its capital was subscribed by many thousands of Chartist working men. And with that capital O'Connor intended to finance the purchase of estates which would at once be divided into smallholdings to be occupied by the company's backers. The project soon collapsed in a welter of scandal and an increasingly vilified O'Connor ended his life in a lunatic asylum. But Murdoch, who always believed that its originator had fallen victim to a concerted campaign of persecution, remained convinced that the Land Company scheme was essentially sound. And in Islay, he argued, such a venture would work well.

When Murdoch came back to Islay as a serving exciseman in 1845, the Campbell ownership of the island was fast approaching its end and the social order he had known as a boy was on the verge of disintegration. Within a few months of his return, the all-important potato crop had failed and Islay's people, like their counterparts elsewhere in the Highlands and in Ireland, were plunged into catastrophe. There had been a time not long before when Highland lairds had obstructed emigration in order to retain on their estates the workforces required by the kelp industry—a lucrative trade in seaweed-based alkalis. But the kelp boom was now over. Farm prices were falling as a result of the repeal of the corn laws and the ending of agricultural protection. And in those circumstances the poverty-stricken tenants of crofts and smaller farms could no longer pay their rents. From the men who took charge of Islay at this time, such tenants received scant sympathy.

'The matter stands simply thus,' Murdoch wrote in 1851. 'The late proprietor, during the existence of corn laws, kelp trade and consequent high prices, raised the rents as high as the people could well engage to pay. Pressed, in the course of time, by his own difficulties, he left the whole property to his creditors who, notwithstanding the repeal of the corn laws and the fall in the price of agricultural produce, continue to exact the same old and high rents—until, as you may naturally conclude, the whole of the people nearly have been thrown into arrears.' In Islay, as in every other part of the Highlands, he concluded, 'the poor people are being reduced to the lowest pitch' and 'are sinking into a state of abject poverty'.[24]

To this crisis Highland lairds responded by embarking on a new round of clearances and evictions which were more terrible and more ruthless than any that had gone before. These were all the more inexcusable, Murdoch argued, because the predicament in which Highlanders found themselves was largely the fault of the region's proprietors. Landowners, he wrote, had appropriated the profits resulting from the kelp business and had 'turned to their own private advantage what should, to say the least, have been divided among all'. The kelp boom had 'afforded the landlords a ground for exacting more than the land was capable of yielding'. The same landlords had evicted the traditional occupants of inland glens which were then put under sheep. The people thus dispossessed were settled on ever smaller holdings on the coast where they were forced to provide their lairds with the kelp from which the latter derived excessive revenues. And because 'potatoes could grow anywhere', the occupants of these newly-created coastal crofts became tragically dependant on that single and precarious crop. 'In this way the Highlanders managed to live from year to year. . . . In this way they eked out a poor, degraded existence in hovels getting every day less fit for the accommodation of human beings and therein subsisting upon one article of food, until the Highlander and his potato had become as if they were part and parcel of each other.'[25]

The landed gentry and their political allies, Murdoch went on, presented emigration as the only solution to the problem they had themselves created. But if Canada and Australia were really 'gardens of pleasure', as landowners maintained, why were the advocates of emigration so conspicuously reluctant to practice what they preached? They were anxious enough to 'send others away to luxuriate in the abundance which awaits across the ocean'. Why did they not go themselves? 'The country can spare them better than it can spare any other class.' Nor was it true that emigration was benefiting the residual population of the Highlands. The 'resources of the country' were not 'so managed as to make the most of them for those of the people who remained behind'. The holdings of evicted tenants were not redistributed among their neighbours. Instead, 'whole townslands and parishes' were 'cleared of people for sheep and deer' and surviving crofters were 'driven to dismal rocks and barren bogs'. Landlords had begun by exploiting Highlanders, Murdoch declared. They had now embarked on their destruction. 'First apply to them a degrading and ruining system; and then make their degradation and ruin an excuse for their extermination. This is the true statement of the case. Knock the poor man down and then kick him for falling.'[26]

Of course Highlanders were in a 'depressed and distressed condition', Murdoch acknowledged. But they need not be. 'The two grand sources of wealth are still there, the land on the one hand and the labour of the people on the other; and with these brought into union, under a just system, there is every reason to believe that the Highlands will yet present the pleasing spectacle of a free, industrious, contented people.' Of Islay's 140,000 acres, for example, 20,000 should be reserved for the bankrupt Walter Frederick Campbell's family and the remainder divided into as many as 3,000 holdings—each of which would consist of about 12 acres of arable and 28 acres of rough pasture. And if these crofts, for which there would be no lack of demand, Murdoch predicted, were to be sold to their occupiers at a rate of some £5.00 an acre, then all the debts with which the Islay estate was encumbered would be cleared.[27]

That particular suggestion, made in a pamphlet which Murdoch published in 1850, unsurprisingly evoked no response from the Islay estate management. And although, a quarter of a century later, Murdoch was still prepared to canvas a similar approach to Highland land reform, the wholesale clearances which followed the potato famine had the effect of inclining him towards a more root-and-branch solution. In a series of articles written in 1852 he ended be asserting that the only way out of the Highland impasse lay in doing away with landlordism and restoring 'the land to the people' who would 'hold from . . . the crown'. Some would call this 'robbery', he agreed. But it was equally criminal that people were going hungry in the Highlands 'whilst the lands upon which their forefathers lived in plenty are lying uncultivated'.[28]

It was at this time—with almost every month bringing reports of some new eviction atrocity from places like Skye, Uist and Barra—that John Murdoch began to formulate the comprehensive critique of Highland landlordism which was to be his hallmark for the next half century. For examples of more humane forms of land occupancy he turned to continental Europe and, in the early 1850s, he was already describing the superior 'social arrangements which obtain in relation to the land' in Belgium, Prussia, Switzerland and Norway. In these countries, he observed, farmers owned their farms and prospered as a result. It was no coincidence, he said subsequently, that Switzerland, where owner-occupancy or 'peasant proprietorship' prevailed, was 'perhaps the most enlightened, independent and prosperous country in Europe'. Nor were the Swiss unique in this regard. 'Casting the eye over the wide world, we see that the rule is for the land to be owned, occupied and laboured by the same class.' But to this rule Britain and Ireland were exceptions. So much for the British people's claims to superiority over their neighbours. 'It is very surprising that we who profess to be in the van of progress, and in the enjoyment of the highest degree of liberty, should be content to be in the most unsatisfactory state, with regard to land, of almost any nation in Europe.'[29]

There could be no 'absolute property' in land, John Murdoch believed. Land was 'not the creation of man' and should not be treated in the same way as 'houses or furniture or ships or manufactures'. 'Land, at the utmost, is a trust, to be administered not merely nor mainly for the profit of the trustee, but chiefly for the production of food and for the maintenance of men.' And that, Murdoch argued, was the way that land had always been viewed in the Highlands. In Gaelic literature and in Gaelic tradition, he pointed out, there was to be found 'a distinct recognition of the fact that the land in the Highlands belonged to the clans as such and not to the chiefs'. A chieftain was 'head of the clan or family, not owner of the great tract of land which that clan occupied'. Eventually, of course, 'many of the chiefs received a kind of chartered right to the land of their clans' and clansmen were consequently 'degraded into feudal tenants'. But the fact that chiefs had thus been 'converted into landlords' did not entitle them or their successors to indefinite enjoyment of that status. 'The landlord class in the Highlands have been but the usurpers of the right which the people there once possessed in the soil.' And the right which had thus been misappropriated could, and should, be restored.[30]

The Irish, too, Murdoch thought, had been deprived of their rights to their own country. And in this he was at one, not only with Irish nationalists, but with John Stuart Mill—one of Victorian Britain's more eminent intellectuals and, in Murdoch's opinion, 'a great social and political reformer'. In a pamphlet published in 1868, Mill made this classic statement of the Gaelic world's view of its own history: 'Before the conquest the Irish people knew nothing of absolute property in land. The land virtually belonged to the entire sept; the chief was little more than the managing member of the association. The feudal idea, which views all rights as emanating from a head landlord, came in with the conquest, was associated with foreign dominion and has never to this day been recognised by the moral sentiments of the people. . . . In the moral feelings of the Irish people, the right to hold the land goes, as it did in the beginning, with the right to till it.' That accorded entirely with Murdoch's opinions—and with those of the crofting and farming tenants whom he championed in both Ireland and Scotland. And it was in belated recognition of the claims made by these tenants that parliament eventually passed both the Irish Land Act of 1881 and the Crofters Act of 1886.[31]

The young exciseman posted to Ulster in 1839 had known little of Ireland and had shown no great interest in its politics. But by 1855, when he was transferred to Dublin, John Murdoch was more than ready to take an active part in the affairs of a nation with which he had come to identify whole-heartedly. This made him exceptional. Most English people, and most Scots also, would then have agreed implicitly with Benjamin Disraeli's characteris-ation of the Irish as a 'wild, reckless, indolent, uncertain and superstitious race'. Their misfortunes, not least those associated with the famine of a few years before, were generally thought in Britain to be the fault of the Irish themselves. Their aspirations to self-government were not taken seriously and, when these aspirations were given violent expression, as in the Young Ireland uprising of 1848, those involved were treated harshly by the British authorities. Irish demands for land reform were, for all practical purposes, ignored entirely. Ireland's Gaelic language and culture, if acknowledged at all, were considered worthless. And, all in all, the Irish were assigned a pretty lowly place in that pseudo-scientific scheme of things which so appealed to Victorians and which viewed Anglo-Saxon Protestants as the most perfect product of human evolution. It was no coincidence that nineteenth century English cartoonists habitually portrayed Irishmen as apes.

There were several reasons for John Murdoch's adoption of a quite different approach to Ireland and the Irish. His growing detestation of Highland land-lordism naturally made him sympathise with the plight of Irish tenants who, in the years following the potato failure, were treated every bit as badly as their counterparts in Scotland. But his recognition of an identity of interest between Highland crofters and Irish smallholders was itself merely one mani-festation of Murdoch's increasing commitment to the concept of the High-lands and Ireland as two components of a single Celtic civilisation. And that commitment was, in turn, the product of Murdoch's steadily expanding knowledge of both the history and the language of the Gaelic-speaking peoples.

The influence of the Gaelic past is evident even in the pseudonym which, as a civil servant, Murdoch was obliged to use when writing in the Irish nationalist press. Finlagan he called himself in conscious tribute to the 'famous place' in Islay which had been 'so intimately connected with the history of the Highlands' as both the administrative and spiritual centre of the medieval Lordship of the Isles—the semi-independent Gaelic principality whose eventual destruction marked the commencement of the long, state-sponsored assault on Scottish Gaeldom. And in thus commemorating his Islay background, Murdoch was well aware that Scotland's Gaels had come originally from Ireland in the sixth century and that, throughout the period of the Lordship of the Isles and, indeed, until the completion of the English conquest of Ireland in the seventeenth century, there had been much cultural, commercial and political intercourse between Gaelic Scotland and Gaelic Ireland. It was this sense of ancient kinship which underlay Murdoch's own attitude to Ireland. And he was convinced that others could be made to share his feelings. 'A little acquaintance with history,' he wrote in the 1850s, 'would make Irishmen and Scotchmen have a better opinion of each other and prepare them for a renewal of the intercourse and good offices of the olden times.'[32]

On arriving in Dublin, which was always to remain his favourite city, Murdoch at once plunged into the Irish capital's flourishing intellectual life. He attended classes and lectures on topics as diverse as Irish history and medicine. He helped to establish the Dublin Chemical Society and became friendly with Charles Cameron, later a well-known scientist, then the Society's young 'professor'. Cameron's mother was Irish. His father came from Lochaber. And by way of illustrating the similarities between the two branches of the Gaelic language, Cameron was to recall subsequently that his parents conversed easily in their different dialects and that his father could readily understand the speech of the itinerant workers from the west of Ireland who then passed through Dublin each summer on their way to England where they helped take in the harvest. 'I often heard my father talking in Gaelic to the harvest men,' wrote Cameron, 'the Connaught and West Highland Gaelic being practically identical.'[33]

Murdoch, too, found it easy to acquire an understanding of Irish Gaelic. When engaged on excise business on Ireland's Atlantic coast he was able to talk freely with the people there in their own language. And not long after he arrived in Dublin he made the acquaintance of the leading Irish scholars of the time, John O'Donovan and Eugene O'Curry. Murdoch was immensely impressed by the way in which these men were collecting, preserving and analysing their country's Gaelic literature and folklore. A similar effort, he believed, should be mounted in the Highlands. 'We have long been of opinion,' he wrote in Dublin towards the end of the 1850s, 'that the Scotch and Irish, instead of being led on either side into the disputes raised by Englishmen who know nothing of the old language of the Celtic people, should work into each other's hands for the purpose of rescuing from destruction such fragments of what is unquestionably common property.'[34]

As was also true of the later leaders of the Easter Rising and the founders of Ireland's eventual independence, Murdoch's interest in Gaelic was part and parcel of his commitment to Irish self-government. Unlike those early twentieth century nationalists, of course, he was a pacifist and, as such, no advocate of armed rebellion against British rule. But that did not quench Murdoch's admiration for the ideals of the Young Irelanders whose unsuccessful uprising was a recent memory in the Ireland of the 1850s. 'Never was there a case in which a body of men set before them a better purpose in regard to a nation,' he wrote of Young Ireland. And although Michael Davitt was wrong in his belief that Murdoch had been in Dublin at the time of the Young Ireland revolution, there seems no reason to quarrel with the Irish land reformer's assertion that Murdoch 'imbibed' the teachings of James Fintan

Lalor, the Young Irelander whose ideas so inspired Davitt himself and who had written, in the 1840s, that 'the entire soil of a country belongs of right to the people of that country'.[35]

Murdoch certainly met that surviving Young Irelander, Charles Gavan Duffy, who, at the time of Murdoch's arrival in Dublin was one of the leading figures in the Tenant League—then pressing unsuccessfully for the security of tenure and judicially-determined rents which were finally to be granted to Irish and Highland smallholders in the 1880s. In collaboration with other Young Irelanders, notably Thomas Davis, Duffy had founded *The Nation*. And it was to the Dublin office of this leading nationalist weekly that Murdoch now gravitated. There he met A M Sullivan, soon to become the paper's editor and, as such, to be responsible for the effective commencement of the Scots exciseman's second career as a campaigning journalist.

Sullivan, said Murdoch, was a 'quiet, mild, young man with a taste for music, for dancing, for poetry'. And soon the two became firm friends. They shared common literary interests. And they shared a passionate dislike of landlordism whether in Ireland or Scotland. Because of Murdoch's influence, in fact, Sullivan became one of the comparatively small band of Irish national- ists who appreciated the extent to which Ireland and the Highlands had suffered in common. Recalling how 'a Highland friend' had 'dwelt with emotion on the spectacle of the evicted clansmen marching through the glens on the way to exile', Sullivan wrote: 'I sympathised with his story; I shared all his feelings. I had seen my own countrymen march in like sorrowful procession on their way to the emigrant ship.' As an Irish nationalist MP in the 1870s and 1880s, Sullivan was to be an energetic promoter of Highland causes in the Westminster parliament. As editor, and eventual proprietor, of *The Nation*, he was equally assiduous in his encouragement of John Murdoch's emergence as a journalist.[36]

Murdoch had first contributed to newspapers in 1843—when living in Lancashire. And in the early 1850s, when stationed in Kintyre, he wrote a number of fairly lengthy, and increasingly contentious, articles on land reform and related topics for the *Campbeltown Journal*, the *Argyleshire Herald* and the *Inverness Advertiser*. In Dublin he helped Charles Cameron establish the *Agricultural Review* and, when that monthly periodical was relaunched as the weekly *Agricultural Review and Country Gentleman's Newspaper*, Murdoch became one of its regular columnists. But it was his work for *The Nation* which gave him his first real insight into the mechanics of newspaper production and introduced him to the techniques needed to publicise and defend a contro- versial point of view. These skills would make it possible for him to keep *The Highlander* afloat by his own virtually unaided efforts. And, more immediately, they enabled him to make more than a minor impact on *The Nation* and its readers. Commencing with a long series on 'The Land for the People', Murdoch went on to make regular contributions ranging from book reviews to leading articles. And in all of these the theme of Celtic unity was uppermost. In one typical editorial, certainly from Murdoch's pen, *The Nation* described resistance to renewed evictions in the Highlands and observed: 'The things which we have noted show that in Scotland the Celt is not going to lie down tamely under the heel of the oppressor; he will be up yet and hand- in-hand with his Irish kinsman will labour for the emancipation of both. May we not look forward to a period not very distant when we shall see the long-separated Gaels of Ireland and Scotland working together for the common good.'[37]

In Dublin, in April 1856, John Murdoch married Eliza Jane Tickell, some 14 years his junior. The couple were to have six children—born in places as far apart as Waterford and Lerwick. And their unsettled style of life was evident from the first; for, in addition to attending to his work, his classes and his journalism, Murdoch had also taken on a key role in a sustained campaign for improved salaries and conditions throughout the British excise service. The staff of Dublin's customs and excise offices had volunteered to prepare a document—some 10,000 copies of which were printed—in support of the service's claims. And its author, needless to say, was John Murdoch—that 'able, energetic advocate for the betterment of this department', as one of his fellow officers described him.[38]

Despite the substantial salary increase which resulted from these efforts, Murdoch continued to press for further improvements—not least by means of the many articles which he published in the *Civil Service Gazette* and *The Civilian*. Murdoch himself made little of the personal consequences of his activities in this regard. In the opinion of his colleagues, however, his 'fearless and able advocacy of revenue reform', to quote the inscription on the silver salver with which these same colleagues presented him on his retirement in 1873, proved an insurmountable bar to his own promotion beyond the rank of supervisor. 'It is pretty generally thought,' said the leader of the deputation who came to Inverness from Dublin on the occasion of that presentation, 'that to a certain extent Mr Murdoch has sacrificed his own interests to the interests of his brother officers and that, had he been more solicitous of his own welfare and less anxious for the welfare of others, his chances of advancement would have been much greater; and this feeling gives him a strong claim on our consideration.' Just how strong a claim was made clear by the fact that the 300 guineas which accompanied the salver was the equivalent of its recipient's annual salary and was by far the most generous presentation made to any retiring excise officer of the period.[39]

His supervisors' desire to remove John Murdoch from the centre of things may have had something to do with his having been posted to Shetland in 1864. But there, too, Murdoch maintained his range of interests. He acquired a croft and put to practical use the farming skills he had learned as a boy in Islay. He urged a wide variety of agricultural improvements on his fellow crofters. And he became the Shetland correspondent of *The People's Journal*, a radical weekly which was published in Dundee and which, with a circulation of over 110,000, was then one of the most widely read newspapers in Britain.

In his *People's Journal* column Murdoch advocated a series of reforms designed to enhance Shetland's economic prospects: better inter-island shipping links, the introduction of flax, the installation of telegraphic communications with the mainland; the import of lime for agricultural purposes, the establishment of a ropeworks, the construction of new piers and the provision of adequate water supplies. He publicised the predicament of crofters threatened with eviction and he came quickly to appreciate, unlike most Scots of his day, the marked distinction between Shetlanders and Highlanders. 'We are often asked,' he wrote, '"Do the people of Shetland speak Gaelic?" No, they do not. . . . So far from being Highlanders, the Shetland people are far from being Scotch even. Whatever we may prove them to be historically, they . . . cherish as antagonistic a feeling towards Scotchmen as exists in any part of the Highlands, or of Ireland, towards that class of Lowland Scotch who come in and take the land from under the feet of the natives. And we could give striking examples of the manner in which Lowland Scots greed has contributed in latter years to keep up this feeling. Whole districts in Shetland have been swept of their peasant population or, as bad, the crofters have been deprived of the hill pasture and left to subsist on the inbye land and what they take out of the sea—without reduction of rent. These cases go far to fan the flame of the desire for re-annexation to Denmark which has survived for centuries.'[40]

While he denounced clearances in Shetland every bit as vigorously as clearances in the Hebrides, and while he sympathised strongly with Shetlanders' longstanding conviction that their Norse heritage differentiated them from Scots, it was to the Gaelic-speaking parts of Scotland that Murdoch still felt most attracted. And when, in 1866, he was appointed excise supervisor in Inverness, he was presented with an ideal opportunity to involve himself in efforts to improve the position of his native language—then regarded as a decidedly inferior tongue by almost everyone in authority. When, in September 1871, a public meeting was called to consider the formation of an avowedly Gaelic organisation in the Highlands, it was John Murdoch who 'moved that a Gaelic Society be established in Inverness. In so doing, he stated that he had himself felt both surprised and ashamed that until this hour the Highland capital should be without such an institution.' Going on to pay tribute to the work of 'the late lamented Professor O'Curry', he urged that any such society should emulate the Irish example and make 'a special effort . . . to rescue from destruction and oblivion all that is valuable in the lore now afloat in the Highlands'.[41]

The still surviving Gaelic Society of Inverness was inaugurated a few weeks later. Soon Murdoch was its honorary secretary. He was also a major donor to the Society's library and the author of a substantial proportion of the papers heard by members in its early years. At Murdoch's insistence, moreover, the Gaelic Society aspired to a role that was more than purely linguistic. Among its aims were the furtherance of 'the material interests of the Highlands' and the 'vindication of the rights and character of the Gaelic people'. And it was to ways in which the attainment of these and other more radical objectives might be assisted by the launch of a new Highland newspaper that Murdoch now began to turn his mind. 'The more patriotic and enterprising of our citizens,' he informed his old Islay friend, John Francis Campbell, in the autumn of 1872, 'are determined to try if a paper in the interest of the Highlands cannot be started in the capital of the Highlands. When the project has got so far, I will send you a prospectus.'[42]

The promised prospectus was duly forwarded to Campbell and other Gaelic enthusiasts in the Highlands and beyond. A number, including Campbell himself, responded with promises of financial help. And it was at this point, indeed, that there began to emerge the loosely-knit coalition of Gaelic revivalists which was to play such an important role in the politics of the Highlands during the following 15 years. Many of the men who gave Murdoch their backing in 1873 were to campaign successfully for greater recognition of

Gaelic in both Highland schools and Scottish universities. They were also to align themselves increasingly with the land reform lobby and to take part in the formation of the organisation known eventually as the Highland Land League.

A prominent member of this group was Charles Fraser Mackintosh, the Inverness lawyer, historian and businessman who was to be elected Liberal MP for Inverness Burghs in 1874—with Murdoch's support. Equally committed to *The Highlander*—which he later described as a 'publication to which all who take any interest in the Highlands and in Celtic literature owe a deep debt of gratitude'—was John Stuart Blackie, Professor of Greek at Edinburgh University and a man with a longstanding and flamboyant passion for all things Gaelic. Still more supportive was John MacKay. A crofter's son who came originally from Rogart in Sutherland, MacKay was a leading member of the Gaelic Society of London. He was also a civil engineer specialising in railway construction. As such, he was that rare phenomenon—a wealthy Gaelic-speaker. And while his politics, like those of Blackie and Fraser Macintosh, were never as radical as Murdoch's, he was to do more than any other individual to keep the latter's newspaper financially solvent.[43]

Murdoch himself, meanwhile, was now set, at the age of 55, on becoming a full-time newspaperman. To the welcome—but always inadequate—funds obtained from the Gaelic lobby's more affluent members, he added the £315 presentation which he received on leaving the excise service in the spring of 1873. And on May 16 that year, from a hastily-acquired office in Church Street, Inverness, he launched *The Highlander* with the characteristically ambitious intention of transforming the region which the new weekly was to serve. 'We this day place in the hands of Highlanders,' ran Murdoch's first editorial, 'a journal which they can call their own. This we do with the distinct view of stimulating them to develop their own industrial resources and of encouraging them to assert their nationality and maintain that position in the country to which their numbers, their traditions and their character entitle them.'

To assert Highland 'nationality' was necessarily to promote the Gaelic language. *The Highlander*, which was considered unusual, not to say peculiar, in always carrying articles in Gaelic, was the paper to give most space to John Stuart Blackie's efforts to raise the cash needed to finance the establishment of a professorship in Celtic at Edinburgh University. And when that professorship became a reality, Murdoch was to take the lead in carrying the Gaelic campaign into the wider educational arena. 'The courage, the vigour, the *success* of Professor Blackie,' he wrote, 'has brought thousands upon thousands who sneered at the first movers of the Celtic Chair to believe in the propriety of giving Celtic philology "and all that" a place in the university; but there is something of the same kind required in regard to Gaelic in the schools. . . . Highland people must show that they are alive to the importance of the matter and they must bring their feelings and opinions to bear on the government and parliament. We must impress our friends with the necessity of making quite a "stir" in this matter. We may as well think of blowing up boulders with rosewater, instead of dynamite, as of getting anything from a Tory or a Whig government, or from a legislature made up of a mixture of both, so long as we are content with begging permission to ask.'[44]

The state schools brought into existence by the Scottish Education Act of

1872, in Murdoch's view, were simply 'instilling' in Highlanders 'alien, selfish, unneighbourly and unpatriotic ideas'. By neglecting Gaelic they were 'inspiring' their pupils 'with respect and love for any place but their own'. The new schools, it followed, were 'rooting out the more active and energetic' members of the communities they were supposed to be benefiting. It was thus the responsibility of these communities to make their views felt by standing up to the 'ministers, factors, landlords' and other anglicised and anglicising individuals who dominated local school boards. And it was the responsibility of the many Highland societies which had been formed in cities like Glasgow, Edinburgh, Liverpool and London to concentrate less on 'dinners and suppers and soirees and concerts' and, instead, turn their attention to 'the righting of the wrongs of the Highlands'. The 'social force of the Celt', Murdoch insisted, had to be 'harnessed' for 'political and economic purposes' as well as for those concerned primarily with entertainment and amusement. Blackie agreed. Gaelic societies and Highland associations, he wrote, should cease 'vapourising about Ossian whom they never read and eulogising Duncan Ban whom they do not sing'—and should 'buckle themselves to serious action in the practical world'.[45]

One centre of the practical world was the House of Commons. And there Murdoch's arguments were taken up by Charles Fraser Macintosh—with the active support, incidentally, of A M Sullivan of *The Nation* in his capacity as Irish nationalist MP for Louth. In order to reinforce these parliamentary endeavours, and after further promptings from the editorial column of *The Highlander*, there was formed a Federation of Celtic Societies to advocate the enhancement of Gaelic's status in the schools and to press the Scottish education authorities to adopt, in Highland schools, a syllabus more closely tailored to local requirements. Not only were these schools 'imparting instruction in a foreign language', Murdoch pointed out; they were doing little or nothing to improve the Highland population's chances of making better use of the natural resources available to them. 'Husbandry is not taught,' he complained. 'There is nothing done to fit the people along the coasts to turning the wealth of the sea to account.'[46]

These were constant preoccupations—Murdoch's interest in Highland development being nothing if not comprehensive. Agricultural chemistry should be taught in Highland schools, he wrote. Crofters and their sons should be equipped with Gaelic instruction manuals on the latest farming techniques. The fishing industry—'one of the great enterprises which awaits the heads, the hands and the capital of our people'—should be expanded massively. Postal and telegraphic communications should be improved. The Highlands should be provided with a textile industry—with the region's inexhaustible streams and rivers supplying the 'motive power'. And, not least, much more should be done to tap the 'enormous fuel resources' of Highland peat bogs.[47]

Murdoch's limitless enthusiasm for Highland tradition, then, was not bound up with wishy-washy romanticism of the type which seeks to make material backwardness a virtue. The crudely constructed thatched houses in which crofters then lived were, in his experience, veritable repositories of Gaelic lore. But they were also, as he acknowledged readily, dirty and unhealthy hovels which ought to be replaced as soon as crofters were able to obtain the security of tenure needed to enable them to make such permanent improvements to their holdings. And while Murdoch was a persistent critic of the factory system and the sprawling urbanisation so closely associated with it, the editor of *The Highlander* was no enemy of economic progress as such. Science and technology were to Murdoch an unfailing source of fascination. And their benefits, he believed, should be spread much more widely. 'For my part,' he told the Inverness Gaelic Society in 1874, 'I look forward to a time when hot air and hot water appliances shall have made our homes ten times more pleasant than they ever were with grates.'[48]

His evocations of a better Highland future, however, did not lessen the esteem in which Murdoch held the past. 'Let us strive,' he exhorted his readers in April 1877, 'to preserve as much as we can of the remnant that is still left to us of a popular lore than which nothing finer probably no race or nation ever had.' It was in this spirit that *The Highlander* praised the folklore collections made by John Francis Campbell. And among regular contributors to the paper was Alexander Carmichael, Murdoch's close friend and fellow exciseman, then living in Creagorry in Benbecula where he was amassing the traditional Gaelic material which, when published eventually in the series of volumes entitled *Carmina Gadelica*, would constitute a worthwhile successor to Campbell's *Popular Tales of the West Highlands*.[49]

John Murdoch always valued Gaelic for its own sake. But his concern for the language was intensified by his conviction that Gaeldom's cultural regeneration was a prerequisite to progress on a wider front. 'The language and lore of the Highlanders being treated with despite,' he said, 'has tended to crush their self-respect and to repress that self-reliance without which no people can advance.' Highlanders had to be made to feel that 'they themselves, and the things which belong to them, are of greater value in the world than they have for some time been taught to regard them'. And that was one of the purposes Murdoch had in mind, he made clear, when establishing *The Highlander*. 'Taking our people as we found them,' he wrote, 'we set about endeavouring to arouse them from the low state of mind into which they had sunk.' The effects of 'alien rule' and the experience of clearance, eviction, insecurity and oppression had been such that there was 'a very provoking fear universally present among the people' and the 'sufferers' were consequently 'afraid to open their mouths'. Highlanders, Murdoch declared, must shed this submissive mentality. 'What is wanted is that they should hold up their heads, speak forth their minds like men and let each understand that the other feels like he does.' Anticipating the strategy eventually adopted by the Highland Land League, Murdoch consequently urged: 'Our Highland friends *must* depend on themselves and they should remember that union is strength. . . . We do not advocate that they should fight or use violent means, for there is a better way of defending themselves than that. Why do they not form societies for self-improvement and self-defence? Why have we not one such in every parish, if not in every village? Did they become thus united, they would become conscious that they possess more strength then they are aware of.'[50]

Between land and language, *tir is teanga*, then, there was, in Murdoch's view, an intimate connection. A people taught to undervalue, or even to deprecate, their own heritage could not but be demoralised, timorous, unsure of themselves. A people encouraged to take a proper pride in that heritage, in contrast, would confidently insist upon their rights—including their right to the land. But restoring the missing sense of self-esteem, Murdoch admitted, was not likely to be easy. 'We have to record the terrible fact,' he wrote in

1875, 'that, from some cause or other, a craven, cowed, snivelling population has taken the place of the men of former days. In Lewis, in the Uists, in Barra, in Skye, in Islay, in Applecross and so forth, the great body of the people seem to be penetrated by fear. There is one great, dark cloud hanging over them in which there seem to be the terrible forms of devouring landlords, tormenting factors and ubiquitous ground-officers. People complain; but it is under their breaths and under such a feeling of depression that the complaint is never meant to reach the ear of landlord or factor. We ask for particulars, we take out a notebook to record the facts; but this strikes a deeper terror. "For any sake do not mention what I say to you," says the complainer. "Why?" we naturally ask. "Because the factor might blame me for it."'[51]

To rid crofters of this 'universal nightmare of the factor and the landlord' became Murdoch's over-riding ambition. It was one that could not be attained, he decided, solely by means of his *Highlander* articles. He would have to spend more time among the people he was trying to help—observing their difficulties, conversing with them at every opportunity, discovering how they lived and what they thought. And so began the expeditions and explorations which, during the rest of the 1870s and well into the 1880s, made Murdoch increasingly well-known to crofters and their families in almost every part of the Highlands and Islands.

It was the John Murdoch of those years that Highlanders long afterwards remembered. And his sheer energy and stamina still impress. He had taken to dressing in a kilt in order to demonstrate his personal commitment to re-establishing a Highland identity. And because kilts, then as now, were seldom worn by ordinary Highlanders, his powerful figure was thus made universally recognisable. *Murchadh na Feilidh*, Murdoch of the Kilt, he was called by crofters. And like the heroes of those ancient Gaelic legends he so much admired, he began to be commemorated in the tales told at winter firesides. On one occasion, it was said, Murdoch was caught in a sudden blizzard while making his way from Balallan to Stornoway in Lewis. The road in question is exposed and windswept—and, with darkness coming on, Murdoch had to dig himself into a snowdrift in order to survive. A night spent in these circumstances, the story-tellers asserted, did him no harm whatsoever. And for several weeks, until the belated arrival of a thaw, his enforced accommodation became something a local landmark—known, in popular recollection, as 'John Murdoch's bed'.[52]

As such tales indicate, crofters were to come to have almost boundless affection for, and faith in, *Murchadh na Feilidh*. Other men had written about their problems. But no one, prior to John Murdoch, had come among them with the avowed intention of arousing them to action on their own behalf. They had little enough to give him in return; but what they had was freely made available. 'I never entered a house without the inmates offering me food or apologising for the want of it,' recalled Alexander Carmichael with whom Murdoch sometimes lodged in Uist. And the editor of *The Highlander*, too, had cause to be grateful for the hospitality he received from families whose poverty both horrified and angered him. Croft houses in the Western Isles, he wrote, on going there for the first time, were typically 'huts without windows or chimneys'. And the single apartments they contained were 'shared largely by cattle'.[53]

Unable to afford a horse, Murdoch travelled exclusively on foot, tramping up to 20 miles a day when well over 60. And although most of the crofters he met initially were 'in such a state of terror' that he had 'difficulty in having a conversation with two of them together', he persisted until large numbers gathered to hear him speak. Murdoch had begun by urging crofters to take their complaints to their landlords in the hope that, once their tenantries' grievances had been drawn to their attention, Highland lairds would undertake some basic reforms. But in those places where, with Murdoch's assistance, crofters took the initiative in this way, not least on the estates belonging to the Gordon-Cathcart family in Benbecula, South Uist and Barra, no worthwhile changes resulted. And Murdoch came increasingly to believe that crofters, if they were to obtain concessions, would have to put landlords under a lot more pressure. 'They were no doubt, as they confessed, afraid of the landlord,' he told crofters at Lochboisdale in South Uist, 'but they were not more so than landlords and factors were of public opinion.'[54]

To speak out in this way was to make enemies. And soon estate owners were going out of their way to obstruct John Murdoch's activities. When he visited Strontian in Argyll in August 1879, for example, the local laird, Sir Thomas Riddell, declared his lecture topic—'The self-respect of Highlanders'—to be 'political' and barred him from the village school. Nothing daunted, however, Murdoch held a more then usually defiant meeting 'under a beech tree at the joiner's shop'. And next day, after seeking out Sir Thomas and informing him of his tenantry's dissatisfaction with his estate management policy, Murdoch was marching off confidently to his next speaking engagement—making for Mull by way of Morvern. This was 'one of the most melancholy districts in the whole country', he discovered. 'You may walk a distance of nearly 20 miles from the head of Loch Sunart to the head of Lochaline without meeting a house that is not either a shepherd's or a gamekeeper's.'[55]

But there were compensations even amid so many reminders of the clearances which had depopulated Morvern and similar locations. There were the rich tales and songs to be heard in even the poorest homes. There was the undoubted progress being made by more independent-minded crofters. There were the beauties of the Highland landscape to which Murdoch never ceased to respond. 'I have not gone a mile out of my way to see any of the "sights" for which Skye is famous,' Murdoch wrote in the course of his first visit to an island he would come to know intimately. 'And yet almost every step has brought me into contact with fresh objects of interest and gone to make me thankful that I have at last made something of an acquaintance with the "Isle of Mist". . . . And although my objects have been social, moral and economic, I confess that I have had extreme satisfaction, and even delight, in the scenery itself and in the objects of historic note.'[56]

His enjoyment of his surroundings was one of the few rewards that the editor of *The Highlander* derived from his work. Certainly he made no money from it. Prior to its launch in 1873, Murdoch had calculated that £3000 would be required to finance his paper. When the first edition went to press, however, only £835 had been raised. And for the rest of its eight-year existence the paper was beset by chronic financial problems which came close to reducing its editor to despair. Murdoch drew little in the way of either salary or expenses from the venture—in which he himself was said in 1883 to have sunk over

£1000. But funds had to be found to pay printers and to meet other unavoidable costs. And because very many advertisers were put off by its aggressively radical politics, *The Highlander* became increasingly dependent on the generosity of John MacKay and the one or two other more affluent Gaels who saw both the newspaper and its editor through a series of potentially fatal crises.[57]

Not the least of these began in 1877 when *The Highlander* carried an account of an exceptionally violent thunderstorm in the northern part of Skye. Worst affected was the Kilmuir estate which was then owned by a Captain William Fraser—whose longstanding policy of enforcing repeated rent increases had made him one of the most unpopular landlords in the Highlands. At the height of the storm, Fraser's house at Uig was partially destroyed by floodwater from a swollen river which had also engulfed the local graveyard. And when the flood subsided both coffins and corpses were found to have been deposited against the walls of the unfortunate laird's devastated home—'as if the dead in their graves', ran the account in *The Highlander*, 'arose to perform the work of vengeance which the living had not the spirit to execute'.[58]

This, and much more in the same vein, was the very stuff of libel. And Murdoch—who admitted afterwards that pressure of work had resulted in his failing to check the offending story which had been supplied by one of the paper's many amateur correspondents—was soon expressing his 'sincere regret that such a paragraph should have appeared'. But urged on by his fellow lairds, who were naturally anxious to capitalise on what seemed to them a heaven-sent opportunity to silence their most effective critic, Fraser sued *The Highlander* for £1000 damages. In the event, Kilmuir's proprietor was awarded £50—together with his costs. That was not a crippling amount. But it was one more substantial debt among many. And it led to the winding up of The Highlander Newspaper Printing and Publishing Company Ltd—which had been formed at Murdoch's instigation in 1873 and which had maintained publication, in the face of mounting losses, for more than five years.[59]

The Company's assets, including publication rights to its newspaper, were offered for sale by public auction on Saturday, November 9, 1878. Not unsurprisingly, there were no bidders; nor were there the following week. The attempt to dispose of the firm as a going concern was accordingly abandoned. It was decided to sell such machinery as could be sold. And, but for John Murdoch's refusal to let it die, *The Highlander* would have ceased publication there and then. At the beginning of December, however, having obtained further financial assistance from friends and having secured the backing of the workforce, Murdoch purchased the defunct company's remaining assets—including its newspaper. 'I have this week secured the copyright of *The Highlander* ,' he announced triumphantly. But in so doing he had also accepted sole responsibility for the troubled affairs of a weekly publication which had seldom if ever made a profit. A fresh injection of capital was urgently required. And it was principally in an attempt to raise the necessary cash from overseas symphathisers that Murdoch set off for North America in September 1879.[60]

Like most other British radicals of the nineteenth century, John Murdoch was a fervent admirer of the United States. In that 'great democratic nation of the west', as he called the USA, there was already to be found, in his opinion, the freer and more open society being denied to Britain's people by their country's reactionary rulers. Closer acquaintance with Americans and their institutions did nothing to diminish his enthusiasm for them. Almost everything about the USA—from its comfortable trains and well-equipped homes to its lack of both aristocrats and landlords—seemed to Murdoch to proclaim its superiority. And those Highlanders who had exchanged tenanted plots in Scotland for their own farms in North America, he thought, had benefited immensely from their acquisition of liberties still unavailable to their counterparts at home.[61]

Murdoch's six-month stay in the United States and Canada, over the winter of 1879–80, provided him with the opportunity to travel widely and to visit scores of Highland immigrant communities—many of them, at that time, still Gaelic-speaking. But it was his contacts with Irish-Americans which were to prove more important—both politically and financially. Through William Carroll, the Philadelphia doctor who was chairman of Clan na Gael, the American wing of the avowedly revolutionary fenian movement, Murdoch was put in touch with the younger generation of Irish nationalists who were then initiating the protest campaign that was to mark the beginning of the end of landlordism in Ireland.

Carroll, who had been conducting a transatlantic correspondence with Murdoch for some months, believed him to be 'the foremost man of a new and nobler era in the Highlands'. And the pro-Irish attitudes of *The Highlander*, in the opinion of the Clan na Gael chairman, made the paper well worth supporting. To be effective, Carroll realised, such support had to take the form of hard cash. And as effective controller of the so-called 'skirmishing fund'—originally established by his fellow fenian, Jeremiah O'Donovan Rossa, to finance guerilla attacks on Britain—Carroll was able to ensure that the necessary cash was made available. When Murdoch was a guest at Carroll's Philadelphia home in the autumn of 1879, therefore, arrangements were made for the visiting Scot to receive some $3000 from Irish republican sources.[62]

Carroll intended that this payment be kept secret—'as *The Highlander*'s weight and influence might be lessened by its editor being employed by the Irish at a salary'. But news of the transaction eventually found its way into the Scottish press—to Murdoch's considerable embarrassment. His own inclinations were such as to make violence genuinely abhorrent to him. And his previous Irish alliances had been with constitutionalists like A M Sullivan—who, incidentally, was cordially detested by O'Donovan Rossa and other revolutionary activists. Murdoch's subsequent denials that he sympathised in any way with republican terrorism are thus entirely plausible. He accepted Carroll's offer of monetary assistance, it seems likely, because both he and his newspaper were on the verge of bankruptcy. And as something of an innocent abroad in the murky world of Irish-American extremism, he may also have been unaware of the gift's antecedents. 'I was too thankful to get it,' he wrote afterwards, 'to raise any questions about it.'[63]

But if Murdoch was anxious to avoid any permanent entanglement with O'Donovan Rossa, whom he was soon to attack in print in Scotland, he had no such inhibitions about associating himself with a parliamentarian such as Charles Stewart Parnell—then emerging in both the House of Commons and in Ireland as the leading exponent of a new and uncompromising brand of

Irish politics. Parnell was also in North America in the early months of 1880. And at William Carroll's invitation, Murdoch accompanied the Irish nation's latest spokesman to a series of enormous and well publicised meetings in different parts of the United States.

Although Parnell apparently suggested at this time that Murdoch should be offered the chance of standing as nationalist candidate for an Irish parliamentary constituency, an offer which Murdoch rejected, the two men were never close. Parnell, not yet the political giant of later years, was both young and inexperienced. He was also a poor public performer. Murdoch, in contrast, dressed as always in his kilt and with a well developed gift for oratory, was the sort of flamboyant figure to whom American audiences responded instinctively. Newspaper reports make clear that in Philadelphia, for example, Murdoch was cheered more heartily than Parnell. And Carroll, for one, was convinced that the Irish MP felt himself overshadowed by his Scottish companion.

A more basic cause of Parnell's failure to warm to Murdoch was his lack of interest in any cause beyond his own. 'Mr Parnell,' Murdoch wrote in 1881, 'is the exponent of the determination of the Irish people to secure their own freedom and the possession of the soil.' And that was undeniably the case. While Parnell's commitment to Ireland was total, however, his interest in Scotland was nil. In this he differed markedly from Michael Davitt—the Gaelic-speaking fenian who, on his release from Dartmoor Prison where he had served seven years for trafficking in firearms, had been instrumental in establishing the Irish Land League of which Parnell had become president. Davitt's sympathies were much wider than those of his chief. And John Murdoch, as the Irish Land League founder's most recent biographer has written, 'was a man after Davitt's own heart'.[64]

Because of its editor's longstanding connection with Ireland it was inevitable that *The Highlander* should have devoted a good deal of space to Irish issues. In the opinion of *The Nation*, indeed, the paper was 'distinguished among British journals as almost the only one which has not degraded itself by distorting the facts of current or past Irish history to suit the ignorant and malignant prejudices which the dominant classes in England deem it their interest to foster against Ireland.' In thus seeking to establish a better understanding of Irish aspirations, Murdoch initially emphasised the need for Scots-Irish co-operation on the linguistic front—encouraging, for example, a steady stream of correspondence from Thomas O'Neill Russell and other founding members of the Society for the Preservation of the Irish Language. On his return from America in the spring of 1880, however, Murdoch—who was by then so close to the Irish Land League leadership as to have attended at least one of their meetings—set himself the task of persuading Highland crofters to follow the Irish lead with regard to the much more down-to-earth matter of land reform. And it was at this time that he earned Michael Davitt's enduring admiration as a 'staunch ally' and the 'truest of true Celts'.[65]

'Twelve thousand persons met the other day in Ennis, County Clare, under the auspices of the Irish Land League,' Murdoch informed his readers in September 1880. 'Mr Parnell reminded the meeting that the firm and independent stand taken by Irish members [of parliament] elicited an increase of respect for them. The lesson, we are glad to say, is not entirely lost on

Scotsmen. They are rapidly coming to see that, whatever mistakes individual Irishmen may make, the Irish as a nation are on the right track, and Scotsmen will soon be following them in demanding a restoration of the land to the people.' Nor would Highlanders be duped by anti-Irish propaganda, Murdoch insisted. They, too, had experience of 'rack-renting, of eviction and of gross misrepresentation; and they can thus all the more readily understand us when we tell them that their brother Celts in Ireland are oppressed, defrauded and maligned by the very classes who have done the mischief in the Highlands.'[66]

The foremost representative of these ruling 'classes' in Scotland, Murdoch noted, was the then Duke of Argyll. And the fact that the Duke had resigned from William Gladstone's cabinet rather than accept the implications of the Land Bill which the Prime Minister had been obliged to prepare in response to Irish Land League pressure, *The Highlander* observed gleefully, was 'one of the strongest proofs of the beneficent character of the measure'. Under the leadership of Charles Stewart Parnell and Michael Davitt, the Irish had organised a mass movement which neither their landlords nor the British government had been able to crush. As a result, Irish farmers and smallholders were to be granted security of tenure. The moral was obvious. 'The Land Bill for Ireland,' Murdoch wrote on May 4, 1881, 'is suggestive of many practical thoughts to every Highlander.'[67]

A week later *The Highlander* at last succumbed to the insistent demands of its many creditors and Murdoch was left to wonder whether his paper had, after all, achieved anything worthwhile. 'Judged by a banker's balance, which is the world's criterion of success,' he conceded, 'it has not. But if our eight years' work has resulted in one, only *one*, of our readers being assisted to raise himself out of do-nothingism, to realise the fact that he is a MAN, born with a purpose in life, then all our eight years' struggles, our eight years' sacrifices, have not been in vain and the paper has been a success.' Murdoch need not have had any doubts. That month, as it happened, crofters on Captain William Fraser's Kilmuir estate employed Irish Land League tactics to compel Murdoch's old enemy to reduce their rents by 25 per cent. Not long afterwards, Lord Macdonald's tenants at Braes announced the rent-strike which marked the beginning of the Highland rebellion against the old order. John Murdoch's long and lonely crusade had most definitely succeeded.[68]

When he visited Braes School in 1882, John Murdoch was 64. But he was not yet ready for retirement. In the course of the months following the Braes people's confrontation with the authorities, Murdoch kept in close touch with events in Skye. In April he arrived in Portree to tour the localities which southern newspapers now called 'disaffected districts'. In September a police report from Glendale, then emerging as Skye's second centre of crofting protest, recorded the local constable's regret that he was unable to provide his superiors with evidence 'that would be any good against Murdoch'. And in the spring of 1883, when the government responded to the mounting unrest in the Highlands by setting up a royal commission to inquire into the causes of the crofting community's grievances, Murdoch extended his activities to all of north-west Scotland—striding from township to township to ensure that crofters took the steps needed to appoint delegates to the commission.[69]

The first such delegate, a Braes crofter named Angus Stewart, set the tone for all that followed. 'I cannot bear evidence to the distress of my people,' he said simply, 'without bearing evidence to the oppression and high- handedness of the landlord and his factor.' In a desperate attempt to counter the considerable impact of this type of assertion, landowners and their representatives assured the commission—chaired by the diplomat and former colonial official Francis Napier, Baron Napier and Ettrick—that both the complaints and convictions voiced by crofters had, in effect, been implanted in their minds by politically motivated men. 'I can state with the utmost confidence,' said Alexander MacDonald, Lord Macdonald's factor, 'that the ideas and sentiments of the people of Skye have to a very great extent been stirred up, influenced and shaped by the action of these agitators.'[70]

Murdoch treated these allegations with contempt. 'For myself,' he told Lord Napier, 'I have such confidence in the truth that I have no desire to warp it; and I was so sure of the good sense and good feeling of the mass of the people that the height of my desire was to have them speak out their own minds in their own native way.' This objective, he continued, had been attained. 'The people themselves have been heard. Not only have numbers of them stated their grievances, their disappointments, their hopes and their own ideas as to the redress of what troubles them, they have revealed a good deal of the character of their minds and given the commission, and the nation besides, a glimpse of the sort of men who have been lying long under the burden of wrong which has at last compelled them to make their voice be heard.'[71]

That assessment of the Napier Commission's significance proved to be correct. Even more important than the commission's eventual advocacy of reform was the contribution it made to liberating crofters from that debilitating 'state of fear' which Murdoch had been struggling, almost single-handedly, to dispel. Crofters in Skye had refused to be intimidated by their landlords. That was why the royal commission had been appointed. Crofters everywhere had participated in the process of selecting men to put their point of view to Lord Napier and his colleagues. And in so doing they were adopting the tactics which John Murdoch had long urged upon them: they were organising themselves in a concerted attempt to improve their own conditions and prospects.

There followed a marked increase in the crofting community's collective confidence in its own abilities. People whose entire existence had been dogged by uncertainty and insecurity were at last taking charge of their own lives. And the resulting transformation was little short of revolutionary. 'We have put up with these grievances for a long time,' said a crofter from Shawbost in Lewis, explaining the illegal occupation of a neighbouring sheep farm, 'but now we venture to lay hold of that piece of our old grazings with the strong hand of the people united for their rights.' As such conduct demonstrated, the men who John Murdoch had found 'afraid to open their mouths' were no more. In their place were people capable of determining their own future. 'The crofters,' a newspaper correspondent reported from Skye at the end of the parliamentary election campaign in 1885, 'were most enthusiastic and each approached the polling station with an air of independence which would have seemed singularly strange to any visitor who had not seen a Skye crofter during the last five years.'[72]

That election was a triumph for the Highland Land Law Reform Association—established in 1883 to give a political dimension to crofting protest. The association was directed by men whom John Murdoch had persuaded to take an interest in the land reform issue. Its numerous branches provided the local leadership he had sought to foster. And its candidates overwhelmingly defeated the landowning MPs whom he had consistently criticised. But Murdoch himself took no part in the association's activities. He still visited the crofting areas. He still corresponded with crofters. He still wrote articles and pamphlets denouncing Highland lairds and all their works. But from his home in Glasgow, where he had gone to live following the demise of *The Highlander*, Murdoch made clear his growing disenchantment with Highland Land Law Reform Association policy—which he believed, entirely characteristically, to be less radical than it should have been.

The crofting community's parliamentary representatives condemned the Crofters Act because of its failure to enforce the redistribution of land lost to crofters at the time of the Highland Clearances. John Murdoch, too, thought such land redistribution to be essential. But he was also convinced, and in this he differed from the Highland Land Law Reform Association and from most crofters, that the security of tenure provided by the 1886 Act would leave landlordism comparatively unscathed. To give guarantees of undisturbed occupation to tenants, as had been done by both the Crofters Act and by the Irish Land Act of 1881, was certainly a step forward, John Murdoch conceded. But it was also to permit landowners to remain in possession of their estates. And not until landlordism itself was abolished, in John Murdoch's opinion, would Irish farmers or Highland crofters be in a position to make good their traditional claims to the land on which they lived.

These convictions, which were shared by Michael Davitt, led Murdoch to identify himself increasingly with ideas developed by the American social theorist and political reformer, Henry George—whose contention it was that all inequalities in wealth and opportunity could be traced to the fact that the ownership of land, humanity's basic resource, was concentrated in the hands of a small but highly privileged minority. George's views were to influence a whole generation of late nineteenth and early twentieth century radicals and socialists. And they were first publicised in Scotland by the Scottish Land Restoration League—formed in Glasgow on February 25, 1884, at a meeting addressed by Henry George and chaired by John Murdoch.

Murdoch became the Land Restoration League's secretary and stood as its parliamentary candidate in Partick in the 1885 general election. Only by supporting his candidature, he maintained, could electors demonstrate that they were 'full-grown Christian men' and not 'mere cogs and wheels in a landlord-made machine—Liberal or Tory'. These appeals for the creation of a third force in parliament proved premature, however. And like other Land Restoration League candidates, Murdoch came bottom of the poll. But he had now identified himself clearly with the cause of attaining an independent, working-class representation in the House of Commons. And when James Keir Hardie and some two dozen other like-minded individuals gathered in

Glasgow in May 1888 to form the Scottish Labour Party, the man asked to preside at their meeting was John Murdoch.[73]

That was the last of Murdoch's many political involvements. But he remained physically strong and active. One of the socialists with whom he mingled in old age thought him 'as sturdy in frame as in opinions'. And as late as 1898 he considered himself to have 'energy rare for a man of more than 80 years of age'. His eyesight, however, had begun to fail. And though, in September 1901, he was fit enough to deliver 'a stirring Gaelic speech' at a Highland Association meeting in Glasgow, encroaching blindness had finally put an end to his writing. Some years earlier, he and his wife had moved to yet another home—in the Ayrshire town of Saltcoats. And there John Murdoch died, at the age of 85, on January 29, 1903.[74]

'The masses are only beginning to learn that they possess enormous power and that that power is valueless unless it is concentrated,' John Murdoch wrote during the 1870s when advocating the establishment of more effective trades unions. It was essential, he asserted in the course of the same decade, that Scotland was not permitted to 'sink into an English province' and was provided, instead with its own national parliament. 'No doubt there are emasculated Scotchmen,' Murdoch continued, 'who would reject the enfranchisement of their own nation just because the Irish demand it for their's; but the thing is getting into the atmosphere and even they will inhale it by and bye.'[75]

Such comments, which could be multiplied indefinitely from Murdoch's writings, were to allow both socialists and Scottish nationalists to claim him as their own. And there is no doubt that he sympathised with each of these often overlapping ideologies. But no such creed was central to his outlook. Throughout his career, John Murdoch's conduct was governed primarily by a profound concern for, and commitment to, the Celtic people—as he himself would have called them—of Ireland and the Scottish Highlands. It was to their liberation he devoted himself. And it was in order to secure their political, social and cultural advancement that he advocated land reform, the regeneration of the Gaelic language and the right of both the Scots and Irish nations to self-determination.

In so doing, Murdoch helped re-establish the ancient links between the two parts of the Gaelic world. Irish nationalist MPs threw their weight behind the campaign for the Crofters Act. Highland Land Law Reform Association and Highland Land League branches passed resolution after resolution in support of Home Rule for Ireland. And when, in 1887, Michael Davitt, accompanied by John Murdoch, toured northern Scotland, there was no mistaking the esteem in which the Irish reformer was held by crofters. 'Irishmen and Scotchmen,' proclaimed the leading Highland Land League newspaper, 'may at last congratulate themselves on having overcome the fierce and brutal prejudices of the past. Mr Michael Davitt, one of the ablest and most persistent of Erin's patriots, has received a welcome in the Highlands which augurs well for the people's cause.' Not least among the indications of the warmth of that welcome was the fact that Skye's staunchly Presbyterian crofters asked this nationalist and Catholic Irishman to become their parliamentary candidate. As a token of the sort of Celtic solidarity which John

Murdoch had preached for nearly 50 years, their gesture could scarcely have been bettered.[76]

James Hunter
Scottish Crofters Union
Broadford
Isle of Skye

February, 1986

1   N MacLean, *The Former Days*, London, 1945, 81–3. These footnotes give sources for quotations other than those drawn from writings reproduced elsewhere in this book.

2   For a detailed account of these events, see: J Hunter, *The Making of the Crofting Community*, Edinburgh, 1976, 131–83.

3   M Ferguson, *Rambles in Skye*, Glasgow, 1885, 122.

4   Murdoch's manuscript account of a visit to Islay in the 1850's, now in the National Library of Scotland, was rescued from a flooded basement in Glasgow. Part of its contents are reproduced below, Chapter 5.

5   *Ardrossan and Saltcoats Herald*, Feb 6, 1903.

6   Information from various family death certificates. See also: J A Nydegger, *The MacQueens*, Baltimore, 1928.

7   *Report of the Commissioners of Inquiry into the Condition of the Crofters and Cottars in the Highlands and Islands of Scotland* (afterwards referred to as *Napier Commission*), 1884, 3093.

8   *Argyleshire Herald*, Oct 1953.

9   Quoted in *Lamplight and Story-Teller*, the catalogue of a National Library of Scotland exhibition on J F Campbell, 1985, 10.

10   *Napier Commission*, 3082.

11   J F Campbell Papers, National Library of Scotland, Adv 50.5.8, f 26. *Napier Commission*, 3082.

12   T Brown, *Annals of the Disruption*, Edinburgh, 1877, Part 1, 10; Part 4, 163.

13   *Highlander*, Dec 11, 1875; June 3, 1876; Oct 19, 1878; Sept 1, 1880.

14   *Highlander,* Dec 4, 1875; Sept 30, 1876.

15   The pamphlets mentioned are *Baptism by Sprinkling* and *Apostolic Succession and Diocesan Episcopacy Refuted from the New Testament*. They are preserved with Murdoch's autobiography in the Mitchell Library, Glasgow, and appear to have been printed in Bury about 1843.

16   *Argyleshire Herald*, Dec 1851. *Highlander*, Dec 23, 1876; Jan 2, 1880.

17   *Highlander*, April 13, 1878.

18   *Highlander*, Feb 19, 1876; Aug 11, 1877.

19   *Highlander*, Nov 1, 1873; Nov 15, 1873; Mar 13, 1875; June 16, 1877.

20   *People's Journal*, Sept 1, 1866. *Napier Commission*, 3022.

21   *Nation*, Aug 22, 1857. *Highlander*, June 27, 1879.

22   *Highlander*, Aug 7, 1875; Nov 25, 1876; Aug 10, 1878; Oct 19, 1878. J Cameron, *The Old and New Highlands and Hebrides*, Kirkcaldy, 1912, 30.

23   *Highlander*, Jan 25, 1879. T W Moody, *Davitt and Irish Revolution*, Oxford, 1981, 21.

24   *Argyleshire Herald*, July 1851. *Campbeltown Journal*, Sept 19, 1851.

25   *Argyleshire Herald*, Feb 1852.

26   *Argyleshire Herald*, March, May 1852.

27   W MacDonald and J Murdoch, *Descriptive and Historical Sketches of Islay*, Glasgow, 1850. *Argyleshire Herald*, Jan 1852.

28   *Campbeltown Journal*, Oct 3, 1851. *Argyleshire Herald*, July 1852. See also Murdoch's account of the Commercial Land Company formed in 1875 with the aim of raising £1 million, through the issue of 50,000 shares, to finance the purchase of Highland estates on the O'Connorite model. *Highlander*, Feb 20, 1875; July 3, 1875; Jan 8, 1876.

29   MacDonald and Murdoch, *Sketches. Campbeltown Journal*, Oct 22, 1851. *Argyleshire Herald*, Jan 1852. *Highlander*, Nov 22, 1873; Jan 10, 1874.

30 *Campbeltown Journal*, Oct 3, 1851; *Argyleshire Herald*, July 1852. *Mark Lane Express*, Oct 10, 1859. *Highlander*, Mar 4, 1876; Dec 8, 1877.

31 *Highlander*, Nov 21, 1874. Moody, *Davitt*, 38.

32 Murdoch M S, 'Queen of the Hebrides', National Library of Scotland, f.68. *Highlander*, Sept 25, 1875.

33 C Cameron, *Autobiography*, Dublin, 1921, 1–2.

34 'Queen of the Hebrides', f.141.

35 *Highlander*, Feb 16, 1881. M Davitt, *The Fall of Feudalism in Ireland*, London, 1904, 228. L Fogarty, *James Fintan Lalor: Collected Writings*, Dublin, 1947, 61.

36 *Highlander*, May 15, 1875; Dec 1, 1877; Apr 27, 1878. A M Sullivan, *New Ireland*, 2 vols, London, 1877, I, 245.

37 *Nation*, Dec 26, 1857.

38 J Owens, *Plain Papers Relating to the Excise,* Linlithgow, 1879, 277, 429.

39 *Highlander*, May 24, 1873. Owens, *Plain Papers*, 436, 528–31.

40 *People's Journal*, Jan 6, 1866; Jan 20, 1866; Mar 24, 1866; June 2, 1866. *Highlander*, Feb 24, 1877.

41 *Transactions of the Gaelic Society of Inverness*, 1, 1872, 1–3.

42 *Gaelic Society*, I, 1872, v, 126–7. Murdoch to Campbell, Oct 30, 1872, National Library of Scotland, Adv 50.2.17, f.23.

43 See J Hunter, 'The Politics of Highland Land Law Reform', *Scottish Historical Review*, 53, 1974, 46–7.

44 *Highlander*, Jan 15, 1876.

45 *Highlander*, May 9, 1874; Feb 27, 1875; Jan 15, 1876. J S Blackie, *Gaelic Societies, Highland Depopulation and the Land Laws*, Edinburgh, 1880, 2.

46 *Highlander*, Jan 19, 1875; May 22, 1875; June 19, 1876; Mar 16, 1878.

47 *Highlander*, May 24, 1873; Apr 25, 1874; June 17, 1875; Dec 18, 1875; Aug 4, 1877.

48 *Gaelic Society*, 2, 1874, 68.

49 *Highlander*, Apr 7, 1877.

50 *Highlander*, Jan 24, 1874; Mar 13, 1875; Dec 18, 1875; Jul 29, 1876; Oct 27, 1877; June 27, 1879. *Napier Commission*, 3083.

51 *Highlander*, July 31, 1875.

52 Cameron, *Old and New Highlands*, 30.

53 A Carmichael, *Carmina Gadelica*, 6 vols, Edinburgh, 1928–1971, I, Introduction, xxi. *Highlander*, June 19, 1875.

54 *Highlander*, June 5, 1875. *Napier Commission*, 3092.

55 *Highlander*, Aug 8, 29, 1879.

56 *Highlander*, June 27, 1879.

57 *Highlander*, April 13, 1878. *Oban Times*, Jan 27, 1883.

58 *Highlander*, Nov 3, 1877.

59 *Highlander*, Dec 1, 1877; Mar 30, Apr 13, Nov 16, 1878.

60 *Highlander*, Dec 7, 1878.

61 *Highlander*, Sept 8, 1877.

62 W O'Brien and D Ryan, *Devoy's Post Bag*, 2 vols, Dublin, 1948, I, 434.

63 O'Brien and Ryan, *Devoy's Post Bag*, 504. *Napier Commission*. 3092–3.

64 *Highlander*, Jan 12, 1881. Moody, *Davitt*, 359.

65 *Highlander*, Feb 14, 1874; May 15, 1875; May 25, 1878. Davitt, *Fall of Feudalism*, 228–9. Moody, *Davitt*, 343.

66 *Highlander*, Sept 22, 1880; Feb 9, 1881.

67 *Highlander*, May 4, 1881.

68 *Highlander*, May 11, 1881. Hunter, *Crofting Community,* 133.

69 *Oban Times*, Apr 29, 1882. *Napier Commission*, 3072. Police Report, Glendale, July 5, 1882: Ivory Papers, Scottish Record Office, GD1/36/1.

70 *Napier Commission*, 1, 475.

71 Napier Commission, 3069, 3073–4.

72 *Oban Times*, Jan 17, 1885. *Scotsman*, Dec 4, 1885.

73 D Lowe, *Souvenirs of Scottish Labour*, Glasgow, 1919, 18.

74 W Stewart, *J Keir Hardie*, London, 1921, 43.

75 *Highlander*, June 21, 1873; Oct 27, 1877.

76 *Oban Times*, May 14, 1887.

A Highland Boyhood
1818-1837

Murdoch begins his autobiography by recalling his boyhood, especially in Islay, and by giving some account of the influences which, in his opinion, shaped his character and interests.

Having been born on January 15, 1818, I am this day 71 years old. I have often been urged to make some record of my life; and, just a few days ago, Archibald Sinclair II, as I may call him, pressed the matter upon me afresh, putting this book in my hand that I might make a beginning. As it is easier to write of another than of myself, and also as it is more or less a duty as well as a pleasure, I may explain that my good friend Archibald II is the worthy son of Archibald Sinclair—for many years the only printer of Gaelic in Glasgow and a native of Mulindry in Islay. From the time of our early manhood until his death in 1870, Archibald I was perhaps the most valued friend I had in the world. But apart from that fact, he deserves more than a passing notice in any such record as I am here beginning.

Archibald Sinclair was a man of the very finest qualities. He was possessed of the highest sense of right and of honour. He was not merely just, he was generous; devoid of every grain of selfishness. Then he was possessed of much vigour and was large of mind. And the gifts which he inherited from God he put to the best of all worship—the service of his fellows. While an ardent Highlander all his days, he entered zealously into questions of religious thought and life; of temperance; of the land; and of slavery. And such were the genial, social elements in his character that he was an attractive centre for many years at 62 Argyle Street, Glasgow, towards which many spirits gravitated. This suggests a narrative which I fear no one but myself will ever complete but which ought to be written. No one ever deserved so well of his Highland fellow countrymen as old Archibald Sinclair the First.

I was born in the old house at Lynemore in the Highland parish of Ardclach, county of Nairn. I say the 'old house' because it was burned and now another white, slated house stands in its stead. My father and mother and my sister, who was older, were living with the Lynemore family at the time of my birth. My father was John Murdoch, the son of John—indeed John was the name, as I heard, for eleven generations at that time. My mother was Mary Macpherson. Her father was Alexander and her mother Eliza MacQueen, daughter of Captain MacQueen of Corribrough. My father was born at Lynemore and my mother at Rebeg between Corribrough and Findhorn Bridge. And I may mention here that on my return to that country, many years afterwards, I found a good many relatives up and down the Findhorn—they being MacPhersons, Murdochs, MacQueens, MacArthurs and MacIntoshes.

Lynemore, whatever the name may mean, commands a very extensive view northward to the shore of the Moray firth; eastward to Dava; westward across the turbulent Findhorn; and southward to the rampart of rocks of which Beum a' Chlaideimh forms a marked feature. Much of this area is brown heath; but in the immediate vicinity there are beautiful clumps of most bewitching birch. Some distance off there are weird old firs, looking lonely as if they were mourning the departure of the primeval forest.[1] And it may be noted here that perhaps there is not another river in Scotland which can boast as much romantic beauty as the Findhorn. From shortly above Forres, up by Relugas, Darnaway, Lethen, Cailmony, Glenferness, Dulsie and away up into Dalarossie, a stretch of at least thirty miles, there is scarce a breath in the succession of interesting scenes.

As I found on my return, in December 1866, all through my life I had images of various objects around Lynemore well preserved in my mind—

although I must have left the spot when I was about three. And so to our departure for Bonskeid in Atholl.

At Bonskeid we lived in a cottage at the roadside, at the foot of the hill of Clochgan, one part of the year, and the other part in Bonskeid House which was rented for the purposes of sport by the Reverend John Sandford. This gentleman was accompanied by a very beautiful woman who was called Mrs Sandford but who was the runaway lady of the Lord Cloncurry of the day. From Bonskeid I was sent to school, at the foot of the Glen of Fincastle, to one David Stewart. He was an old man married to a young, strong wife and had a grown-up son who also helped him to teach.

Just above the schoolhouse was Ballinealich the farm of Charles Forbes. Of this man I have all my life preserved a vivid picture. He sat in an angle formed by a table and the wall. The table was round. But it had an articulated connection with the wall and was supported by a broad leg attached by a joint. A dish with mashed potatoes was laid on this table and a bowl and spoon for each person were placed. These things arranged, the father of the family took off his very broad bonnet and, with his shining bald head exposed to the light which came in through the chimney, he gave thanks. This done he put on the bonnet and proceeded with the horn spoon, like the rest, to partake of the simple fare before him. When the meal was over, and the vessels removed, the table was folded up against the wall and the leg fell flat against it.

The fire was on the floor a little distance from the end wall and was overhung by a large, wide funnel which terminated above in the hole in the roof. I think this funnel is called the 'hallon' in broad Scotch.[2] I have an idea that the fire at Lynemore, in the old house, was overhung in the same way and that there was a large stone near on which tapers of bog pine burned and gave light by which the women carded and spun.

I am reminded of one of the Atholl institutions of these days. Young women from different houses, to the number sometimes of a dozen, shouldered their spinning wheels and marched, in their clean but homely attire, to some neighbour's house where they competed who should spin the greatest quantity of linen yarn. The Atholl women of these days spun with both hands. The wheels had two bobbins and combs, as they were called, and the maidens sent down a thread with each hand as well as other women did one thread. In the evening young men gathered and the day's labours terminated in a dance to the music of pipe or fiddle—or of both alternately.

My parents being bent on having me educated to better purpose than was likely in David Stewart's school, I was sent to that of John MacCraw at Moulin above Pitlochry. When Candlemas came round I remember being provided with a fine, big red-breasted and black-winged cock which I carried that morning all the way from Bonskeid to Moulin. The owner of the best fighting cock was king of the school. How long he reigned I do not remember. The reign of the tawse was so very visible in this school that no one was at all likely to carry another sceptre long. To all appearance John MacCraw held that the rod or the tawse was the chief factor in education. He literally thrashed terror into our flesh. Whether he was equally successful in imparting knowledge to the boys, I cannot say.

The catechism was at that time, as it is now, one of the instruments of education in Scotland; and I remember being kept religiously locked up in one of the big rooms at Bonskeid House so that I could not stay away from learning it.[3] There was some feeling of dislike for the book implanted within me by the confinement. I question if any good came of it.

The surroundings of Bonskeid, as well as those of Lynemore, were very favourable to the growth of Highland sentiment. We were surrounded by woods, some old and some recently planted. We were in the angle formed by the meeting of the Tummel and the Garry. A short ramble among the trees and rocks and boulders and bracken took us to the bank of the Tummel where I gathered quantities of what appear to me still to have been very large hazel nuts. Across the river came the strains of the pipes played by one John Scott, I think. My father had a fiddle. And he and others helped to make the little house in the wood musical.

At that time the district was full of music and dancing—defiled, I am sorry to say, by the droppings of the still which was a power in the glen. I remember being in bothies quite near in the wood where the malt was masking. And ponies, with their whisky kegs, going down to the *machair,* as the lowlands were called, were frequent after nightfall. On one occasion a man with a white pony and two kegs sought concealment about us for the day. When night fell he departed with his contraband. On another occasion I was sent up the glen for a bottle of whisky; and although I met the 'gauger' on my way back, I made myself believe that I succeeded in concealing the smuggled goods.[4] At any rate, I was not taken prisoner!

Our removal from Perthshire to the island of Islay took place in the year 1827. I remember our staying for a night in Perth, also the steep and narrow bridge at Stirling—but not much else along the way to Glasgow. I do remember Tarbert, then a very small place. And well do I remember the voyage on a small sloop to Port Askaig on the Sound of Islay. The steamer *Maid of Islay* was off the station; and, there being no wind, we were at the mercy of tides for I do not know how long. It was summer when we reached the 'Queen of the Hebrides'. But I do not feel as if I caught the enthusiasm which the designation should have kindled. Coming as we had done from a richly wooded district, I at once felt the absence of trees. No doubt the island was elevated to the rank of Queen on account of its superior fertility—not on account of its beauty.

The absence of trees was remarked by old Mrs Birnie, the blacksmith's wife, at the time of the marriage of Colonel John Campbell with Lady Charlotte, the then Duke of Argyll's sister.[5] Donald Ban MacGillivray rehearsed the woman's speech to me when he was past middle life.

Looking about, she said: 'Donald, you see how bare all the country about is. But before you are my age all that country will be under wood.'

'How do you make that out,' said the boy.

'Shawfield's heir,' said Mrs Birnie, 'has married one of the Inveraray ladies. Nothing suits the Campbells of Inveraray but wood, wood, wood everywhere; and as soon as the Inveraray blood has got into the Shawfield veins tree-planting will begin. And what I have told you, you will see.'[6]

And indeed planting went on—the most notable planting, perhaps, being that of *Lag buidhe.* In those days the Shawfield mansion was a great, plain white house—named, accordingly, *An Tigh Ban.*[7] It was exposed to the wind and 'scud' from Lochindaal and in 1829, when a severe storm crowded the loch with ships and other craft in distress and stranded numbers of them, several of the front windows of Islay House were wholly blown in. The distance between the house and links was not more than a good gunshot. Along the head of the links was the public road. Above this stretched *Lag buidhe*. This was the great gathering place for district shinty matches and from far choice players came to prove their powers in the grand game— famous and classic since Cuchulainn outplayed all the chieftains of Emhain. [8]

By the time that I speak of, Walter Frederick Campbell, the son of Colonel John Campbell and Lady Charlotte, had been some years in possession and, true to Mrs Birnie's foresight, planting had been going on under the care of John Gray, the head gardener. And the planting propensity must have been very strong to have led to the planting of the favourite shinty ground; for, although a self-willed man, Walter Frederick possessed all the elements of a popular character and I am surprised he went so far against the wishes of the people.

The planting of *Lag buidhe* deserves more than a passing notice for the reason that it was attended with great difficulty. The wind and spray from the sea seemed to be too much for the young trees and setting after setting withered. But whins were both sown and planted and they afforded shelter. [9] Different kinds of trees were tried and they were put in thickly and in rapid succession so that if one plant failed there were two or three beside it. The struggle with the elements was kept up with such success that, by the time the Shawfield family had finished their course in the island, the Inveraray blood had made its wooded mark abundantly on the face of the country and the mansion house has been for many years sheltered by the trees which have taken firm root in *Lag buidhe*.

I am tempted here to mention things which may have had but little to do with my life and character. So largely do they bulk in my memory, however, that they must have had some effect. No doubt I was at the most susceptible time of my life there; and also there was a body of men, yes and of women, in the island at the time which stands out grandly, I may say, in comparison with all the corresponding masses of people I have seen since.

At the time I speak of, Walter Frederick Campbell, laird of Islay, was in the prime of his early manhood. He was really a handsome man, possessing good features, great vigour and a love of what are called manly sports. Around him were mature men of which such a man might be proud. And that he was animated by a good Highland feeling is shown by the training he arranged for his son, John Francis.

I found John Francis a young, soft, gentle, growing boy in the charge of *Am Piobair Mor*.[10] This was John Campbell, a Lorne man of quiet, steady character, well informed and a good piper. He wore the Highland dress and spoke good Gaelic; and, from what we read in *The West Highland Tales*, he must have had some Highland lore in his head. Such was the early tutor which the then laird of Islay placed over his son. One result was that the son spoke the language of the country from his youth and took part in all the hardy exercises of the people. And without making a long story of what followed, this part of John Francis Campbell's education formed his great inheritance when he came to man's estate.

An outer circle of educative agencies which must have told upon me as well as upon him was provided by the splendid population of the island at that time. There was a stock of gentry there of which any chief might have been proud: Duncan Campbell, Rockside, and his household; William

MacDougall, Ardbeg; MacNeill, Lossit; Johnson, Lagavulin; Campbell, Bale-martin, with his sister and brothers; the MacEacherns, Daill; John Simpson, Bowmore; George Campbell, Kinnabus; Godfrey MacNeill, Ellister; John Campbell, Ardmore; the Campbells of Carnbeg.

Then there were families a little above the common folk; the MacTaggarts and the MacWilliams, the Campbells of Machrie and the Hunters of Glenege-dale. These were looked up to somewhat although they were really working folk; while these first mentioned were quite above work and those of them who had families brought them up in idleness which no doubt led to their ruin.

The third class constituted really a stock of people which can hardly be equalled anywhere. They were all on one social level and lived in a rough sort of way—many of them having the cattle going in the same door as themselves, the fire on the floor and the hens roosting overhead. But some of them had money in banks before there was a branch in the island; and numbers were creditors of the laird when he came to grief.

No doubt some will be inclined to charge me with partiality in representing Islay men and women as being so large, strong and handsome. Let me explain a little. In the first place, I have to state that, at the time I speak of, there were about 1100 tenant farmers in the island as against 230 or so the last time I looked up the Valuation Roll. In reality, the best of the stock emigrated—and the result was exhibited many years later at Bowmore when a number of Portnahaven fishermen with their boats were driven past their own port by a squall which caught them outside the mouth of Lochindaal. The fishing industry kept up the stamina of the people there for some time after the population elsewhere had fallen off in physique as well as in numbers. So there was quite a contrast between the fishermen and the Bowmore people who crowded to see them. The crews of those boats were such big, able men that the villagers were but as children beside them.

After two or three years we removed to a house which was enlarged and improved for us at Claggan. But I dare say I should mention that during our stay at Islay House I became well acquainted with the workmen about—although I was only a small boy. How this came about I do not know. But I remember remarking to myself that those men condescended to enter so fully into conversation with so small a boy. I am not sure whether this was characteristic of the Islay people as a whole or not. But casting my mind back as well as I can, I think it really was. At any rate, it was my experience and I think it had one very marked effect on my character: that of awakening within me a fellow feeling for men of whatever degree in life.

This is the more to be noticed inasmuch as my kind, warm-hearted mother had a strain of Highland pride in her composition which she perhaps inherited from her grandfather, the laird of Corribrough. Add to this that she had a good deal of ambition for her boys and girls. Both these elements working in the family circle were counteracted, however, by the intercourse which I had with those nice, kind genial people. I loitered among them at their work in the stackyard, in the barn, in the stables and even out in the fields at the plough. And if there was any way of doing it, I would preserve several of these men in some shape so that others might be able to realise what sort of persons and characters these humble but potent teachers of mine were.

Let me at any rate remember the names of some of them. Donald MacLean and Dugald MacCuaig were the men who drove our furniture from Port Askaig. Donald was very shrewd in the management of horses and he was very ingenious in several respects. I remember being struck with the ingenuity which he showed in the use of a very limited English vocabulary. Donald would manage to answer a question, or to shape his account of anything he had to tell, so as to avoid blundering. This, of course, he did by framing his speeches so as to require as few words as possible.

John Campbell, or *Iain MacThearlaich*, was a man with whom I liked to spend some time.[11] John was remarkable for his swiftness. Dugald MacGregor, an older man, said of John's running, that he was not at full speed as long as one could see his feet. At his best his feet became invisible.

John MacLugash was the leading ploughman and was said to be so good that he could split a potato in the line of his furrow with the plough. Peter MacCuaig and Neil Shaw were next in this line. Of strong men, there were several. And, as there were public competitions, questions of strength and of skill in athletics soon came to be solved and settled.

John Bell, a sort of game preserver or watcher, was one of the champions in those days. He had been a smuggler and got condemned to imprisonment at Inveraray on one occasion. During his incarceration, Walter Frederick Campbell was on a visit to Inveraray Castle, and, coming upon a number of athletes throwing a heavy stone, the laird, who was very proud of his vassals, laid a bet of £30 that he would bring an Islay man into their midst who would out-throw the best of them. The bet being taken up, the laird went straight to the jail and paid the fine which was just £30. And in one easy throw John won the £30 for his liberator and indemnified him for the amount of his own fine.

One of my inostensible teachers was Margaret MacLeora. I never knew her but as an old woman and it was said afterwards that she got a fresh set of teeth when old and that she attained to 109. She was employed to card wool, to knit stockings and perhaps to spin. And in our house she entertained the young with tales of the Kings of Lochlann, Ireland and Rome.[12] That she had good teeth as well as a good tongue is proved by the fact that the reward we boys gave her was nothing more tender than horse beans.[13] She munched them as well as any of us and preferred them to anything else. Besides being a reciter, she was a bard; but I only remember that she sang for us a lament which she had composed over a sheep which she lost. Many a time I have regretted that I did not preserve the old lady's tales.

My next teacher in the same line was Lachie MacNeill, shoemaker and fiddler, Bowmore. He came to work for our family when there was a stock of leather available. He also was a man of good memory and of rigorous learning powers. I have listened to him reciting the *Arabian Nights* in Gaelic; and to this day I wonder at the command of letters which he brought to bear upon his task.

Lachlan was the only person from whom I heard *Sgeulachd Cois O'Cein*, the example mentioned by Dr McNicol of Lismore of the lengthy compositions which he knew to have been preserved in Gaelic.[14] This also I was negligent enough to let slip although I had many opportunities of writing it. However, when John Francis Campbell brought out his first issue of *The West Highland Tales*, I wrote to him telling him that Lachlan was likely to be found in Paisley. Some years later, he and Hector MacLean, so well known for his literary and scientific attainments, found Lachie in Paisley and committed the *sgeula* to writing.[15]

I cannot pass on without expressing dissatisfaction with myself for not committing to writing these and many other valuable portions of what ought, by this time, to have formed part of the literature of the Gael. And by implication, I pronounce censure upon others who, having had opportunities of the same kind, neglected them. Vast treasures have been lost through such negligence on the part of thousands; and all that can be hoped for now is that what still exists may be preserved.

The little farm of Claggan had been selected and conferred on my father, I have no doubt, as a favour. The spot was choice in many respects. It was retired and yet not far from people. There was a wood just in front; but the wood being on lower ground, there was a considerable extent of country to be seen over and between the trees. From here I went to school to the Red Houses—all the way through the wood and along private paths, hung in the season with woodbine and fragrant also with meadowsweet, thyme and bogmirtle. Wild raspberries were to be found and black bramble berries were abundant. Here also could be found sticks with natural crooks which could be finished off into clubs for the game of shinty.

This school was kept by James MacNab, the son of a farmer, and was very successful both as to numbers and to progress. The furnishings were of the rudest description and the floor was simple clay. But the teaching was done with great vigour. I have known over 120 pupils attending; and many a time I have wondered how well both the boys and girls read, parsed and calculated although they did not know a dozen words of English consecutively—and the teaching was in English. I remember that there were, from time to time, children of excise officers attending and that they were thought cleverer than the native boys because their English was better. I learned to read, write and count and was about an average learner, nothing more.

Right across the river from the school at the Red Houses was Moylea, or some such name, where old George Shanks lived. When Mary Shanks and Dugald MacLarty were getting married the festivities were kept up for so many days and nights that I feel as if they lasted a week. And as the dancing was indulged in outside as well as in the house, much of the rejoicing was participated in by the children at school.

The Red Houses were a few small tiled houses which sheltered five families of the laird's workmen. I remember on an Old New Year's Eve, *Oidhche Challuinn,* going along with Kate Terry to her father's house there. Kate was a servant with us and a fine, hearty, good-looking girl she was. Well, the festivities began with old George Terry taking his bottle and glass, his bread and cheese, and setting out duly accompanied by others. This company went to Donald MacLean's and, when the household was roused, drams and bread and cheese were exchanged; then on from house to house until the round was completed at the house of Peter MacCuaig. Whether the visiting extended to the houses of James Bannatyne, of Angus Campbell, or Rob Roy Campbell across the river, I do not know. It was a favour for me to be allowed to go so far.

James Bannatyne was a Kintyreman who kept a small but-and-ben dram shop. He had, I should say, about two acres of ground behind the house. This little lot was kept going, always under crop all my school time; and, I found it the same when I got back to the island 20 years later. He had oats in the one half, potatoes in the other, the crops changing sides every year. And he kept a cow—mostly grazed along the roadside. James gathered all the scrapings off the road and also the bits of sward which were cut by the roadkeepers. These were put on the land. And the returns from his little bit of ground would tell a tale worth remembering in relation to the system of national economy which leaves the land idle.

New slated houses now occupy the places of the old tiled and thatched ones of my day. But the most of the houses within a radius of two miles have crumbled away. The lands are partly under wood—but are mostly absorbed in the great farm of Daill.

Although attending school, I gave much attention to the affairs of the little farm at Claggan. This would be partly from a sense of care which my father's necessary absence during the day suggested—and partly from the good feeling which always existed between myself and the servants, both male and female. I saw what they did. I heard what they thought and what they could tell of other places and their farming; and they always had something old or new to relate pertaining to a sphere outside the range of farming.

I hoed potatoes and turnips and soon became a good reaper with the sickle. I could thresh with the flail at an early age and my mornings were pretty often devoted to preparing the straw thus for the beasts. I am very thankful today for all that experience. I was even at an early age able to plough; and one season, although still in my teens, I was allowed to do all the ploughing. This was something to be proud of. But it was not all enjoyment. A good deal of the land had its end to the public road. Thus every furrow was exposed to criticism and I was sensitive. So I had very often something else than the satisfaction of feeling that my work must commend itself to the eye of the passer-by. But on the whole, from what I heard years afterwards, I think I did wonderfully well.

I have since learned that all the Murdochs of Lynemore were possessed with the ambition to excel all competitors at whatever work they engaged in. My father had a good head and a neat hand and could do everything thoroughly well. This was in my favour; and I have reason to believe that my labours and my care were, on the whole, well pleasing to him.

I know that I was not vindictive. But I know also that I did aim at doing things better than others; and, having a good mechanical turn of head and hand, I think I succeeded pretty well. I was always ready and even able to do joiner work and even mason work. And many of the permanent works done in and about the house were the work of my young hands. I even went to the smithy and was readily entrusted with jobs which required neatness of hand and painstaking. I remember making a cheese press, woodwork and ironwork; and it was on a new principal which differed from anything to be seen on the island. In the same shop the smith had an order for a brand with letters—and he was complimentary enough to entrust the execution to me. There were few things to be done on the farm that I could not do, although the tools and conveniences were not always of the recognised type. Harness and shoemending and even tailoring were all in my way.

I am aware of the prejudice which exists to the effect that farming is an unintellectual life. But I am ready to say that it is more natural, more healthy and far more intellectual that most of the professions which young men are ever preferring to it. I can now see how vastly the interest of the business had been enhanced had I some hints on botany and chemistry. But limited as my range of thought and experience was, I carry with me from the farm of Claggan some of the more important parts of my education even as a public man.

Before leaving this, I may state that, in the course of a year or two, I was sent to Tigh na Coille to be under the tutorship night and day of Hugh Ross, Assembly teacher then.[16] Mr Ross was a delicate little man of no great ability. But he was very earnest and painstaking to a remarkable degree. And he took much more to do with the moral character and religious interest, not only of the pupils but of the whole district, than was done by some abler teachers.

Mr Ross was a native of Croick in the parish of Kincardine in Ross-shire and he brought with him the ingrained religiousness which is so characteristic of the men of the north. And so he was a missionary as well as a dominie and held meetings for preaching and prayer all round the district. I do not think there was an ordained minister in the parish for many years who made so deep and lasting an impression on the mind of the district as was made by Mr Ross.

Mr Ross read on every subject which he thought would enable him to teach those under his charge. To the tilling of his bit of ground, just an acre in extent, he brought the same vigilance; and I had the advantage of being permitted to work with him on the ground. The first lesson I received was as to the extent of an acre. And for many a year the measure of an acre in my mind's eye was the *doid*, or crop, at Tigh na Coille. The next lesson was in turning up the subsoil. Mr Ross had caught up the idea and he turned over the whole of the garden to the depth, I should think, of 18 or 20 inches.

When the potatoes and the oats were to be put down, as many of the farmers from Conisby, Kintra or Uisgeantsuidhe as could find room came with carts and ploughs; and the sowing and planting was done in a few hours from sheer goodwill, all idea of reward being repudiated. It seemed to be a recognised duty with the farmers that they should give a day of men and horses to put the croft under crop. It was the same with cutting and stacking the peats.

As elsewhere, stone throwing, shinty playing, leaping and running were leading pastimes. Donald Ross, a grown up man and a brother of Mr Ross's followed the trade of shoemaker under the same roof. His lapstone became the stone for 'putting'.[17] He, of course, was above and beyond the reach of us boys. But Walter Turnbull, a lad about my own age but of larger growth, was there, and some others. All of us persevered at the stone. And one day I managed to throw the lapstone further than any of them to their great surprise and chagrin. They could not understand it and they were determined that the feat should not be confirmed. But it was. And from that day it was only good hands among full grown men who could top me.

I had a teacher at home, Archibald Currie, a manservant, who threw beautifully—lowering his hand to behind his very heel and then, forming a correct arc from that over his shoulder, he sent the stone forward not only with all the force that could be imparted by the long bow formed by body, leg and arm, but also with that exact elevation which made sure that the projectile touched the ground as the momentum was exhausted.

Coming home from school on Saturdays, we had quite a field day at Traigh an Luig at shinty playing. This was one of the best fields possible for the game and the players were good. My great delight was to play at this game; and soon I became not only a good player but came to be recognised as such.

Shortly before I got home there was a New Year gathering for a shinty match. The 'chiefs' were John Francis Campbell and Colin Campbell, Balnaby, who was very often with the young laird. I remember I was the first person called by John Francis. Whether this had anything to do with what I am going to notice or not, I do not know. But there were famous players on the ground, among them David Crawford. David and I were on opposite sides and, even in a scramble with him, I justified the selection made by my chief. This did not go down well with David whose temper had not been improved by the drams which were going in the morning. So he made at me and when nothing else would do, he raised his club to strike me. I, however, kept my temper, seized him, by the wrists and held him. And trying to pacify him, I said, 'Of course you are better than I am.' But Finlay MacArthur, hearing my protestations of inferiority, came forward and protested in his turn that I had proved in the play that I was better than my assailant. The story of the scuffle got abroad and it put a feather in my cap.

These reminiscenses are in striking contrast with the present state of things along that part of the country. Traigh an Luig is silent under the feet of cattle. And the small farms from which the keen shinty players of these days came are consolidated into the large farms.

I would like to say a word or two about the dumb animals about us at Claggan. The black mare would form the leading character in a long story. She was bought, a pretty old beast, at the Sinclair's sale at Mulindry after the failure of the distillery there. It was in connection with this transaction that I first saw Archibald Sinclair I. Some time after the sale he was sent to receive payment of some portion of the price. I think the sum was £5.00.

Archibald was the son of Neil Sinclair, the oldest of that generation of Sinclairs. And when he came on that occasion to Claggan he was a mild faced, bright eyed, intellectual looking young lad still in his teens. He was a good height—above the average—with a good, lithe figure and every sign of having the free and effective use of his limbs. And this accords with what I heard of him.

At that time all sorts of feats of agility and strength were tried and I heard it said that *Baldi Neil*, as he was called, could catch the rope which then stretched from side to side of most houses in the Highlands—for drying things—and vault over it twice before coming to the ground! That is to say, he would vault over the rope, come back under it and go over the second time and then come to the ground. On the occasion of my first seeing him, he wore a common, homemade blue suit, a good deal the worse for wear, and his feet were bare. But he had an air of modest independence about him which commanded attention and respect.

He told me, years afterwards, the story of the distillery at Mulindry. John, his youngest brother, was the pushing man who kindled the ambition of the rest of the family to make money by whisky making. And his father, Neil, who was a man of conscience and character, had been induced to sign a bill to help to keep John on his feet in the distillery. Some time afterwards, Neil died, leaving his little farm divided between Archibald and a second family. Archibald took upon himself his father's responsibilities, including the bill to the bank, and went on farming.

He was not long before got married to an active and willing young woman, Ann MacEwan from Cruach above Bowmore. Then in the course of some conversation he had with Mr Cheyne, the factor, the latter said he had taken a step towards the devil in getting married. 'Well,' said the young man, 'we are both able and willing to work our way and I think I have done rightly.' But Mr Cheyne followed up his Malthusian censure with something more of the same nature and my friend turned on him and said: 'If you think I am going to the Devil, you can keep your land. I can do without it.'[18] And before long he left the island and went to work as a farm servant out from Glasgow.

It was out of his humble earnings on the farm that he paid up the amount of the bill to the bank. After this he went into Glasgow and got a job driving a printing machine which was worked by hand. If this was not exactly paradise to him, it was the threshhold. By paying attention to what was done about him, and taking advantage of spare moments, he learned some typesetting. He had thus began to handle the key of knowledge and that, for a man who was from his early youth only kept by the narrow limits of his existence from indulging in the love of books which was in his very nature, was something which could not fail to send a thrill of new life through his frame.

So he put up with many wants. And his wife helped him, bore with the privations, cheered him on and shed over him the sunshine of a happy, kindly, loving heart. He got employment in the office of the Glasgow *Saturday Post* where he worked as a compositor. After that he was with William Gilchrist, a good, kind Highlander from Kintyre. It was here that he first adhibited his name to a piece of printing. Although he was only Mr Gilchrist's journeyman, he was allowed to issue the little *Sketches of Islay*, by Dr William MacDonald and myself, with the imprint: 'Printed by A Sinclair, 145 Argyle Street, Glasgow.'[19]

About 1852 Alexander MacEwan, bookseller, Campbeltown, started a small monthly *Argyleshire Herald* in which I had a hand. I advised Mr MacEwan to engage my friend, there being no one in the town to be trusted with such a job. Mr and Mrs Sinclair, Jessie and young Archie came to St Ciaran where I was living at the time. But as soon as the first number of the paper was out, Mr MacEwan intimated that he would not require Mr Sinclair's services any longer. This was a great blow—for he had come to the country for the sake of his children's and his wife's health.

It had the effect, however, of setting him on a resolution never to be at the beck of an employer. So he returned to Glasgow and in company with John Gillies, a Skyeman who was an amateur in the art, he set up a small shop or office in which he served the many rather than the one. In the course of time, Gillies left and the nucleus developed into an office which enabled Mr Sinclair to follow the business of a general printer.

Mr Sinclair was not only a Gaelic reader and writer but a true Highlander. So he not only did the most of the Gaelic printing which was done in Glasgow, his office became a place of gathering for Highlanders—particularly such as were patriotic, literary and given to welldoing. He kept up a close connection with the Highlands and his wife and children spent weeks and months in Islay from time to time. They all learned to speak, and to love, Gaelic. And Archibald II was early initiated so as to be a good writer and compositor of the language. So that most of the Gaelic work of recent years has gone through the office of father and son.

But I must return to the black mare, the paying for which brought about my seeing Archibald Sinclair for the first time. There was nothing remarkable about her exteriorily. She was a good sized Highland animal with a thin neck and slender legs. But she was lively, spirited and ambitious. Although she was considered an old animal when we got her, she had not given up the idea that, were there an opportunity, she must show her superiority to any other of the horse kind. Crossing the strand, where there was room, she would, with a cart and a small load, make a point of keeping ahead of any competition—even if only weighted with a gig or even a rider. In cart, in gig or in saddle, the black mare was equal to the occasion.

On one occasion she was loaded with her complement of whisky casks for the schooner at Port Askaig, a distance of 15 miles or more from Mulindry. Whatever put it into her head or heels, my lady set out at full speed to get to the front of the other carts. In the attempt, she upset the cart, burst the casks and let the spirits free over the road. But she was freely forgiven and cherished as a jewel of a horse. She was so full of life and so serviceable. For any work out of hours and out of season, the black mare was always the resort—to cart, to gig, to ride.

An excise officer of the name of MacDonald had her away on some hurried expedition and on the return journey, in the dark, he sent her head over heels into a quarry. Getting home himself, halt and maimed, he proposed to go back and end the faithful beast's pains by shooting her. But no; no one who knew her and no one who owned her would agree to such summary execution, even out of mercy, when there was any chance at all. So she was brought home and the accident, like the exploit of spilling the whisky, was only an additional feather in her cap and another item in the song which some of the bright sports made to celebrate her fame. To the last she kept up her spirits and literally died in harness at the age of 26. Turning quickly with the plough, she broke a leg and was put out of pain by the means with which MacDonald would have put an end to her usefulness perhaps 14 years earlier.

There was another mare which was, I will not say as celebrated, but as notorious, as the black one was famous. She had been hand fed from her foalhood and in her fillyhood was a great pet. She would trot after a person like a dog, eat bread or anything out of hand or even take it out of pocket. She was such a pet and such a model that she was to have been the riding pony of the boy John Francis Campbell—and had been imported from Coll, I think, for the purpose. But while she was loose in a field where thoughtless men and boys had to cross to and from work, they teased her and provoked her until she became a terror to them and would chase anyone out of the field, squealing and letting fly at them with her heels.

The result was that she was handed over to my father who was one of the very few who could make anything of her. She was of a fine, nervous temperament, great speed and great endurance. She was a rare roadster in the saddle; and in the plough, after a good deal of trouble, she did the work of a full sized horse. But all the ingenuity of man, and all the might of men, could not get her between the shafts of cart or gig. Although as a small boy I came in for a bad wound in the head from her, I came later on to be another of the very few who could manage her. But poor thing, she had a bad name and some man, more brutal than she, injured her spine with a heavy poker and left her lame. Even so, she fought her way along the road, never giving in to the last.

I am reminded of another passage in that early part of my life. I was drawing home slates from Bowmore with two carts and two very good beasts: old Lyon, a stout grey horse, at that time nearly white; and Lilly, a fine young mare, a daughter of the black mare. They were pulling up the brae towards Garnatra, and a bad brae it was with a deep and unfenced ditch on the lower side. Lilly was taking the ascent skilfully, going from side to side to ease the pull. But she went too near the lower edge of the road and the wheel sank a little in the softer substance not usually trodden. She pulled and pulled again, directing her force to the object of taking the sinking wheel out of its hold. Every side effort thus made, the other wheel was being used as a fulcrum. And there being nothing to stop it, it was getting round towards the precipice—I all the time with my shoulder to the wheel on the brink of the ditch.

There was a little boy passing and I shouted to him to bring a stone and put it against the wheel that was on the hard road. And had this been done, the mare could have levered the other out. But the poor boy came to me with the stone where there was no room for it. And all the time the other wheel was coming round until at last it was actually parallel with the one which I was holding.

At this juncture, several men were in sight from Gartnatra at the top of the brae—and they shouting to me to get out of that. But I held on in desperation, my feet somehow holding the face of the bank. Among the men was Angus Mackay, the piper at Islay House and after in the same post with the Queen. Poor Angus, seeing the predicament in which I was, shouted to me with a fierce oath to come out of that or I should be killed. Somehow I let go and sprang aside. Down went the cart, the two wheels going at the same time into the ditch so quickly that it almost looked as if my poor shoulder had been all that was keeping the wheels up. The poor mare was suspended by the neck, her feet playing in the air.

But with the exception of a little grazing on one of her hind legs which she had got between the spokes of a wheel, there was no damage done. I mounted the front of the cart and unyoked her. And after a good deal of trouble the men got her leg free. We got her up on the road, poor thing, and she trembling with the shock. Next day we got cart and slates out of the ditch and Lyon pulled them home. So imminent was the danger to myself, and so narrow the escape, that for years after I shivered when I remembered the crisis.

There were many things to excite my interest in home affairs at Claggan besides the variety of cares and occupations on the farm. The very spot was charming. The house was about a sixth of a mile from the public road leading to the glen. It was by itself and yet it commanded a view of the homesteads of a large population. The garden stretched down a gentle little slope from the house to a stripe of wood which stretched away on each side and which was a great shelter as well as an ornament to our home. In the garden itself were several large ash and plane trees and a bit of hawthorn hedge. On the other side of a ditch between the garden and the wood were the best of bramble berry briars. In the wood itself were queen of the meadow, honeysuckle and wild roses—but no hazel nuts!

Looking to the right, we had a view of the upper parts of Daill and the hills above. Beyond the eye went right away behind Baletarsin and all that populous country until it reached the mountains, Beinn Bhan and Beinn Bheigeir, which were regarded as the great boundary between the two sides of the island. We talked of the Kildalton side as over-the-hills until we came to know the different divisions on the other side.

To the left of Claggan, we looked over Springbank to Lochindaal which formed a very good feature of the landscape. Across it we took in Kintra, Conisby, Gartacharra and on to Port Charlotte. Straight across from the front of the house, which looked westward, we took in a view of the strath through which the River Sorn ran, with its fringes of trees through which, here and there, the waters of the stream gleamed. Fields came in sight beyond; and then hedges; and then strips of wood; and then the fast growing woods around the mansion with the roofs of the steadings and the corn stacks at a respectful distance.

All these places and objects possessed a beauty at that time which no longer exists. Hillside and hollow, and even hilltop, were alive with groups of people moving north or south. The ridges in the landscape were everywhere occupied with houses. Whichever way we looked from Claggan, we saw houses so situated—although, since then, numbers of them have fallen and the materials are in the stone fences of the larger farms.

And so I come back to dear, quiet little Claggan and gather together around me, in my imagination, father, mother, sister Betsy, a couple of years my senior, George, three or four years younger, Mary Ann, Charles, Walter, Alexander, Jessie, one of twins, and David who was a small boy when I left home. Both father and mother were healthy, active, live persons. He was square built, dark complexioned, with a broad chin and well formed roman nose—and with an air, among us, of authority. He was careful, thoughtful, welldoing in every way. Justice would be thought to be the leading feature of his character. But I knew that he was patient, kind, obliging and neigh-bourly. He was fond of reading, knew well the value of education and made a point of letting us have all that the place afforded in that way.

My mother was even more anxious, I think, on the score of education because she was more ambitious. She was also more ready to show her temper. She had had far greater advantages in her training than he had had. But my impression is that he was able to turn his fewer advantages to better account. He was better balanced, more under mental control. She was the source of whatever of social ambition appeared in the family. She kept her own head just as high as she well could and she wished her family to be able to hold their heads above the level of poor peasant farmers.

I was always rather quiet. I did not say much. But I was very active, able and willing to do anything. My brother George was outspoken, rattling and full of fun and tricks—but was not nearly so willing to exert himself or to accept responsibility as I was. He was more careless in every way. While I did the heavier work on the farm, George did the herding. Of this sort of thing there was a good deal to do where there was a rotation of crops and but few fences. One of the contradictions with which one meets is that George had the patience necessary for herding while I had not. And the cows knew the difference.

In the face of all the shallow teaching of the day, I say that the family feeling, the family tie, the family home should be cherished so that old and young should have the moral benefits of strong natural affection. There is no place where the right feelings can be so well cherished as on a farm, a concern which is capable of almost unlimited expansion. It is true that even farming is handicapped by the evil power of landlords. However, that is not a reason why it should be avoided—but rather that the evil power should be removed.

There is a part of the education of these islands which deserves more than a passing notice here. Despite my predilection for farming, the false elements raised within me a hankering after something 'better' than tilling the ground.

Instead of qualifying for the greatest usefulness at home, I qualified for something abroad—and on leaving the country I set my mind. In fact, it was accepted as a matter of course that any lad of intelligence and proper ambition should look beyond the island for his sphere. And as the years roll on, what was then thought by the few has become the ruling idea.

Besides the contrifugal force developed by the ordinary school teaching, I had a desire for travel awakened within me. Among the Assembly schools were movable libraries. I do not remember how long one of them was allowed to remain in one school. But I know that they existed. I know also that I read lots of these books when I was at Tigh na Coille and that even after I left school I was privileged to get the loan of them. I think I must have had a strong desire for reading at an early age. I have an impression that it was upon books I spent my first pence—and I can remember stitching the small treasures together until they formed a thickish volume.

And so I had vivid pictures of distant lands created within me—and ere very long I wished to see the places, and move among the objects, described. Then the sea gleamed or swelled or raged before me every day. Ships rode at anchor in Lochindaal and vessels came over to the poor old quay at Bowmore. It became easy to form the design of sailing in quest of adventures and to see the regions of which I had read.

I cannot help saying here what an invaluable means of education would not such a book as Martin Doyle's *Hints to Irish Farmers* have been to me and to many others.[20] The minds of boys were inflated with ideas which drew them away from home when they should have had their interest in things around them excited. Today it is still worse; and, as a result, the good soil, the fine climate, the glorious scenery, the language, the history, the literature and the living lore of our country are all to a great extent despised. I know that in my own case I had the idea of leaving home pretty strongly established in my mind. It was only away from home that one could 'get on', could 'rise in the world' and so forth. This idea was encouraged by everyone in authority. But I am inclined to think that it would have been better for my father's family if I had stayed at home. I could have kept them together on the farm after his early death—whereas they soon got dispersed and none of them got the benefits of home which I think they would have had if I, the eldest son, had been kept at their head.

1 The word *fir* was applied in Scotland to the Scots pine, one of the dominant trees in the ancient Caledonian forest.
2 The *Scottish National Dictionary* gives *hallan* as a partition or screen erected in a cottage between the door and the fireplace.
3 The catechism was a manual of religious instruction, in question and answer form, used in Scottish schools well into this century.
4 *Gauger,* literally 'measurer', was the name commonly applied to an exciseman.
5 The marriage took place in 1776.

6 The Campbells of Islay were descended from Daniel Campbell of Shawfield who bought Islay in 1726.

7 This was Islay House. *An Tigh Ban,* the white house.

8 Cuchulainn, a legendry fenian warrior, singlehandedly defeated 150 others in a game of hurling or shinty.

9 Whins, gorse.

10 *An Piobair Mor,* the big piper. For John Francis Campbell, see Introduction.

11 *Iain MacThearlaich,* John, son of Charles.

12 Lochlann, Norway.

13 Horse beans were large, coarse beans used to feed horses and cattle.

14 *Sgeulachd Cois O'Cein,* one the longest folktales in Europe, is, like the *Arabian Nights,* a series of stories within a story. The Rev Donald McNicol, minister of Lismore, was an eighteenth century Gaelic scholar.

15 Hector MacLean, an Islay schoolmaster, was one of John Francis Campbell's folklore collectors. Campbell records how, in 1870, he visited Paisley and found MacLean and MacNeill 'installed in a small public, both rather screwed, Hector the worse'. The tale being recorded by MacLean then stretched to 260 foolscap pages. J H Delargy, 'Three Men of Islay', *Scottish Studies,* 4, 1960, 127.

16 Assembly Schools were established in many Highland parishes in the early nineteenth century by order of the General Assembly of the Church of Scotland.

17 A lapstone, as its name suggests, was a stone which a cobbler placed on his knees to provide a surface on which to work leather.

18 Thomas Malthus, whose *Essay on Population* was published in 1798, favoured checks on population growth.

19 This pamphlet contains Murdoch's plan for the division of Islay into crofts. See Introduction.

20 Martin Doyle, was the pen-name of William Hickey, 1787–1875, Protestant rector at Wexford. Hickey wrote a series of instruction manuals for Irish farmers. The one mentioned by Murdoch ran through many editions.

An Exciseman in Scotland, Ulster
and Lancashire
1838-1844

Murdoch joined the excise service in 1838. Here he describes his training, his initial postings, his early religious experiences and his first dabblings in public controversy.

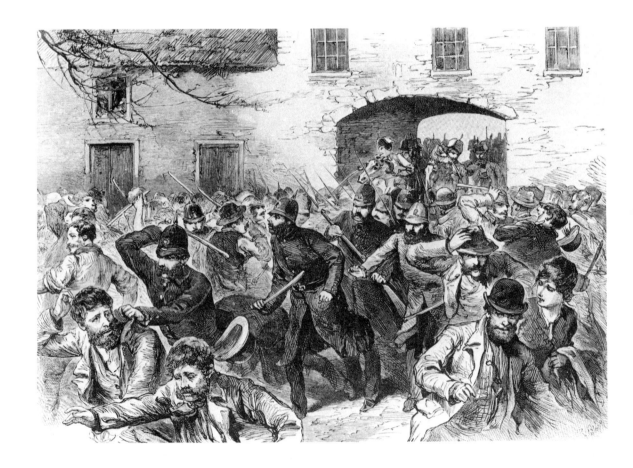

The extent to which my ambition to see the world seemed destined to be gratified was my being sent to serve in the shop of Mr William Boyd, grocer, in the High Street, of Paisley. This occurred early in 1838. The season was cold, dry and frosty—and the frost lasted so long that people seemed to have come to regard frost as the normal temperature.

Mr Boyd was an earnest and a prominent radical in politics. But my stay in Paisley was so short that I did not even know that it held so important a place in the political world. Many a time I have regretted that I did not have the good fortune to know and to hear Mr Patrick Brewster, the radical minister of the parish church.[1] I could just hear exchanges of opinion between my employee and the kindred spirits who came to the shop—and I felt as if he and they were living under a power which they regarded with something like defiance.

Before I had been quite six weeks in the place, there was a letter from my father stating that he had been favoured with an appointment for me in the excise. I wrote at once stating my dislike to be called an exciseman—I presume because I had imbibed in my boyhood some of the smuggler's feelings towards those who interfered with his operations. In the course of a day or two, however, I resolved to go home and hear what could be said in favour of a vocation in which I would at once come in for an amount of pay which I could not expect ever to reach as a grocer's assistant.

When I reached the home circle, the general feeling was that the offer was very good; and being so good I gave in—on the ground that if I declined the boon I might be doing an injury to the younger members of a large family which was in need of patronage. If I refused, the gentlemen who had interested themselves so far in my father's family might decline to do so another time.

So steps were taken to have me admitted to the excise department. My first certificate was duly made up and signed by the two Justices, Colin MacLean, Laggan, and William Campbell, Balemartin.[2] And on my own application, Mr Samual Aris, then an officer in Edinburgh, was appointed to instruct me. Mr Aris was an English gentleman who had strong Highland sentiments from his serving some time when a young man in Islay. He was a great friend of my father and he was married to Charlotte Hamilton of Bowmore.

In due course I set out for the capital of Scotland and, arriving in Glasgow in the evening, set out that night from Port Dundas by the night boat on the Clyde and Forth Canal. There were no railways then with trains and engines rushing furiously about. But my transit to Edinburgh was a speedy one—attended by no discomfort and beset by no dangers. The morning was a little wet and from that day to this my normal impression of Edinburgh has been the sheen of the wet streets on the morning of April 4, 1838.

Mr Aris was like a father to me and Mrs Aris like a mother. He was well pleased that I had accepted the post and he pointed out what an advantage it would be to a young man, who could command but little from home, to have right off about £100 a year coming to him—when many with more to do and with greater responsibilities had not a third of that amount. This told upon my mind; and I soon jumped to the conclusion that I would live on the one half and save the other. In a short time I would have a good sum laid up; and if my distaste for the service continued, I would have the wherewithal to start in some other business.

I went to lodge near to Mr Aris. And before long I was under instruction.

With Mr Aris himself I had malt and the minor matters of public houses, tea and tobacco dealers, auctioneers, horse hiring, stage carriages and distillery. For paper and snuff I went to Juniper Green. Glass instruction I got at the Canongate and perhaps it was the most interesting part of the whole course. It was a strange sight. Sand, white lead and other ingredients were put into a fireclay pot and fused until they could be run, twisted, blown and moulded into any shape. But the business was trying for the men—they were so hot.

One of my trials was that they claimed as a privilege to be 'treated' by the young gaugers when they were being instructed there. They tried me. But I refused. They came at me again. But somehow, although I was not then an abstainer from strong drink from principle, I held out—although I was told that they meant to injure my clothes with their hot metal. But they did not even do that. And when any games were tried I used to beat them— although there were some active men among them. That obtained some respect for me.

In due time I got through the hands of the examining supervisor and was certified as a fit man to be entrusted with the public revenue. I am very sure I was far from fit for much requiring knowledge. But Mr David Smith, the examiner, was friendly to Mr Aris and to myself and the passing of me was made easy. He had been an officer in Islay and, by the bye, a natural daughter of his—Mary Smith, a nice, round-faced, fair girl—had been at school with me at the Red Houses. Her mother was one of the Shanks.

I was hoping that, on completing my course of instruction, I might be appointed expectant to the Edinburgh Collection. I had a great liking for the classic city and felt, in an ignorant sort of way, the influence of its many associations. But I was disappointed—an order coming sending me to Stirling.[3]

Here I was fortunate in having a spell in an easy station, officiating for old Peter Morrison. Among the duties were soap, bricks and carriages—on all of which there were duties. Tea shops and tobacco shops, besides spirit shops, were under frequent visitation by the excise—certain measurements and calculations being gone through which have long since been seen to have been of no earthly use. Toll gates also were under the visitation of the excise. Persons letting horses were required to give tickets to the hirers. These were delivered to the toll keepers as they went through and, being gathered up again by the excise, were checks upon the entries which the horse owners were required to make in their books and on which duty was charged.[4]

There was a big, strong man, an officer there, who had been in Islay. From him I got some rough anecdotes about smuggling—including adventures with the Bells. Among these was their being put to flight by a young woman of the family who sprang naked out of bed on them and struck such terror into them that they never looked back. This officer's name was James Oswald and I think he was along with one Black and that rough tyke Joseph Thomas— both of whom I remember seeing coming back to Bowmore with their heads and faces cut and bandaged.

At the beginning of October I was sent to Doune in Perthshire, some eight miles north of Stirling, to take charge of Doune Ride—the proper officer being set at large to hunt down smuggling. I had a wide range of country to travel and I had this to do in the autumn, winter and spring months—so that, for a 'greenhorn', I had enough to do. I went north to Callander, west to Thornhill and all over Blair Drummond Moss.

Doune was an old little village fast losing its Highland character. The old knew Gaelic, the middle-aged knew some and despised the language—and the young ignored it. It was an old town with no ancient feeling about it. But the country about was interesting and I was just in time to witness the annual Doune Fair and to see the droves of cattle and sheep which gravitated to it.

In a short time I got a pony and this brought me to David Brice the blacksmith. Here I was much more in my element than in taking in information. My pony was very difficult to handle and, but for my own determination and iron grip, it never could have been shod. This led to other trials of strength. I did what no other man could do who visited; and David Brice made something of a boast of me. I took the two forehammers in one hand, turned them up and kissed them.

On May 27, 1839, I was removed to Kilsyth. Here I lodged in the High Street, in a large thatched house, along with David Jack, a master weaver. Helen, his daughter, was a young, handsome girl with auburn hair and a lithe graceful figure. She had fetching ways which were not very easily resisted and they were all the more potent in that she did not mean to make use of their spell. For myself, however, I considered myself safe in the keeping of another whom I had left in Islay.[5] The rest of the family I do not remember— excepting the parents who were decent, hospitable people.

Weaving was the chief business in Kilsyth. Mr Jack was one of a class who got yarn from the Glasgow merchants and gave it out to the weavers to be woven. There were several looms in his own house and his family, as they grew up, plied the shuttle—although I remember the mother ambitioned something better for her offspring.

The most remarkable circumstance in connection with Kilsyth and myself may be begun with the statement that the parish minister was Mr William Burns. Although regarded as a very dead and alive sort of minister, Mr Burns was the father of a more famous man. I had not been very long in the place when the sacrament was to be held and young William Burns, who was officiating in Dundee, came to help his father.

The young man preached with great vehemence and caused much excitement. He was in great favour with the Methodists and they crowded to hear him. When he came out with anything more than ordinarily striking, they responded—some of them even shouting. The more he was encouraged thus, the bolder the young preacher became—his language and his pictures of hell and the sufferings of the damned becoming unusually vivid and terrifying. People began to shout and to cry and, by and bye, the report got about that there was a great revival of religion in the place. The Methodists fanned the flames and kept up meetings all through the night. This sort of thing spread into the other churches and the Revival of Kilsyth was now a worldwide topic. Scores were believed to have 'got religion' and to have 'crossed the Jordan'.

Many anxious souls came from England, Ireland and even America in the belief that there really was there a clearer opening from earth to heaven. Men and women, young and old, came to regard the 'seeking of the Kingdom of God and His Righteousness' as their chief end and their immediate duty. And all possible time was given up to attending religious services, outdoors and indoors. The whole dispensation was regarded as a sort of pentecostal visitation to the gentiles.

I was fully impressed with the whole proceedings and I confessed that my first interest and duty was in seeking the Kingdom of God. But I was always held back from the vortex of excitement and confusion by the words of the angel to Cornelius: 'He shall tell thee words by which thou and thine house shall be saved.'

It was not upon words of God at all that the converts in Kilsyth laid hold. They were churned up by terrible descriptions of the state of the wicked in hellfire and so roused by denunciations of sin that they felt themselves as if suspended by a hair over the mouth of the bottomless pit. They were thus thrown into a state of alarm—into agony, confusion and darkness streaked with lightnings sent forth to lick the unpenitent from the face of the earth. Young Burns was an adept at this sort of conjuring.

Then another process was tried. Heaven and the affairs of the Kingdom of God were described with ability to equal that with which the people had been filled with terror. And when the poor victims or subjects of the first process had these bright pictures spread out before them, and when their minds took them in, they became conscious, of course, of a change of feeling. This change came, in the case of many, to be accepted as a change from death into life. And they went forth rejoicing that they were 'new creatures'. But not one of these could give a 'thus saith the Lord' for what they thus rested their eternal hope upon.

While all the preachers in Kilsyth referred to the Bible as the word of God, and as the only safe guide, they seemed to be in the most hopeless state of confusion as to what that guide taught on the question of life and death. While they had the Bible in their hands, they relied upon another means of salvation— the means which threw people into a state of fear and then raised them, apart altogether from knowledge, into a state of hope. Feelings of pain and sorrow and alarm on the one side, and feelings of gladness on the other, constituted the main things. And the agencies by which these feelings could be produced were 'the means of grace'.

I dwell upon these things because the main question around which people danced, as in the smoke arising out of a cauldron of ignorance and superstition, is too important to be passed by in a word or two; and because, although I admit the want of divine light among the dancers, the ultimate effect on myself was of a serious nature and lasting in its consequences.

I had been taught to read the Bible before I left home and I made a practice of doing so. I remember being struck, even when a child, with the difference between the procedure under the teaching of the Holy Spirit as recorded in the New Testament and the methods followed under the direction of the ministers. By degrees my mind was having a marked distinction established within it between the exact and authoritative utterances of the men sent by God to teach us and the confused and uncertain preaching which was passed off as the gospel in the pulpits. I was drawn nearer to the Bible and further away from the preachers.

It came out clearly in my mind that the word of God placed salvation beyond the doubts and fears which were essential elements in the Kilsyth conversions. Christ died for sinners or He did not. Why get into states of feeling when forgiveness of sin was offered to him who believes as clearly as bits of bread and bits of fish were offered to the hungry?

From that time I determined to let no human opinion or authority come between me and God's word. If the compilations of men were in accordance with it, so much the better. But there was no guarantee that any of these human books were correct and so there was no sense in relying on them. The only safe guide was that which all agreed in acknowledging to be such—the Bible.

I think I am safe in saying that the Bible teaching seized my mind and conscience and raised me to a platform of thought and duty far above that of the selfish and unbelieving world around. And I forthwith set about learning what it taught that I might know from God Himself what He would have me do. If I can say nothing else, I am safe in stating that any positive good which has shown itself in my character, and any service which I have rendered to my fellows, are to be traced to the influence of the divine teaching which is found in the Bible.

It was under this teaching that I dropped the idea which possessed me on entering the excise that I would amass wealth. It was under this teaching that I adopted the conviction that we were not to fight but to leave God to do the avenging in His own way. It was under this teaching that I dropped the clerical fraternity out of the category of God's ministers. And from the same inexhaustible fountain of knowledge I came in time to receive the truth that God means to fill this earth with His glory, sin and sorrow and death itself being destroyed, and that it forms no part of His plan that the vast majority of His human creatures should writhe and curse and suffer in indescribable torment forever and ever while a handful should be brutalized in heaven itself witnessing the torture of their fellows and seeing evil gain the upper hand of good.

These hurried passages will help to an understanding of the readiness with which I appeal to the Bible on the land question—although it may seem to many to be a very wordly sort of thing. Further than this I will not go at present except to say that the leading idea which now occupied my mind was that whatever I had, or could acquire, was to be devoted to the service of God through doing my best for my fellows. I had no right to hoard up money, no right to think of myself as anything better than an instrument in the hand of God to do whatever good work came in my way.[6]

From a professional point of view, my sojourn in Kilsyth was quite uneventful—unless my first attempt at still-hunting is to be regarded as of importance. Passing a place some few miles out of Kilsyth, the name of which I now forget, I saw signs of whisky making and went off to Kirkintilloch to have the advice and help of the supervisor. But Mr Fulton seemed to think nothing of it and would take no steps—so, being late, I went home. But early in the morning I went alone to face the smuggler.

The utensils—all but the still—were there. So I proceeded, quite confidently, to break and spill what I found. This I did without any interruption. When all was demolished, I went into the poor man's house and, having had my clothes and shoes well defiled, I asked his little daughter to bear a hand in cleaning them. She did this quite meekly. All this time Mr Boyle, for such I think was his name, sat in a corner resting his chin in his hands and his elbows on his knees. All he said was: 'It's a good thing for you I am not drunk today.'

Perhaps it was. But I was not much afraid. The hold which the gospel had got of me gave me a measure of boldness which was not to be accounted for otherwise.

With this exploit off hand, I made for Kilsyth. And what did I find but a young gentleman sent by the collector to take charge of the station—at the same time giving me a letter intimating my promotion to an assistancy in the Middletown Ride in Armagh Collection and County in the Kingdom of Ireland.

These two events occurred on October 29, 1839, and the thought that I was going to Ireland was not very pleasant to some of my friends. There was a great deal of prejudice against the Irish—just as there was against the excise. But all my father said to me on the subject was not to meddle with their religion.

The first impression I received on going into port in Belfast is not likely to be effaced as long as I live. The steamer was besieged with beggars. They came, I should say, to the number of a dozen or more in boats—scrambling up the sides of the steamer asking for ha'pence. They were more like heaps of rags tied round the middle than anything else. Of the town I saw little and have no impression of what is now a very proud city than that of those sheaves of rags.

I got out of the town that same day, making for the nice little city of Armagh. Here I had to wait for the Bianconi car which started in the morning for Monaghan, passing through my destination, Middletown, where I was received very kindly by Mr James Gray, the ride officer, and Mr Thomas Reilly, the other assistant.[7] James Gray was a steady, faithful officer and what you might call a sturdy Scot. Tom Reilly was an Irishman, a very sedate looking man, inclined to be stout. But he was really a hearty fellow, full of frolic and fond of good company. He took his dram and his punch and enjoyed himself among the good people of the district.

I drank none—even though I boarded in a public house. But the people soon got to accept the fact that I was not given to riotous living and they put up with me. It was a very unusual thing for a gauger to abstain entirely from drink and to devote his days and his nights to study. But all these oddities were borne with in a kindly, liberal spirit.

Middletown was a poor, sprawling village, lying half way between Armagh and Monaghan—somewhat similarly placed to Keady on the one side and Caledon on the other. Caledon was a nice town, Tynan a good village in a rich country. Glaslough was the same. Monaghan, eight miles away, was a good business town with a crowded market once a week. Indeed, all the towns and villages were something which they are not now. They were surrounded by large populations and crowded by them to sell their corn, their potatoes, their pigs, goats and asses, their hens also and their eggs.[8]

The country about was very fine—rich, dry land resting on limestone rock and capable of yielding the best of crops. Such potatoes as grew there I have never seen since. The oats, wheat and the barley were all good; and most of them were the outcome of spade husbandry. There were a great many smallholdings and, instead of horses, asses abounded. The land was turned over in great style with a long spade worked by a long handle; and a good sight it was when half a dozen men, with their coats off and their knee breeches exposing the muscular calves of their legs, applied themselves in a row to turning over the soil. This was a country which was capable of being turned to good account and, whenever the land got anything like justice, the produce was highly satisfactory.

I remember being struck with the very large sums which the holders of small lots of land asked and obtained for them. These lots were all subject to a fixed rent to the landlord. But the tenant right was bought and sold.[9] I thought the sums thus paid very high—as much as £7.00, £8.00, £9.00 and £10.00 an acre for the mere tenant right. But the land was very good and I was equally surprised at the quantities of produce which were obtained from it. The people came into market with their small carts drawn by asses—and some with bags on the backs of these small animals. And there they stood, heedless of the passing time, and seemingly never afraid but that they would get their prices in the end.

On every side were mansions of proprietors. Sir James Strong's, called Tynan Abbey, was a fine place whose woods, hedges and gardens seemed to burst with the fulness they took out of the land. Hard by was the rectory of the parish of Tynan, no less rich looking. There was an avenue of trees leading up to the rectory such as I have not seen anywhere—and the rest of the grounds were in keeping. Lord Caledon had his place near the nice little village of Caledon. It also was good and possessed all the appearance of being well looked after. The tenants also were said to be well-to-do.

So fine was the physique of the gentry all about that one could not help remarking. The Youngs of Knockbane, the Porters, the Bonds of some other place; all were fine looking men. And they made great turns-out, cantering about at one time, foxhunting another and the next at a steeplechase. The Bonds, of whom there were three powerful young fellows, were given to horses. The father was always in jail for debt and would come out, they said, to spite his creditors. The young men went on as if they had an inexhaustible income.

The common people were about an average stock. At the monthly and weekly markets they came in crowds to the village and had their fun drinking and capering about. I soon came to the conclusion that these men made more noise under the inspiration of two glasses of whisky than my countrymen would make after taking half a dozen! The Irish seemed to be like boys who thought it becoming to show signs of indulgence for which they had not the means. From my previous training of mind, however, I was surprised at the absence of serious quarrels—even at a market when drink was flowing.

They had not at this time lost a sense of the enjoyment of physical exertion. They had their contests at leaping, lifting weights and stone throwing. One day at the Middletown distillery James Johnstone, the distillery manager, and Tom Reilly were handling a 56 pound weight and they tried who would throw it furthest. They were both bigger and stronger looking than I was by a good deal. But, to their astonishment, the best they could do I beat them—although it was a thing I had never tried before. Some of the more active men then tried a stone. But they were all far behind the barefaced Scot.

Another day Ned Grey, the cooper at the distillery, came and asked me to have a throw with him. He was a square built, wiry man—in the decline rather, but full of spirit. He used to be a crack hand and was thus much chagrined when he was beaten. I was thus quite a surprise to the population.

About a month after this, Ned came obsequiously where I was and hoped I would not be offended but would I do him a good turn? He had been up the country a bit and been beaten at the stone by the champion of that district. On the spur of the moment, he had backed me against his victor, Christy, or Christopher, Hughes, and laid a bet on my head. 'He'll be back in a day or so with barley and I depend upon you.'

Christy came and a fine, strong, round, flexible young fellow he was—a year or two my senior. He was an easy minded, pleasant person who did not look upon a contest of that kind as anything more serious than it really was. It was play and nothing more.

We soon got into the arena. Knowing as I did how Irishmen threw, and that they followed the stone over the mark, I seized a hawthorn branch which lay by and placed it as the toemark. And selecting one of the ugliest stones I saw lying about, one which one person would draw and another push from the shoulder, I swung it over the shoulder and planted it in a safe place a good distance beyond. Christy took it, poised it nicely on a level with his ear and then sent it off with all the grace and ease of an active and a strong man. But it came short of my throw. I threw again and increased the distance between us. He threw again and inproved upon his first throw. But after a couple of throws more, he gave up and Ned won his wager.

These notes show, without my making any confession, that there was in my nature, or in my training, or in the influences with which I had been surrounded, something more physical than intellectual in my composition. And the fact of my going with such relish into such matters shows that I am still fonder of bodily exercise than is quite consistent with a high standard of intellectual or of literary excellence.

Inconsistent with these proclivities as it may appear, and dangerous as it might have been thought by many, I spoke out distinctly on moral and religious questions. I was among a people who possessed very active minds. And being so well meshed in theological and ecclesiastical differences, they were all the more ready to take up any question which presented itself. I very soon found that I was much more free to express myself than I had thought.

There were Roman Catholics, Episcopalians, two kinds of Presbyterians at least and Methodists in the place.[10] The Methodists were the most zealous and outspoken and it was with them that I had the earliest exchanges of opinion. But it was not long until I found that I had lances to break also with the Presbyterians who, I think, were the most conceited. In due course it became my good fortune to come into conflict with some zealous Roman Catholics. And it was remarkable, after all I had heard of their bigotry and of their being kept in such ignorance by their priests, that they were able to make a very clever defence of their own belief and could quote scripture with great readiness and with wonderful appositeness.

In the course of some time a number of us got into the way of coming together on Sundays, and on other days, that we might, by patient and personal study, know what the scriptures really taught—independently of what uninspired men might say. Old John Lister, James Bryans, a Mrs Hughes and her daughter and one Helen Paton are the only names I remember— with the exception of Bob Maxwell who only came once or twice for sheer controversy. Yes, there were John Higgins and his wife, two excellent characters. These, and several others, betook themselves to the teaching of the word of God, not caring how much or how little it agreed or disagreed with the teachings going on about them.

Bob Maxwell was a hot, anti-Irish politician and an Orangeman who could not stand anything which went to create a feeling of independence in the people. One day he was in our meeting and, when I produced scripture which went completely against what he had said, he got up in anger exclaiming, 'Is it a man from the Highlands of Scotland, where they do not know how to make trousers, who is to teach me religion!'

These small doings among the people caused uneasiness among the clergy. The perpetual curate of the place went to Miss Connor, the woman in whose house we met, and told her she would be turned out of the house if she persisted. And when the trouble was at its height, Bob Maxwell made an appeal to me to desist from what I was doing on the ground that I was affording the Roman Catholics the satisfaction of witnessing the divisions between Protestants.

One thing came out: that the Protestant clergy were quite ready to resort to cruelty, injustice and other forms of persecution when their crafts were supposed to be in danger. I never heard that the priest, Father Lochran, went further than to denounce my heresy and warn his flock against it. I paid him the compliment of going to his church as I had done to all the others. The poor people—who were paying to keep up fine houses for the Episcopal ministers—were crowded into a great, rough, barn-like house with an earthen floor and only a very few seats for those who could afford to have them.

I heard much, of course, about O'Connel—but took no interest in the Repeal agitation.[11] There was some excitement in Ulster at this time over a challenge which Dr Cooke of Belfast had sent O'Connel to discuss the question of Repeal. This was something for Ulster to be proud of.[12] And when Dan declined, Ulster exulted. Dan declined on the ground that he was not going to do anything which might have even the smallest appearance of his being in antagonism to his fellow countrymen of the north.

Of Father Mathew and his work I heard much also.[13] He was causing much alarm among the makers and vendors of strong drink. His progress through the island and the conversions and the cures which accompanied that progress were little short of miraculous. And I have long since seen what I did not see fifty years ago: that if the Repeal movement had been immediately successful Ireland would have been in the same category with the State of Maine, would have been the pioneer among the nations in the cause of prohibition. Ireland was ripe for the entire stoppage of the manufacture and sale of strong drink. But she was under the dominion of an ignorant and immoral nation and the traffic was kept going.

This is a matter on which the English will have to reckon with Ireland yet. Who can calculate the loss and injury to Ireland from the drink traffic; and, what is the same thing in regard to the last fifty years, from Ireland not having the management of her own affairs? Had she been self-governing at the time I speak of, the distilleries and the breweries would have been put down and Ireland, which had become a sober nation by moral suasion, would have been kept sober by Act of Parliament. The nation was ready for such a grand and salutary stroke. But it had not a government to give effect to its views.

The season at the Middletown distillery being over, I was 'dropped' and reduced to the rank of assistant. However, in 1840 I was sent to do business for a short time in the town of Monaghan. Thence I was sent, as assistant again, to the Londonderry Collection and to a little place called Dunnamanagh in a hill district of Tyrone County about five miles from Strabane and nine from Londonderry.

This was a remarkably Scotch settlement and, although several generations had been born in the country, the distinction was kept up with all the arrogance of conquerors by the Presbyterians. I think they were the most numerous professors. They had two large churches, well filled, a short way off, and two ministers, Messrs Porter and Chambers, of considerable ability and standing.

The parish rector was no other than the Honourable and Reverend Archibald Douglas, uncle to the Marquis of Abercorn. The Marquis was the leading proprietor in the district and Mr Douglas was ecclesiastical cock of the walk. He had a rich living and could afford to keep a good stud of horses. He was a leading foxhunter and steeplechaser and enjoyed society outside and in. He sometimes ascended the pulpit. But he kept a curate of the name of Colthurst who did the drudgery and managed to live on a small salary.

So there was a considerable mixture and some friction. But I never knew any real enmity to be shown to me excepting by the curate. He had said or done something which, as I thought, gave me a right to write to him. I forget the offence. But he went the length of actually complaining to the government against me.

When off duty I devoted myself sedulously to study. So greedy was I in this regard that I neglected going to sleep in the daytime despite being up all night. I am sure also that I neglected my food—and there was no one to insist upon my taking better care of myself. Add to these things that the place I spent every third night, the Dunnamanagh paper mill, was windy, dusty and smoky. The stove blew downward as often as it blew upward and I was frequently in a cloud of smoke and dust. So bad was it that every morning I had a tough job cleaning my eyes, my ears, my throat and lungs of the soot and dust which the night had driven on and into me.

I was hardy, or rather foolhardy, enough to pay no attention. But when spring came round I found my health so impaired that I began to think that something must be done. I who was really the strongest man at every exercise in the whole country began to lose flesh and to show signs of failure.

Add to this that news came of my father having met with an accident. He and Cuthbert Campbell had been out with their guns down about Blackrock. And somehow he got a grain of shot into his head—how no one that I ever met could explain. My poor father fell by the roadside unable to proceed further and, before the intimation of the accident reached me, the wound proved fatal. I never saw him again.

Just as I was thinking of giving up business on account of bad health, my promotion to a Ride in Lancashire arrived. And on June 30, 1841, I set sail from Londonderry on one of the steamers to Liverpool. It was early in the morning and the succession of scenes as we passed down the Foyle was really enchanting.

Derry itself, with all its historical associations, was interesting. And leaving the district awoke feelings which made me think more of the surroundings than I did when I had time to make acquaintance with them in detail. The banks of the river, and away back for miles beyond, were looking their best.

Rich fields were made to appear still more rich by the luxuriant trees—in clumps and strips and hedgerows—which adorned them. And still more beautiful did the two countrysides look from the presence of the many homesteads which then studded the country. At that time there were over eight million souls in Ireland, Ulster having its fair share. Now there are not five million and Ulster, for all its adhesion to the power of the alien rulers, has suffered its share of the loss.

Leaving the Mulls of Kintyre and Galloway on the left, and the Isle of Man on the right, we got into Liverpool next morning. My first impression of Liverpool was very confused. There was an election in hand and mounted soldiers and police were dashing about on the pretext of keeping the Lancashire roughs in order. I remained but a short time in Liverpool and that night was in Bolton. From Bolton I travelled to Bury and thence, in due course, by coach to Shuttleworth, four or five miles further north-west.

Shuttleworth was not even a town or a village. It was just a district which, until comparatively recently, was a badly formed rural mixture of plain, hill and moorland. The village was Banklane, consisting of some houses here and there on the sides of the road leading from Manchester through Bury, and on to Edenfield, Haslingden and Bacup, to Colne and Skipton in Yorkshire.

A busy road this was. All the raw cotton, rags, wool, dye stuffs and bleaching materials used up the country were conveyed northward in carts; and the yarn, the cloth, the bleached and dyed goods and paper were carried south to Manchester in the same manner, as there were no railways then in all that region.

I dropped off the coach at James Haworth's *Pack Horse,* a big beer shop, the equivalent of an inn elsewhere. I was Scotch enough, and even Irish enough, to dislike my new location very much. It would take much time and space to write the half of what I felt among the rough, untutored and unmannerly 'Lankies'. The *Pack Horse* was typical of the rest—my meals on a bare table with sawdust for a carpet and my sleeping room in keeping.

However, I could put up with the place till I should see about me. I soon saw Thomas Lambert, whom I was to succeed, and soon after that I was taken to the paper mill which was to furnish my chief source of labour. This mill was not on a very large scale. But it was a castle to the establishment I had left behind at Dunnamanagh. The firm was Broadbent and Hughes.

Mr Broadbent was an artificial-looking man with a shaven face and a dark wig—that is, he took off the hair where it was willing to grow and where it would not grow naturally he replaced it by artificial means. He was an active member of the Methodist body and his wife, who was very deaf, was a devout worker in the same connection. Although I formed the impression which I have mentioned, I do not remember that I found Mr Broadbent to be anything else than a man of truth and honour. He had a large family who lived, I thought, fully up to their means and were above engaging in any kind of rough work.

Mr James Hughes was a quiet, civil, unpretending man with a large family of daughters—four, I think—and no mother at their head. He made no profession such as his partner did; and he even went the length of coming home from Manchester sometimes with a good cargo of strong drink on board. Martha, his eldest daughter, was a very excellent young lady in every sense that one would like to attach to the word. Alice, the second, was also a fine girl, just nearing 17 at that time. She was a pretty girl, too, and pleasant company. It would have been quite easy to cultivate more than the ordinary sentiment of simple gallantry towards her. But I did not. We were all on good terms and I derived a good deal of pleasure from the intercourse.

The pleasure was all the greater from the roughness of the majority of the people about. To me there was a positive contrast between these Lancashire folk and the more polite folk whom I had left behind me in the north of Ireland. Perhaps I was prejudiced. But I did feel that I had fallen among comparative savages after leaving the more polite Irish behind me—even in Ulster which is not by any means so refined as Leinster and Munster. So marked did I feel this difference between the two peoples that today I suspect I was guilty of a measure of intolerance towards my new neighbours.

Of course, some of my duties brought me in contact with some of the roughest people. Besides the paper mill, I had to visit public houses of different classes and a multitude of what are called Tom and Jerry shops[14]—also toll gates, brick makers and a class of manufacturers who used soap in finishing their goods and who therefore got back the duty then paid on soap.

In the course of my visits to the drinkshops, I met with the lowest class of Englishman and I cannot help repeating that they were a disgusting lot. Nor was their character improved by their surroundings. The Tom and Jerry shop was often no more than a kitchen with a scullery on the one side and some sort of sleeping place on the other. In this kitchen the water was boiled and poured on the malt in a mash tub in the middle of the floor. This was the first stage in the making of the beer. The mash was then run off by a faucet in the bottom of the tub and lifted into a cask where it was supplied with yeast and allowed to ferment.

The mashing, fermenting and the cooking all went on among a number of men who sat or stood where they could, drinking and smoking. This was the kingdom, generally, of the housewife—the husband being at work in the factory. In this thick atmosphere of carbonic acid gas, tobacco smoke and other foul effusions, the young Lankie, as the Lancashire man was often called, was brought up. And one can imagine the kind of education which girls received in such schools, the discourse over the pots of beer being in keeping with the rest.

'Here, gauger, wilt sup?' This was often the salute I met with—the words being followed by the fellow pushing his mug of beer up towards my face. I was not a total abstainer at the time I went there. But I was so far advanced towards that position that I do not think I ever accepted the gruff offer.

Then someone would undertake to amuse his fellows at my expense by telling how a gauger was found in a state of hopeless intoxication and taken down by the colliers into their dark domains. When he begins to show signs of returning reason, he is asked: 'Who are tae, fellow?'

'A wur a gauger in t'other worl', but a'll be onything thee likes, Mr Devil!'

Perhaps the next thing was, if I stayed long enough: 'Now, gauger, wilt stand hand?'—out of which I got as well as I could when my survey was finished.

When the stereotyped story was told by a collier, as it often was, I sometimes made reprisal by saying: 'If I were you, I would not repeat a story which conveys that your class were taken for devils.'

'Hae,' the answer might be, 'we don't want none o' thy sort. There be monny black coals gaw-an aboot an' we workin' hard to keep thee up. What wad 'ee do but for us drinkin' t' beer and payin' tax? By ——, we'll dismiss a lot o' you idle gents!'

The same roughness showed itself in almost every form. Sometimes a fellow thought to frighten me. And in most cases they conveyed that I was idle and useless and sometimes that I was incapable. One fellow was particularly bold in this direction. He had a cart with stones on the road. So I put him to the test in his own line. I took the shovel out of the cart and asked him to stand on it. This he would not do. 'Well', I said, 'I'll stand on it and let you try and lift me.' But he could not stir me off the ground. I now got him to stand on the shovel and, to his surprise, I lifted him easily—because while I had stood at the point of the shovel and held myself upright, he stood far in towards the handle and bent over me, reducing the leverage. But he did not know that the difference between us lay in knowledge and not in physical strength. This, and my taking a big stone from the roadside and throwing it a distance which astonished him, put an end to his boasting and set a report about which won for me a measure of respect which a diploma in science would have utterly failed to secure.

Cotton was the staple industry there. But there were others such as woollen mills at Edenfield and Ramsbottom and Rochdale. And of course these industries created work for engineers and iron and brass founders. But while there was much energy put forth in these artificial industries, the land industry was in a very backward state. The husbandry was slow and wasteful and unproductive—and there was very little of it.

This, in connection with the periodical depressions of trade which threw so many out of employment, first fixed my attention on the land. On the one side were broad acres in need of workmen to turn them to account—while, on the other, were men by the thousand going about in quest of employment. I even began to write a little on the subject—mostly in reference to the desirableness of bringing the labour and the land together.

It was while witnessing the destitution of the unemployed that I made up my mind to abstain from strong drink—discerning it wrong so to spend and my fellows destitute. The foundation was not very broad. But it was a good beginning. And what was thus right on account of others was found to be right and sound in my own interest.

All the time I attempted to keep close to Bible teaching and in this connection I met with William Haigh of Huddersfield and we had meetings together to preach the gospel as it was and is worded in the New Testament. I was brought into contact with the followers of Robert Owen; so also with the Mormons who were busy there at the time. With the Owenites and with the Mormons I had some debates.[15]

On one occasion one of the Mormonites was preaching in the street in Bury. He said that he had received the power to work miracles. I asked him: was it not to enable him to prove the truth of the gospel he had received this gift. He said it was. 'Then,' I said, 'you will be able to tell us what the gospel is.' He gave his answer as to what the gospel was. But, rightly or wrongly, I satisfied the crowd that his answers were not correct. He was left in this predicament: while God had endowed him with the power to prove the truth of the gospel, He had not taught him what the gospel was!

But up comes a spruce, clerical gentleman and he attacks the poor Mormon on another point. Correctly enough, and in the words of the New Testament, he had said to the listeners that, on believing, they must repent and be baptised in the name of Jesus Christ for the remission of sins. This did not go down with the sprig of a parson and he said: 'How can that which is immaterial be affected by that which is material?'

The Mormon was not metaphysical, or perhaps learned, enough to understand the question. So I made some remark to that effect and asked the questioner if he would address his question to me. He did so and I said that I presumed him to mean that material water, in baptism, could not affect the immaterial mind of the baptised. 'Let us see,' I said. 'There is a material lamppost beside you there. If you run your head against it, it will affect your immaterial mind will it not?'

When I drew him on to scriptural ground and pressed him with the practice of the early Christians, and with the laws in which baptism and the remission of sins are spoken by the apostles, he had to drop the matter. But just on this, up comes one of the followers of Joanna Southcott—who were known at the time by their uncut beards and hair and by their green, broad-brimmed hats— and he said to me: 'You have the best of the argument. But you are both wrong!'[16]

What with these things, temperance meetings and my business, I never rested. I was led away even to Yorkshire and once or twice into Cheshire to attend meetings.

These were busy times in the political world. And although I did not go much outside the letter of the Bible, I did come in contact with the Chartists and heard some of their public men. I might have heard Feargus O'Connor— but I did not. I am now sorry I did not; for I sympathised much with him when he was assailed on every side for his attempt to plant colonies on the land in England. I never met with Ernest Jones or Bronterre O'Brien. But I took in their teaching in regard to the land and see no ground today to reject it.[17]

The Anti-Corn Law League was then in full force and I had the privilege of hearing and seeing Richard Cobden and John Bright.[18] Cobden was a fine, genial, generous, sound man. But Bright was a veritable full-blooded John Bull—and, in addition, a passionate and pugnacious man. He was also, I could see, ambitious as an orator—but at that time was so impatient with himself that he was not making the impression he deserved. The fighting element was stronger in him, I suspect, than he ever thought. He fought, of course, for cheap bread and Free Trade. And it was while doing battle with the protectionists that he won his spurs. ·

I have all along retained my first impression of the man. And that impression has been to me a key to the John Bright who allied himself with his old enemies—the Unionists and the Tories. He fought at the outset for a class, the mercantile class, against the men who would restrict trade. But he never rose above that. When Home Rule came on the platform, he ranged himself alongside the old foes of Free Trade and fought against the Irish. He was the bull. And power in the hands of the Irish was a red rag which made him lose his head.

1   Patrick Brewster of Paisley Abbey Church was a leading Scottish radical and Chartist.
2   A certificate of competency and character—signed, in Murdoch's case by two justices of

74

the peace—was needed to obtain entry to the excise. In the manner of an apprentice, the entrant was then attached to the serving officer appointed to instruct him.

3 For a list of excise ranks, see Introduction.

4 The duty was one penny per mile travelled or one shilling per horse hired.

5 This, no doubt, was Eliza Turnbull whom Murdoch refers to elsewhere as his 'old and first sweetheart'.

6 The implications of Murdoch's religious views are examined in Introduction.

7 Bianconi cars or carriages provided an Ireland-wide coach service. Their name commemorated the service's Italian originator.

8 'Which they are not now': Murdoch is referring to the well-populated Irish countryside of the period before the famine of the 1840s.

9 Ulster tenant right, or 'Ulster custom', gave tenants a semi-permanent interest in their holdings and enabled them, on leaving a holding, to sell its permanent improvements to an incomer. Its extension to other parts of Ireland was demanded regularly by reformers.

10 Episcopalian here refers to the Anglican Church of Ireland which was, at that time, Ireland's established church.

11 Daniel O'Connell, the leading Irish nationalist politician of the early nineteenth century, forced the British government to extend the franchise to Catholics. He then campaigned for the repeal of the union between Britain and Ireland.

12 Dr Rev Henry Cooke was a leading Presbyterian clergyman.

13 Father Theobald Mathew was a formidably successful temperance campaigner.

14 Tom and Jerry shop was the common designation of a cheap drinking establishment. The origins of the phrase are obscure.

15 Robert Owen was a pioneering socialist. The Mormons were extremely active in English industrial districts in the 1840s. Murdoch always remained favourably disposed to them. See, for example, *Highlander,* July 6, 1878.

16 Joanna Southcott, a Devon farmer's daughter, published *The Strange Effects of Faith* in 1801 and became the founder of a religious sect which had considerable support in Lancashire.

17 O'Connor, Jones and O'Brien were among the leaders of the Chartist movement.

18 Cobden and Bright led the campaign for the repeal of the corn laws and the introduction of free trade in food. Bright later opposed Irish home rule—hence Murdoch's dislike of him.

Smugglers, Shipwrecks and Journalism in Islay, Kintyre and Dublin 1845-1856

Murdoch returned to Islay, as a
serving excise officer, in 1845. He
was subsequently posted to Kintyre
and then to Dublin where he was
soon involved in journalism and in the
politics of Irish nationalism.

In Lancashire I was very nearly married to an attractive, nice young girl. But my mother coming spoiled that project. My mother had got into hot water with William Webster, the factor, in Islay. He wished to victimise her and to secure to himself some effects which my father had left. She lost Claggan and it was thought well that she should come and reside with me. She and Jessie and David came. And, I having a house, there was nothing—excepting the removal of two lodgers—but to let her settle down nicely there.

However, a vacancy occurring at Bridgend in Islay, I asked for the Ride and was sent there. Thus we got back to Islay in the autumn of 1845—and, after some knocking about, took up our abode in Bowmore. John MacLachlan was settled in Claggan and we could not get back there. Had we done so, it is not improbable that I should have stuck to the farm and left the excise.

From whatever cause, I must confess that I did not make that use of my time in Islay which I should have done. There was no dissipation, not even extravagance. But there was no close application to many things which should have been attended to and which are now beyond being done. Of course, it was not for many years afterwards that John Francis Campbell gave an impetus to the movement for saving folklore. Had he begun at this time, I could have rendered him immense help and saved many tales which have since been lost beyond all recovery. However, I did collect some tunes and I made a good deal of acquaintance with the people of the island in an idle sort of way.

There were some promising materials at Bowmore—such as Dr Alexander Currie, then in practice, and John Taylor, just reaching manhood. Then there was Gordon Clunas, a policeman from Helmsdale and a fine fellow. We were all radicals and drew towards each other. We read science, history, poetry, theology and politics—getting a monthly parcel of books from Glasgow by the efforts of our good friend Archibald Sinclair. After so many years, I confess that if we had divided the island between us at that time and made a point of collecting all the lore then existing, we should have done ten times the good we did.

We spent the time mostly in each other's houses—the society sweetened by the presence of young ladies of whom there were a good many in the island at the time. We had at Bridgend a little gathering at which papers were read and subjects discussed. What these subjects were, I do not remember. But I know the land question was under discussion in the autumn of 1847 when the laird of Islay failed.

One of the positions taken up by me was that all rent should go to the Crown for national purposes—or that all taxes should fall upon the land. Hector MacLean and the Rev James Ross, now retired in Inverness, were among the disputants. I have no doubt we could have worked out a good scheme of land management had we followed the discussion up. But we all had so deep a regard for the feelings of the laird and his family that we desisted—out of consideration for the blow which they had received.

The laird was now away. The trustees were in Edinburgh. And Webster was more master in the island than ever. He had not even a co-factor, as he had previously in Mr Cheyne, and he drove things pretty well as he chose. The case as between himself and the laird was remarkable in that the master went bankrupt—while the servant had nearly all the best lands in the island in his hands.

He had got himself planted in the best house in the island when he came at first. And now that things were getting into a state of dissolution he was taking farms in every direction—until I remember old Sandy Campbell and myself making up one day that he had farms which had been held by 37 substantial farmers in former times. It was observed, too, that when any men who came about could be turned to account, he encouraged them. And then, when they were no longer likely to be of service to him, he threw them aside and let them sink.

The failing of Walter Frederick Campbell came as a great blow to many a one. For all his extravagance and passionateness, he possessed all the natural elements of popularity. He was a fine looking man with a ruddy complexion and brown hair. He was strong and active, too, and took much delight in promoting manly sport. To the folly of shooting and game preservation, however, he was devoted to an excessive degree. He carried this craze so far that there was no offence so great, in his eyes, as to meddle with game and salmon.

But he also desired to promote good husbandry in the island and once, if not more, he had a professor in the country lecturing the people on the best way of using soil. It was said also that it was not so much for direct gain that he encouraged south country farmers as for the purpose of having good examples in farming set to the native tenants.

It is doubtful, however, if these farmers succeeded in making money them-selves—or in teaching others. The first of which I knew anything was Mr White, a Fifeshire tenant, who came to the excellent township of Kilchiaran.[1] First, the laird got into trouble and loss by removing the tenants, who were welldoing, before the end of their lease. Second, he laid out much money on a dwellinghouse and outhouses. Third, the tenant was laughed at by his neighbours for what he was doing and—in the course of three, or else four, years—White left, convinced that he was not fit for the place and that the neighbours were right and he was wrong. White came to Kilchiaran about 1829. And unless the present tenant, who is the first Islayman who ever got a chance of it, makes it pay, it has never paid anyone since the native tenants were removed—and he is the fifth man since then.

There is one thing clear: pay or not, the island is not now put to the purpose of keeping up a fine people such as I saw there. At one time I counted 230 families which lived and had land in the glen. In the place of these 1100 souls, I then counted just six families. So whatever may have been in the laird's mind, he did not succeed in making a large population go on increasing in numbers and prosperity.

It was while the Islay estates were in the hands of trustees that I drew up a plan for the sale of the properties. I had in view the setting up of a peasant proprietary in Islay and leaving, after all debts were paid, 20,000 acres to the late laird—of the annual value of £2000 or £3000. The population which was to be provided for then was 15,000. So I proposed that 120,000 acres out of the 140,000 should be laid out in 3000 lots averaging 28 acres—of which 12 should be arable. To make the plan more interesting, Dr William MacDonald was asked to write a historical sketch of the island. This was done. And after I left Islay in 1850 a small volume of 36 pages was printed by Archibald Sinclair and his imprint attached.

I founded my scheme for the sale of a large part of the island on the supposition that men would buy small portions and be able in time to pay the price. Feargus O'Connor proposed a similar scheme. But his clients were townsmen who had no knowledge of any kind of tillage and who had little capital to go on with. Besides these things, Feargus had nearly all the British press yelping at him and representing him as a swindler—so that many likely to have means and intelligence were restrained from joining. Otherwise, in a large population like that of England, quite enough supporters could have been drawn into the enterprise to make a limited but substantial success. But the newspaper men kept at O'Connor and he was driven mad.[2]

When I arrived in Islay, in September 1845, everything looked beautiful. But before many days were over the blight fell on the splendid crop of potatoes which promised so much. This was the year also in which the new Poor Law came into operation.[3] An attempt was made to have the Act carried out in Islay under a combination board—and Mr Dugald MacTavish, son of the Rev Mr MacTavish, Kildalton, was appointed secretary and inspector. Of course, the work was new and the inspector had no men of experience about him to help him over the difficulties of the situation. Things got into confusion.

By and bye, when a board was to be chosen, there was a struggle. As in all such cases and places, there were a few men of means and of position who meant to have the management and the patronage, such as it was, in their own hands. Somehow I was dragged into the contest—mainly, however, to try and have the right men appointed. I believe I incurred some ill-will among the monopolists by my action. And all we got on to the board was one farmer, Alexander Sinclair, Kilchoman.

Then came the weight of the potato disease. Meal and an inspector from the Relief Committee came to the island.[4] The inspector was a weak man and—he having at once fallen into the hands of the potent few—the work, the meal and the seed were largely thrown away. There was scope for the doing of much good in the way of extending tillage and in making drains on the farms held by the poorer husbandmen. But, so far as I remember, the works which would yield productive results were done for those who could afford to do them for themselves.

One of these was the bringing of water to the distillery at Bowmore. Clearly, the proprietor or the distiller should have done the work required. But I remember speaking to Mr Stewart, the parish minister, when Simpson, the Relief Committee inspector came along guarded by Webster, the factor, and James Mutter, the distiller. I just said, as they went away from the manse door: 'That poor fellow has fallen already into the hands of the thieves.' And events proved that I was correct.

In fact, the Poor Law was used much more as a terror to keep the poor from applying for relief than as a means of ameliorating their condition. In too many cases, in the Highlands, the administration was in the hands of extensive sheep farmers, factors and the like. And, instead of endeavouring to find out deserving poverty and relieving it, they rather sat in judgement on the poor and condemned them to immediate want or to perpetual pauperism.

So completely was this the case that in those regions where Gaelic is the universal language of the people their applications must all be made in English to accommodate the ignorance of their guardians. The constitution which the Poor Law has given the parochial boards renders any other class of men ineligible for the office of administrators of the relief which it affords. Heritors, or proprietors, are members *ex-officio*. No one else can be elected unless he be assessed at a certain high rate. So that everything has been done to place the working of this pauperising engine as completely as possible in the hands of those who are least likely to know anything of the actual condition of the poor and who are least liable to have any sympathy with them.

On April 27,1847, the brig *Exmouth* was wrecked on the rocks at Sanaig and her unfortunate passengers, 240 Irish emigrants, were lost. They had set out a couple of days before from Londonderry, bound for Canada. But after clearing the coast of Ireland, they encountered a storm which compelled them to put back. And, according to the testimony of the three of the crew who escaped, the pilot mistook the Rinns of Islay light for that of Tory Island. They lost their course and, before morning, the *Exmouth* was dashed against the rocks and her unfortunate cargo of living beings shared the fate of the thousands of other evicted Celts who were shipwrecked in rotten vessels to be out of the way of more highly favoured sheep and cattle.

The vessel was literally reduced to atoms—for she was an old craft fit only for the timber trade. She had, in fact, been chartered to bring a cargo of timber from Canada. But it was turning a double penny to take out a cargo of 'mere Irish'. Their passage money was paid. And although they and the ship went to destruction, the owners were no losers. And the landlord who cleared out the people thought no more about them than if they had gone quietly to rest in their beds. In Ireland they were in the great man's way. At the bottom of the sea they ceased to trouble him.

The first intimation of the catastrophe was given by those three sailors who scrambled over the rocks on which they had been cast from the mast of the vessel ere she was rent to pieces. They wandered inland and soon came upon the habitations of men by whom they were taken care of. But ere the country people reached the scene of the wreck, the vessel was beyond recognition. Not so much as would make a table held together of her. And the poor passengers were beyond the reach of aid or pity. There was nothing that could be rescued excepting the clothes of the doomed people which floated to the shore.

All that could be done was done, however. John Francis Campbell, Colin Campbell, Balinaby, and others, including myself, worked for days rescuing the bodies. These were carefully picked up and carried ashore. And I think about 160 of them were lapped up in the clothes of different kinds which were washed ashore and buried on a green slope facing the sea about half a mile to the south of where they met their death.[6]

There they rest—well on to 200 of the millions missed in the Irish census of 1851. And when the day of reckoning and of retribution comes, the loss of these people will be laid at the door of the supporters of the British feudal land system. And these supporters, coronetted and gartered though they may be, will be arraigned at the bar of justice for the murder of these poor Irish men, women and children.

The same year there was a trip to Portrush and I went across— visiting the scenes of my previous abodes. I was told in Derry that the emigrants in question were the remnants of previously emigrated families from about Limavady. But although I came through that district, and made inquiry, I could not hear of anyone belonging to the unfortunate people. In fact, it was with the Irish in those years: 'Anywhere, anywhere out of our own country.' I found the greatest changes. The potato disease had worked a great revolution.

The people had lost their little holdings and consolidation of farms had closed over them.

I petitioned to be allowed to remain another year on Islay but I had to remove under the old general removals to Campbeltown in Argyll—taking mother, Jessie and David with me.[7] There we stayed until I had the residence shifted to Muasdale some 14 or more miles up the Largieside. I never took to Campbeltown. But I soon became acquainted with the more advancing young men of the place. There were some debates carried on in an informal way. And when there was any literary work to be done in the town I generally had a hand in it.

The *Inverness Advertiser* was then in its early vigour and I wrote paragraphs to it and sometimes more ambitious papers. The *Advertiser* was a Free Church organ. But it also took up something of the attitude of the *Northern Ensign* and did noble work in the cause of justice and mercy.[8] In Campbeltown itself there was a *Journal* conducted by Willie Clark who was a student and expecting to be licensed by the Established Church. But he also printed, sold books and did some daguerreotyping to help himself, wife and bairns on the way. He was a shifty, scheming little creature. But he having the paper, we were so far disposed to make use of each other.

For the *Campbeltown Journal* I wrote a long series of papers on Islay.[9] Had Willie not been advised to avoid treading on the toes of Webster, the factor, I most likely would have made a pretty complete thing of what I was then writing. The plan was to begin at the north end of the island and write what I could about each place as I went southward. Getting down to Daill, I was noting the expansions of the factor. But someone whom he met on the steamer suggested to Clark that it would be impolitic for him to do anything which Webster would not like—as the factor might give estate advertisements and possibly printing. So Clark held over the copy he had of mine and I never wrote more for him.

However, there started up a monthly *Argyleshire Herald* and I wrote eleven articles under the general heading of 'Highland Destitution'—a subject which was attracting attention after the potato failure and at a time when expatriation was on the brains of leading, or rather misleading, men. H S Paterson was editor. After both of us left, the *Herald* became weekly and subsists as such to this day. Now there is a *Courier* also which, I think, does the Tory side of the business—the *Herald* being a mild Liberal. So far as I have found, they are both opposed to any great advance on the land question. And when I have been in Campbeltown on a lecturing visit, they have lent their aid to the enemies of the people.

Although I had a part of the town to survey, my excise duties were mostly in the country. One of the first duties which devolved upon me out of the ordinary routine was to try and execute a warrant against Angus Robb, Achapharick, for smuggling—he having been detected shortly before my coming to the station.

For twelve months, I think, we were making attempts to apprehend him. But warnings reached him of our approach long before we could reach him. On one occasion, Neil MacCallum, cuttersman, who was my assistant, came on Angus while I was away. But he would not come for Neil and, when coercion was tried, Angus appeared with an apronful of stones and Neil had to give up the attempt before I got on the scene at all. It was late in the day that Neil gave me his report. However, I determined upon bringing the tedious business to an end.

So I went away to Ayr by the steamer and remained on the mainland for a week—returning by the north end of Kintyre. I landed at Tarbert about 1 pm and walked south. By the time I reached Tayinloan it was dusk—the month being April. And I did not get to Achapharick until 11 at night.

I tried Angus's door. But it would not open. And, after a while, I got afraid he might be getting out of a window on the other side. However, a run round the house settled that fear and I tried the door again. After some time it gave way and I was inside speedily. I put my head into a bed—and found I was apprehending the man's sister.

'Where is Angus,' I said.

'He is not at home.'

However, I made a quick march into another apartment and I found my lad there in bed—with a good fire in the middle of the floor.

'Well,' I said, 'I have found you at last.'

'Oh yes, and if you had let me know you wanted me, I'd have come to you at any time.'

'It does not matter. It will do now.'

'But I am not well. I am not fit to travel.'

'I am sorry you are not well. But I am not in a hurry and can wait.'

'You need not wait. You dare not take me out of this.'

'It is all right. I will wait as long as you stay. We are not going to part any more till I am done of you.'

So I sat and got warm at the fire. And I needed it—for it was a cold night. Angus and I had a word now and again; he pleading the one time and defying the other; I all the time as untroubled as a man sitting comfortably, at a good fire, has reason to be.

After some time spent in this diplomacy, Angus called to his sister to get his clothes ready. And, this being arranged, I asked her to go to John Macsporran, the farmer, for the use of a horse and cart to take us to Campbeltown. When we were ready, however, Angus himself thought how cold it would be sitting in a cart and proposed that we should walk. And out we set for a walk of 17 miles.

After walking for some distance, and we becoming chatty, he said: 'I rather than fifty pounds that you came by yourself. I would not have gone with MacCallum and I alive.'

About five next morning we arrived at Campbeltown and went for some breakfast to my mother—as the prison would not be ready until six. I sent for Neil, thinking that he could manage the rest of the business and that I might go to bed. But ere I was halfway stripped, Neil and Angus were at each other like cat and dog and I saw it would not do to trust them together in the street—that all my stratagem would be in danger of being in vain. So I dressed, let Neil go home and handed Angus over to the jailer without any more ado.

I then drew up a petition to the Board of Inland Revenue on Angus's behalf and got his friends to have it put in form and signed. In about three months Angus was a free man and his name out of my books.

There was another man near Barr whose apprehension became incumbent upon me. On my telling him that I wanted him, he pleaded not to be taken that day. It would be very inconvenient for him—as he was on the point of having his crop secured. This itself was against any grace being extended to him. I might have insisted on selling him out, reducing him to pauperism and, if the penalty was not covered by the proceeds, imprisoning him as well.

But I always aimed at letting even smugglers have a good chance of making a new beginning. And I did not wish to injure him by the loss of a day at housing time if I could safely avoid doing so. I just scrutinised the man to see whether or not he was to be trusted and then I said: 'I will trust you. But if you fail me I will be revenged on Kintyre—for I will not trust another after you.'

'Well,' he said, 'I will be down with you tomorrow at half past eleven o'clock.' And, at the minute, the poor man came, with a high step and a low, past the window.

The awkwardness of having the smuggling in the parish of Killean and Kilcalmonell kept under by men living in Campbeltown was, after strong representations by myself, admitted at Somerset House; and the residence of my station was appointed to be at Muasdale.[10] To that little place James Stewart and Neil MacCallum and I were removed in due time—we getting a small house there which we conducted on shipboard principles. This reduced the toil and the expense and it made us masters of the situation.

We had an easy life at Muasdale. I found that I had time saved from the company I met with in Campbeltown. I think I read more during the six months we were there than I had done during the previous six years. I many a time afterwards regretted that I had not remained. I could have read so much and become fitted for greater usefulness.

It was during my stay in Kintyre that my sister Jessie—who was one of the most lovable girls living and beautiful at the same time—went to the house of old Alexander Cowan to teach his third family to speak and read Gaelic. With them she went to Airds in Appin. By and bye, she was awarded a school at Penicuik. Then my mother went to her.

But at Muasdale things went on very pleasantly—with walks across the hill to the east side, northward to Clachan and southward to Barr and Bellochantuy. Smuggling could not show its head.

Neil MacCallum, though not an abstainer, disliked tippling. He was afraid that a Mr Langlands who lived near would be a drinking intruder. And he was deeply concerned over the manner of preventing such an infliction. On the return of James and myself one day, Neil, who had stayed at home, met us rubbing his hands and his eyes sparkling with glee.

'I have disposed of Langlands,' said he.

'How did you manage that?'

'Well, Mr Langlands came to see how we were getting on and I could not but show him some hospitality. I bustled about to get him a dram. But when I made the proposal, he said: "No, no, I never drink before midday." "Dear me," I said, "what a pity;, for I never drink in the afternoon and so we can never have a taste together."'

Neil was one of the most solemn looking men, with a thin, swarthy face and great command of visage. He was rich in jokes and anecdotes. He and a girl in a farmhouse were being coupled for sweethearts. 'No,' said Neil, 'we are both so thin and hard that our legs would ring together like the poker and the tongs.'

James Stewart was co-cuttersman with me. James was a decent, sensible man who should have had a commission but for red-tapery. He knew the country and the people well and could enjoy himself in a neighbourly way among them. Sometimes he was left in the house while Neil and I went on survey. Neil was housekeeper—like the steward of a ship. But very frequently, when we came home, he found fault with James.

'I might as well have a cow in the house as him,' he would say. And he would put off his coat and proceed to remove dust and smuts which James had allowed to rest on the few articles of furniture. 'I do believe,' Neil used to say, 'he was out the whole time gossiping with the women. He knows everyone. I believe he knows the very hens.'

While in Campbeltown I tried, through my friend John Anderson, collector, to get to the Somerset House laboratory. But I did not succeed. I had a strong desire to know chemistry and this would have been just to my purpose. However, I picked up scraps of science. And hearing that a vacancy was to occur in the Dublin First Ride, I applied in pursuance of my oft-repeated desire to get to a seat of learning. At the beginning of March 1853, I left to take up my abode once more in Ireland.

I got into Dublin North Wall early in the morning. I had never been in the capital before. However, I soon found myself at home. I found James Craddock, whom I was to succeed, and he did all he could to put me into the way of getting on—and most kindly warned me against plausible persons with whom I was likely to come in contact.

The Industrial Exhibition in Dublin was in hand and causing some stir. I had not seen the London one of 1851 and I do not suppose that Dublin could at all compete with that. But it was a splendid spectacle and was also most instructive. It was on the occasion of their visit to open the Exhibition that I saw the Queen and the Prince Consort and the Prince of Wales. I saw them all three very well without any effort to gain a sight. The Prince of Wales was only in his teens, I think, and a good enough looking lad. Prince Albert was a fine, manly-looking man—more so that the engravings of him suggest. The Queen had nothing queenly about her that I saw. She had an inflamed-looking face and did not look at all amiable.

But what chiefly attracted me to Dublin was the plenitude of its educational institutions. I do not mean schools in the ordinary sense. These were institutions where, during spare hours, one had access to classes, lectures and museums.

The Royal Dublin Society had meetings for the discussion of scientific and industrial subjects. Courses on various subjects were given by competent men. I attended a course on drawing and one on anatomy in connection with art—all free. Professor Sullivan lectured at certain hours at the Museum of Irish Industry in which all materials and finished products were to be seen.[11] I attended when I could.

Then there was the Royal Irish Academy with its libraries and antiquities—including numerous volumes of Irish manuscripts. There I was introduced to Eugene O'Curry, the famous Gaelic scholar, and to the still more learned Dr O'Donovan.[12] I had the good fortune to attend some of O'Curry's lectures in the Catholic University—then under the presidency of Dr, later Cardinal, Newman. No one knew so much of Gaelic manuscripts as O'Curry—although he was a very plain, country-looking man. His mother, he told me, was a regular repository of Gaelic lore.

Eugene O'Curry was then on the Ordnance Survey—as was Dr O'Donovan. In this way both had rare opportunities of extending their knowledge of their country and of making the Ordnance Survey more correct. Professor O'Curry was a Clare man. Dr O'Donovan was from the County of Kilkenny. Anthony O'Curry, a brother of the professor, was in the library of the Chamber of Commerce. He, too, was a good Gaelic scholar and wrote Gaelic beautifully.

The Royal Hibernian Academy was for the promotion of art. There were also several medical schools. And just as I arrived in Dublin, the Chemical Society was being formed—having for its object the affording to young men of opportunities of following their chemical studies in the laboratory. A very young man, Charles A Cameron, was the professor.[13] I joined at once and did my share of the work of establishing it.

By and bye, the Chemical Society started, very properly, an agricultural department and I prepared and read the first paper—on the application of chemistry to husbandry. It was in this department that the society achieved its greatest success. Seeds, articles of food and manures began to come within its scope—and the value of the skill thus brought to bear on the ingredients used in farming was not long in asserting itself.

The agricultural department grew; and our professor grew along with it until he became known in different parts of the country as an agricultural chemist. I should say a little about the man himself. In the first place, he was the son of a Highland father and an Irish mother. When I knew him, his mother only was living—and an enthusiastic Highlander she was. He had no grand appearance. But he was, as proved, a keen observer and his memory was unfailing. His powers of discrimination and of discerning colours were to me a positive wonder. Then his command of figures and proportions—as shown by his grouping of the constituents of different substances—was an equal amazement. He seemed to have no trouble picking up details. And his retention of them was all that could be desired.

What he knew Charles Cameron could impart with the greatest facility. At the same time, he had no pretension to any of the elements of oratory beyond the ordinary powers of speech and understanding. At the time I knew him he spoke in the flattest of Dublin accents. And any time I have seen and heard him since, he has exhibited no improvement—although he has mixed with the best of speakers largely for many years.

After some time the *Agricultural Review* was started and issued monthly, Charles Cameron and Thomas Baldwin, teacher of agriculture at Glasnevin, being chief contributors—I making some contributions and passing their's through my hands. This led to a weekly *Agricultural Review and Country Gentleman's Newspaper*. For this I wrote a good deal and revised more. I think I may safely say that, besides supplying articles for other columns of the paper, I wrote nine of the leading articles. But Dr Cameron was responsible editor.

A particular department of mine was the weekly summary of parliamentary and other news. Whatever of news, of statistics or of science passed through my hands was made to enforce a social requirement—so that, while information was always furnished and everything given in a clear and intelligible style and as often as it could be in a pleasing form of words, all was made use of as far as possible to enforce the claims of justice and humanity.

Another thing which I never forgot was that we were in Ireland and writing to promote the good, not of a class, but of a nation—so that the country gentlemen whom we supplied with pabulum had their better feelings toward Ireland kept as much awake as I could manage. And I have no doubt they have been the better of the gentle infusion of right feeling which was conveyed in the *Agricultural Review*.

Among the contributions to the *Review* was a series of articles under the heading, 'The Hardships of the Horse'. They appeared under the name of a Captain de Vere and at first they contained information and incident. But the poor fellow needed whatever they yielded in money and he went on spinning them out. One of the consequences was that I had often to insert backbone and to rewite a good deal of them. Under the general heading, I got a tribute inserted to the little black mare at Claggan—written as if by herself. This was the most readable of the series, I am conceited enough to think.

The use of sewerage as manure was one of the subjects to which I endeavoured to call the attention of the municipality and the surrounding farmers.[14] The sewerage was much in the way in the city and it was doing serious injury to the health of the inhabitants. On the other hand, it was much needed on the land. The aim was to have the value of the article made clear to the farmers. I pointed out spots to which, for example, the sewerage of Mountjoy Prison could go by gravitation. An acre here, half an acre there, luxuriating in the fertility produced by the sewerage would be a practical lesson not easily resisted. Gardens producing two or three, or perhaps four, successive crops in the year would have set the farmers who passed out and in to think how they could get such quantities of sewerage in the town as they could carry home in carts when returning after selling their produce—as the farmers of Flanders and even clayey Holland do.

I did my share in trying to get the peat industry into the public mind—writing and speaking on the subject. Of course, in Ireland, as in Scotland, there are great stretches of peat mosses. And at a time when coal was at a high price, there was good prospect of turning them to account. For a time, the manufacture of paraffin was carried on at Athy and the business seemed to prosper. But somehow it did not in Lewis, Dumfries and elsewhere. It came to an end and the plant lay about for years as mere wreck. In Ireland this industry may yet be revived under a native government.

Another stroke of mine on the *Review* was the report on the Royal Agricultural Society's show at Leeds. As it turned out, I wrote the best and most original report of the affair that appeared in any newspaper. Having been in Leeds a few times, while resident in Lancashire, I was able to put in more local touches.

It would have been very convenient for me to keep to the Chemical Society and the *Review*. But my engagements were getting multitudinous. I was attending lectures and even the medical classes as well as taking my share of the temperance work in Dublin. And then, early in 1858, I also got entangled in the salary agitation in the excise.

In this connection, I did a good deal of writing in the *Civil Service Gazette*—

no outsider knowing who did it. And the movement was going on satisfactorily until a meeting of the excise in Dublin was called for the purpose of pressing the government for an answer to what they meant to do towards redress of the excise grievances. This was a false step and should not have been taken. Up to this time, everything in the movement was initiated and pushed on by William Lavender, a division officer in the city. He was ready and forward. And, being in favour with the Collector, he got all the pupils to instruct. So at meetings he had his young followers who swelled the vote in favour of his motions. Ultimately, the wiser men in the department withdrew and he had his own way.

On the day of the proposed meeting, I had a talk with these wiser men—John Wilkinson, Francis Moon, Robert East and Thomas Drinkwater. We agreed not to mix in a matter which we could not mend. Mr Moon, however, walked with me all the way across the city to Dorset Street. And at the last moment he and I agreed that the thing was so dangerous that it should be attempted to be prevented. He was to hasten back and gather the others and I would follow as soon as I could.

The position was this. I had been doing what I could to enlighten the public on the questions affecting the excise and wished to have a proper statement prepared and put into the hands of Members of Parliament, editors and others—so that when the matter came before them they would understand and help. If Lavender's question were put, we would be checkmated. If the answer was favourable, our further preparations would be uncalled for and would be discouraged. If the answer was adverse, then our agitation, if persisted in, would place us at issue with the Treasury and the Board of Inland Revenue.

The men met, Lavender told us what he meant to do. Let us go on assuming that the Treasury and the Board are not against us, we argued, and as soon as we have prepared the public the government willl be glad to meet our demands. But Lavender persisted in putting his motion. There was nothing for it but to run the risk of a division. I moved a direct negative and the negative had it—to the astonishment of Lavender and to the rousing of the anger of his pupils. Various devices were tried to set the vote of majority aside. But none of them succeeded. The next thing was to appoint a committee to draw up a 'Statement of the Claims of the Officers of Excise to an Increase in Salary'. Meantime, we had deputations appointed to wait upon such Members of Parliament as were to be found in Dublin.

What we soon found to have been a great mistake was made in appointing the committee. To keep him out of mischief, we made Lavender honorary secretary—it being understood that I would do the work. It would have taken a number of men to stop the honorary secretary from continually thwarting our efforts, however. He even went and stopped the printing so that the statement I had prepared should, if possible, be prevented from getting into the hands of the public. However, it got out and got into circulation. And before the year was out, the greatest draft ever made on the Treasury was made for behoof of the claimants.

I should mention here that, as far as my championship went, the aim was to improve the position of the staff concurrently with increasing the efficiency of the service—and with increasing, too, the smoothness with which business could be done with all who yielded revenue. There was one improvement which took place, as I may say, unconsciously. The whole body of the service was improved in tone and character by a movement which implied that the men were intelligent and responsible—for, unless their character was upheld by themselves, their claims to amelioration would not have all the force intended.

Just before I left Dublin in 1861, a movement was started to get up a testimonial to me. And shortly after my settlement in Waterford, there came a beautiful silver tea service and a very flattering address—not, however, without Lavender putting in his claim to the compliment. I was, of course, proud and grateful for the present—more especially as it was valued much by my wife who had suffered a good deal of neglect and some privations. While I was busy working for others, she had many heavy hours with very little of my company; and, even when I was at home, my head was often down in a very unsociable manner.

Although so busy with the excise, I was kept hard at work outside. I took part at an early date, I think 1853, in the affairs of the Celtic Union which was intended to revive the spirit of the race. The O'Gorman Mahon, Charles Gavan Duffy, Dr Hare, Kilkenny, Cashel Hoey and Professor Sullivan, after-wards president of Queen's College, Cork, were among the personages I remember. Yes, W M Hennessey was one of the active spirits and perhaps the only one who matured as a Celtic scholar. He is in the Public Record Office, Dublin.[15]

It was about the same time that I was introduced to Maurice O'Connor Leyne of the staff of *The Nation*. Charles Gavan Duffy was MP for New Ross and I did not see much of him. Leyne went away to edit *The Tipperary Leader* and soon died. Duffy went off to Australia and A M Sullivan came to take his place on *The Nation*.[16]

One might almost say that the figurehead of *The Nation* at this time was George Piggott, a remarkably well made block of a man. He was as much the sign of the paper as ever a wooden Highlander was of a snuff shop. He was large and respectable. He came at a certain hour, or rather at a well-known minute, of the morning—and as regularly went away in the evening. At every point along his line of march, from Lower Affrey Street to Portland Street, North Circular Road, the inhabitants might swear the hour and minute of the morning, or of the evening, when they saw him pass.

In no other way was Mr Piggott of *The Nation*. He was the head cashier. But beyond that sordid office he had nothing in common with the rest of the staff. If a bit of literary matter did fall into his hands, it was instantly shaken out as if he had by mistake taken in a spurious coin. This was the father of the unfortunate Richard Piggott.[17] I do not know how it happened that I did not know even the appearance of Dirty Dick, as he was called. All the same, I knew him as a treacherous fellow. He had a special spite at A M Sullivan and never lost an opportunity of attacking him—mostly under cover.

I became intimate with A M Sullivan and wrote a great deal for *The Nation*—leading articles, reviews, letters and so forth which would make volumes. This went on while I also wrote for the *Agricultural Review*. There was one class of article which served for these two papers with a little padding and pointing. These were founded on the hitherto neglected statistics served up to the public at great labour in the *Agricultural Returns*.[18] Having ascertained how they were got up and having assured myself that they were fairly reliable,

I began to examine them and to make use of what they contained to show the public how the husbandry of the country prospered.

Every now and again I worked out a point and gave the figures from the *Returns*. I gave the figures as pointedly as I could in *The Nation*. But in the *Review* they were rounded off and the pace of the retrogression suggested gently to the country gentlemen whose newspaper it was. It came out that while Lord Carlisle was singing and speaking to assure the world that Ireland was making the most remarkable progress in husbandry, her land was rapidly going out of tillage and that which was cultivated was falling off in fertility.[19] Five years compared with five preceding showed a decrease—as did 10 years compared with 10. The counties which showed the greatest emigration showed the greatest decline in fertility. And still greater was the decline where most public money had been expended on 'improvements'. These things were established by means of facts which could not be set aside unless the *Returns* themselves were discarded.

In September 1856, I began a series of letters to *The Nation* under the caption 'The Land for the People' and continued them as such until I had free access to the leading columns.[20] I took things as I found them. Repeal had failed. Young Ireland was prostrate. Republicanism was defunct. And there was no hope of anything being won by the Tenant Rights League. I showed the respects in which the three countries of Ireland, Scotland and England suffered in common and I urged that they should work as if the cause was a common one.

The land question was, I always held, *the* question for the Irish people to solve. And I confess that so much was my sympathy with the Irish as a nation that I found it easy to write and to speak for the people. I discussed almost every phase of the land question and I think I did a little towards priming public opinion on the subject. One thing I know was done: the Irish were made acquainted with many things in Scotland previously unknown to them. And I may say that the signature of Finlagan, over which I wrote, came to be well known and respected. This was proved when, some time later, I began to write on the Sutherland clearances for *The Mark Lane Express*.[21] All my letters were copied into *The Nation* and thence a good many of them were reproduced in the provincial papers.

1   The full story of the Kilchiaran clearance is told in Chapter 5.
2   For Murdoch's land scheme and his view of O'Connor, the Chartist leader, see Introduction.
3   The Poor Law Amendment (Scotland) Act, 1845, established the local boards referred to by Murdoch.
4   For an account of the potato famine in the Highlands, see Hunter, *Crofting Community*, 50–72.
5   Timber ships were notorious hulks. They carried emigrants in very bad conditions on what would otherwise have been profitless westward passages.
6   A poem about the loss of the *Exmouth*, reputedly written by one of the survivors, was published in *The Oban Times* in February 1958. For a copy of the relevant cutting, I am indebted to Mr Gilbert Clark, Port Charlotte, Islay.
7   Until 1857 every excise officer below the rank of supervisor was posted to a new station every four years—to mitigate the risk of corruption.
8   The *Northern Ensign*, published in Wick, took a strong anti-landlord line during the clearances of the famine period.
9   These articles are referred to in the Introduction—as are those from the *Argyleshire Herald* mentioned below.
10   Somerset House was the London headquarters of the excise service.

11 William Kirby Sullivan, a professor of chemistry, was the museum's director.

12 See Introduction.

13 See Introduction.

14 This was a topic to which Murdoch returned in *The Highlander*.

15 James Patrick O'Gorman Mahon was an Irish MP and adventurer. Duffy had founded *The Nation*. John Cashel Hoey was one of the paper's sub-editors. William M Hennessey, an Irish scholar, was also on the staff of *The Nation*. The Celtic Union mentioned by Murdoch may have been the Ossianic Society founded in Dublin in 1853 to publish traditional Gaelic material.

16 For Sullivan, see Introduction.

17 Richard Piggott forged the letters which *The Times* published in 1887 in an attempt to implicate Charles Stewart Parnell in nationalist terrorism. Parnell was eventually vindicated. *The Times* was discredited. Piggott committed suicide.

18 These government-collected agricultural statistics were first produced for Ireland in the 1850s and for Great Britain in 1866.

19 George William Frederick, Earl of Carlisle, was Lord Lieutenant of Ireland in the late 1850s and early 1860s. There was a general switch from tillage to pasture in Ireland in the post-famine period.

20 Selections from these articles are reproduced in Chapter 4.

21 *The Mark Lane Express* was a farming weekly published in London. Murdoch's articles on the clearances appeared between October 1859 and January 1860.

The Land for the People
1856

In a series of articles published in *The Nation* in late 1856 and early 1857, and here much abridged, Murdoch argued the case for a joint Irish, Scottish and English campaign for land reform. The series, under the general heading of 'The Land for the People,' was also intended to inform Irish readers about events in Scotland where the Highland clearances were continuing and where there was, at the time, some evidence of a resurgence of national feeling.

Most English and Scotch, and very many Irishmen, think that Ireland ought to settle down and become, as quickly as possible, an assimilated province of England. This I should be sorry to see—sorry to find the people of Ireland consenting to be anything but Irish or surrendering one fragment of what of their nationality misfortune has left them to cherish. Better expatriation itself; better a dispersion as wide and lasting as that of the Jews than that a nation, founded by God and stamped with features of its own, should allow itself to be thus swallowed up by another. But how is Ireland to maintain what remains to her, or to recover what she has lost, of her nationality? Repeal has failed. Young Ireland is prostrate. Republicanism is as defunct in Ireland as in France. And what of Tenants' Right—even after the uphill struggle of seven or eight years?[1] Is there any hope in the world of that right being secured by the present course of procedure? I see none; although I see no reason why it should not be carried triumphantly and in a very short time.

But why is 'failure' thus written in every one of these enterprises? The great reason, of course, is that you have not a sufficient number of courageous and independent people to create, sustain and command a noble band of representatives in every place in which representation is required—whether that be in or out of parliament. But why are not the people in sufficient numbers thus heroic and independent? They have natural feelings and wants which bind them: family and property, wives and children, houses and land. They are only ordinary mortals who may eat, drink, clothe and house; for all of which they are, in the present state of the law, dependent on the goodwill of landlords having opposite political leanings.

The people may be nationally inclined. They may wish and pray for the independence of their country as ardently as for their daily bread. But when we know that, in the great majority of cases, the bread must be sacrificed in the struggle which must precede the realisation of their sentiments, what are we to expect but that the sentiments should fade away before the stern necessities of the body? A few heroic men will be found to act otherwise—especially if sustained by a steady conviction of the consonance of such a course with their religious duties. But the Irish nation is not made up of such materials. And the religious, or at least the ecclesiastical, sanction which would sustain them is, to say the least, divided against itself. A great proportion of those whose approval they would consider the highest sanction which their acts could have frown upon their patriotic efforts and paralyse the arm which would strike the effective blow for liberty.[2]

We may, then, say that everything national fails because the people are so much in the power of the landlords who, being of the lawmaking class, make and maintain laws to keep the people in their power. This is the vicious circle which girdles the devoted people of Ireland. In one sentence: the people, being in the power of the the landlords, groan under anti-national laws, and anti-national laws keep the people in the power of the landlords. Ireland seems thus in a deadlock—kept so by a kind of self-acting double political machine. And the great question is how the balance of this machine is to be upset.

How is this to be accomplished? Certainly not by the representatives of a small portion of the Irish people going to the British parliament with a 'mere Irish' question. It is absurd to think of accomplishing anything by such means under such circumstances. A very small proportion of Irish members, unsupported by a unanimous and manly pressure from without, contending with the great mass of Irish, Scotch and English legislators! The hope is absurd.

You want a greater amount of popular force in this direction than you have as yet been able to bring into action. Now where is this force to be found? Not at home. You must look elsewhere for it; and we have seen that, as yet, elsewhere is not the British legislature in which we may say that the people of one country contend with the landlord power of three.

This British legislature—composed of, or at least represented chiefly by, the class of men in England and Scotland from whose grasp we want to set our people free—is, in fact, as alien to the people of Great Britain as to the people of Ireland. Certain circumstances have helped to modify the effects of their doings in England in such a manner as to divert the attention of the world, in some measure, from the courses which have been in operation. But it requires no great penetration or research to enable us to see that the people of England and Scotland are in a great measure as much the victims of inquitous land laws as the people of Ireland. The great mass of the rural population of England—all the bombast about 'merry England' notwithstanding—have the mark of the heel of the landlord oppressor on their forehead, and in their inmost soul, as deep and deadly as it is in Ireland. The sullen, stupid patience with which the Saxon boor bears it is only the stronger proof of how oppression has done the work of degradation; and not, as some would have us suppose, a negative evidence of the comparative absence of grounds of complaint.

To those who have looked into the working of these iniquitous land laws in England, it is well known how they drive the ejected country population to compete with their brethren in the towns for employment in factories, foundries and other scenes of urban overtoil, underpay and moral degradation—although it is equally well known that they yearn for their patrimony, the land, with an instinct as unerring as it is just and salutary. The latter is evidenced in the many land societies which the manufacturing population support with their little savings—cherishing a hope that, with patience and perseverance, they may one day have a spot of their own on which, like Adam, they may earn their bread with more legitimate labour than that of the unwholesome and demoralising factory. The avidity with which poor Feargus O'Connor's Land Scheme was seized upon by the people, like drowning men throwing themselves on a raft, is another illustration of how they feel their position and of the direction in which they look for relief.[3] They want to go back to the land from which they and their fathers were driven by grasping landlords and their co-labourers in the work of adding 'field to field'.

In Scotland the same system of oppression is at work. It may almost be said that in the Lowlands the work of depopulation is complete. The land is now in the hands of extensive farmers and what of the people remain are eking out a brutal existence as mere day labourers. In some of the Lothians the men who actually do the agricultural labour, which there commands the admiration of the world, live in what are called bothies—cooking their own food, doing up their own dismal habitations and likewise not being allowed to marry or have about them, to cumber the ground of their lords and masters, wife, mother or child.[4] Nothing is cherished in these men but brute force. The British land system has attained to maturity there and reduced men to the level of a machine—without feelings, privileges or rights, interests, hopes or fears—for which the lords of the soil care one hundredth part so much as for the comfort of an ox.

Following the introduction of the same vandalising system into the Highlands, Sutherland may be said to be one vast sheep walk—the miserable remains of the original inhabitants being condemned to patches of ground which were not considered good enough for the more highly favoured sheep. And a recent writer in *The Times*, who had travelled through Braemar, says that 'along the course of the Dee and its tributaries there stretches for a length of fifty miles a range of deer forest nearly unbroken on the south side of the river and often diverging from it to spread far on the north. If anyone penetrates these tracts of old primeval firs, brushwood and ranges of granite hills he will hardly find a scene more impressive and yet more melancholy; for over this enormous tract, in glens once busy with hamlets, not a house is to be seen but the smart lodges of a few gamekeepers.'[5]

I need not tell you how this state of things was brought about. I need not state the particulars of the wholesale evictions under Sellars, Loch and other agents of Sutherland cruelty—of which one man says: 'I ascended a height about eleven o'clock at night and counted 250 blazing houses, many of the owners of which were my relations'.[6] This was in 1816. Last month, and even last week, the columns of the patriotic *Northern Ensign* were occupied with some of the details of similar doings in the year of grace 1856 and by the agents of the very Duchess of Sutherland who matronised Mrs Stowe, the advocate of negro liberty.[7] I need not detail the horrid particulars of the Barra clearings a few years ago under Colonel Gordon; or the more refined doings in the same line in Mull and Tiree by the agents of the clever, intelligent and popular little Duke of Argyll of the present day, the son-in-law of the aforesaid Duchess of Sutherland.[8] It is enough to know that in England and in Scotland the people suffer under the present feudal land laws and they exhibit pretty strong signs of their being willing to make a desperate effort to rectify their relationship to the soil.

This supplies a cord which stretches across the three kingdoms and which in England, Ireland and Scotland will yield the same harmonious response when touched by a judicious hand—a response whose notes will be strong, loud and long enough to drown, for the time being, the clamorous voices of rival ecclesiastics and hush the warcry of brothers kept alien by traders in the bodies and souls of men. Strike this cord and you will call forth a voice to which legislators dare not turn a deaf ear. I care not whether the people who make the demand are enfranchised or not. The *united people* of these three kingdoms can *command* the Lords and Commons. There, then, is the popular force which is required to upset the unjust balance of power of which I complained—the force of the people of England and Scotland ready to be added to that of Ireland.

I am not altogether ignorant of the seeming obstacles which stand in the way of such a union. I am well aware of the so-called religious animosity which has been kept up between the people on each side of the channel. But although churches have, unfortunately, been more or less engaged in the war of creeds which has raged so long, I refuse to accept the term 'religious hatred'. There is no such thing as religious hatred. Religion is love and I am confident that the slightest knowledge of the principles of the Gospel will satisfy any honest man that such a war never could have a really religious origin. If this melancholy antagonism had a positively religious origin, we should naturally expect to find the subsequently contending parties at peace when both worshipped at the same altar; and history would date the commencement of hostilities at the period of the Anglo-Protestant Reformation. Before that period, however, we find the same spirit of war at work and producing exactly the same results; modified, of course, by different circumstances and manifested under different pretexts. The Anglo-Norman barons who had crushed their South British co-religionists, and taken possession of their land, attempted to do the same thing in Ireland. In thus tracing the so-called religious animosity to its source, we see that the real original dispute is not between the British people and the Irish but between the *class* of Anglo-Norman landlords on the one hand and the *people* of the three kingdoms on the other.

However, we must not ignore the actual antagonism which does undoubtedly exist between the people of England and the people of Ireland. No small measure of this feeling is excited in the Irish breast by the fact of the feudal laws and their authors and agents having come originally from England. Of this I have in some measure disposed already in showing that the feudal system has victimised the English as well as the Irish people; and that, instead of its being a bone of contention, it ought to be a bond of union.

Antagonism is stimulated in England, however, by the numbers of Irish who crowd the labour market. The ignorant multitude there feel agrieved, of course, by the 'Hirish' taking the wages out of their hands and beating them, in many cases, out of their own field.[9] But even here we must make a distinction. It is only the labourer who is agrieved here. What does the employer care for this! Nay, the employer has latterly *complained* that the Irish have not been so numerous in the English labour market and that he has had to pay so much higher wages. But even the competing labourer can easily be shown how the law, which keeps him from owning a clod of English land, compels the Irishman to pass over to England for money which he is to pay as rent to, perhaps, an English lord in order that he might have his cabin for his wife and children at home—if poor Paddy is not in the still worse predicament of having been crowbarred out and been condemned by feudal laws to be a vagabond on the face of God's earth and to seek employment in the land of inhospitable strangers.

It will take but few facts to show that the self-same laws drive the Englishman and the Irishman thus into competition in the English and other labour markets; and that the former has a direct personal interest in the equitable settlement of even the 'Hirish' land question. In this way John Bull's stomach can easily be touched; and once that organ is fairly reached, ethnology and theology may both go to the dogs for anything he cares. In short, we see that the irritation to which we refer is traceable to the land laws which drive the downtrodden people to seek employment from others when they ought to be working for themselves on the land which God gave them; and that it is to the removal of the feudal system which we must look for the removal of those hostilities which have been unjustly ascribed to blood and creed.

But while I would thus endeavour to smooth the path to union between the British and Irish people, it is to Scotland that I would turn for the first link in the golden chain which we hope yet to see adorning a united people. There we find, in the glens and on the hillsides of ancient Albyn, a people among whom the feudal system has made just about the same destructive progress as it has done in Ireland. Still cherishing their language—studded with gems of traditions, proverbs and poetry—they live in an atmosphere charged with those ideas and feelings of freedom and brotherly love which once had their embodiment in their patriarchal institutions. In the light of these, they not only feel the cruelty of which they are the victims but they can understand the wrong which prepared the way for it. So that thus, besides speaking the same language and having the same Celtic blood in their veins as the Irish, they can at once see eye to eye with their fellow-sufferers here. They not only feel and understand the wrong which the present system imposes upon them; they have a positive idea of a genial system under which, even in darker times, their forefathers lived in plenty, security and independence. Falling back thus on their ancient rights as clansmen, their minds are prepared to impeach those who at present aspire to the dignity of chiefs and who claim the substantial privileges of feudal lords for usurping what neither the sword of the conqueror nor the will of the people ever conferred upon them—the absolute ownership of the soil.[10]

Relying on this oneness of race, of language and of traditional right, as well as of present pressing wrong, let the erstwhile separated Celtic brothers meet with *ceud mille failte* on the broad ground of *the land*.[11] Let it be their high privilege, as it is their duty, to erect the standard around which the whole British people of whatever race, creed or name shall yet rally for the purpose of casting off forever the accursed feudal yoke which has bound them as slaves to the care of the Anglo-Norman oppressor. From the plains of Erin and from the Highlands of Caledonia, the stern cry for justice will soon be heard and will readily meet with a suitable response from the toiling serfs of Saxondom. And what was wrested from the English by means of the sword, and from the Irish and Scottish Celt by falsehood and fraud, will thus be won back by means of an enlightened public opinion.

Under the land laws established in England by conquest and transplanted into Scotland by fraud, the property and power of the country are being concentrated in the hands of the one absorbing, monopolising class of landlords. The estates and farms get larger and larger, and the country is depopulated, all to the same end of aggrandising this class. By this arrangement rents are drawn in thousands, instead of in driblets of units and tens, of pounds. And the enterprising farmers who are thus necessarily ousted are thrown themselves into the market to become the tools of the same glorious fraternity—as land agents and stewards and so forth—to screw every possible penny out of the land and people of England and Ireland.[12] And the economic philosophy of the day affords it a place in its records, as one of the provisions of a wise Providence, that those educated in the high farming schools of Lowland agriculture in Scotland are thus sent out to discipline the Saxon boor and lazy Irish in that approved system by which the earth and its fullness are made to serve the purposes of their lords and masters.

And when we add to these things the Highlands being laid out as sheep walks, deer forests and grouse moors, the grand end of the existence of Scotland and its people is accomplished. The land, the skills, the industry and the capital of Scotland all exist for the honour and gratification of this one landlord fraternity. And as *The Times* has so forcibly told the Scottish people in its recent article on the Wallace Testimonial Movement, and on many other occasions, they have their reward: the highest offices, civil, commercial and industrial, are open to them, even in England, if they can show that in them they will serve the same grand purpose of their existence, that of serving their Anglo-Norman superiors.[13] When thus exercised, the steadiness, the perseverance and integrity of the Scottish character are commendable virtues. But when these traits exhibit themselves in any other interest they are foibles to be sneered at. And if shown in securing their own or their country's rights and interests, they are propensities to be instantly checked; and those who show them are so many miscreants to be duly punished for daring to think that they are anything else than the lower extremities of the English body politic.

Nor can I say that this contemptuous treatment is altogether unmerited by an important section of the people of Scotland. They have brought it on themselves. They have shown their sympathies to be much more with the English in power than with their own countrymen north of the Forth. Besides rendering themselves directly subservient to what are called English interests, they have lent a steady hand to bring under the same yoke the more national and independent Celtic inhabitants of the Highlands who, in times past, never allowed the common country to fall prey for any length of time to the invaders.

Little wonder, then, that when they show a disposition to be anything else than useful appendages to this monstrous English corporation, they should be snubbed for their unwonted temerity; particularly when, after ages of the tamest submission, one of their first exhibitions of national life and feeling should be one calculated to call forth recollections, feelings and distinctions which they had long laboured to bury in the depths of oblivion. The movement which is to serve as a prop to the declining tree of Scottish nationality is to commemorate a victory gained 500 years ago over the English. And in the wisdom of some of the moving spirits it is to be a 'bronze lion looking defiance at England'—at the country and power which they have been hugging to their bosoms and enriching with their industry for so many generations.

In view of such antecedents, and of their reputed long-headedness, one would scarcely expect to find them giving such a tone and direction to their occasional attempts to play at nationality. One would expect almost any manifestation of spirit rather than one calling forth feelings of hostility between themselves and their nearest and dearest neighbour. For dear as well as near must that neighbour have been during the many years of cordial co-operation which have passed since the war torch was extinguished in the Tweed. And if so, why, on a mere occasion of stretching the national body, should old war cries be revived and a molten image of Scotland be cast to frown at and threaten this long sworn friend?

Perhaps, if well looked into, it will be found that there is a serious cause, though a badly understood one, at the bottom of this seemingly erratic movement. Do the movers begin to feel that the bargain with England was a partial and a one-sided one? That it was only a bargain between the heads of the Anglo-Norman power on both sides of the Tweed—in which the people had little heart and less interest? That it was an arrangement by which the people of both countries could be made the more perfect slaves of the one ruling class? Possibly some such idea, ill-defined but pressing as in a nightmare, haunts them and makes them, in the resulting excitement, call upon one another to rise and shake a bronze fist in John Bull's face.

Where, then, and how, does England interfere with Scottish nationality that it should be expedient to show this defiant front? In what way has Scotland been put into the train to subside into a mere province? And how is this denationalising progress to be checked and the country preserved in its integrity and character? Those who have entered with me into the question of The Land for the People are prepared to look to our land laws for these things. Everyone who knows anything on the subject knows that the feudal laws derived by Scotland from its connection with England have, in the first place, produced their denationalising effects by depriving the great mass of the Scottish people of their native soil; thus depriving them of all rational interest in anything proper to their country. When, instead of looking to their own country as their home, their wealth and their pride, they can be told with truth that their greatest interest lies in developing the industrial resources of England, where their efforts will be better rewarded than on their native soil, with what show of reason can they be asked to cherish anything more than a mere visionary sentiment of nationality—a sentiment which may derive some support from the past but in the stern and sad realities of the present can find nothing on which to subsist? The nation does not belong to the people; and why should they cherish the feeling of nationality?

The laws in question not only deprive the people of the land, they set up positive denationalising institutions in the country. What are the demesnes of the landed gentry in Scotland generally but so many Anglo-Norman centres of denationalising effluences? If there be many of these gentry who are not themselves members of the great body of the landocracy of England, there are very few indeed who do not ambition to be such and who do not aim at being classed as belonging to it. This is not in any measure invalidated by the fact that the English nobility often look with contempt on those who thus ape them.

Every demesne, every estate, every one of these alienating institutions has its staff of underlings, all basking in the light which issues from the master who himself derives all his lustre from his connection with the great body whose centre may be said to be in London. From the land agent downwards, these underlings are generally recommended by some adaptability to English demands and their tenure of office, of course, depends on the success with which they smoothe down all local asperities to an alien taste and cast everything around them in the mould of the presiding genius. This is the sphere of flunkeyism proper. But it does not exactly terminate here. If all these, even if they happen in any proportion to be Scotch, have to live, move and have their being as if they were only the menial parts of an Anglo-Norman institution, so also have the outer circles of tenants and labourers to do the same thing in a somewhat mitigated degree. They must, more or less, endeavour to forget their country, its interests and peculiarities; and endeavour to please the landlord in order that he may let them live.

Nor does the flunkeyism terminate even here. It has made its way into the Established Church of Scotland to such a degrading and polluting degree that, generally speaking, the clergy of that once national and honoured body are found co-operating with those who are depopulating and denationalising the country. They have their stipend secured to them by the same law which has deprived the people of the land; that stipend is increased as the price of the people's food rises and is paid them, I may say, in the land agent's office. They are thus, in their degenerate days, embarked not with the people as at Bothwell Bridge and Drumclog, but in the same boat with the denationalising landlords.[14]

In such a state of things, how could nationality exist? And as long as they are in operation what could restore it? The usual exhibition of it is an occasional Braemar gathering for the amusement of those who look on genuine Scots in kilts as an interesting curiosity and, perhaps, for the edification of such as would keep up the ancient Highland spirit and people as a military nursery for England—but nothing higher. The Queen, too, by dressing in tartan and turning out her boys 'in the garb of old Gaul' has done something to make such exhibitions fashionable on holiday occasions.[15] Alas, it is all but making that honoured garb the livery of flunkeys instead of the means of preserving the spirit which was wont to animate the ancient wearers thereof. And how far will a Wallace testimonial go to remedy the evil may be guessed from the absurdity and futility of attempting to preserve, by such means, the spirit of nationality after the people have ceased to own the nation.

Indeed one of the very movers in the matter of the Wallace Monument, Sheriff Logan, who seems to be a good and honest Scot though of an anti-national order, gives two reasons for his enthusiasm in the cause. The one is that he was born on the very land where Bruce won the crown of Scotland. The other is that he owns that land. Give the mass of the people the same kind of interest in their native soil and their national spirit will require no column to lean upon. Make Logans of them, in that respect, and they will themselves be a national movement.

Such also would be the most appropriate testimonial to Wallace. He led the people of Scotland to fight against 'Edward's power, chains and slavery'. But it is well known that that power consisted in no small measure of the Scottish nobility who looked with anything but favour on a movement so popular and led by one whom they regarded as so nearly of the people. A couple of centuries before Wallace's day, the feudal system had been introduced into Scotland by Anglo-Saxon offshoots. As, however, it had not exactly the edge of the sword to help it on, it had not completely prostrated the people—although it had rendered the nobility little better than the facile tools of the king of feudalised England. Wallace was not the champion of an aristocratic Scotland, but of the cause of the people—for the liberty of whose persons and land he fought exactly against that power and that interest with which the present friends of Scotch nationality have to contend. Accordingly, if he fell a prey to Edward's cruelty, he was also the victim of the treachery of his own—so called noble—countrymen. And I feel perfectly sure that the oneness of the ancient and modern enemies of Scottish nationality will be found exemplified in the kind and extent of support which the Wallace movement will derive from the magnates of the land.

The land of Scotland, then, being in the hands of an alien power, and the people being merely suffered to exist on it in the capacity of 'hewers of wood and drawers of water' for the benefit of their lords and masters, anything approaching to nationality is a mere fiction. There is scarcely anything of the kind in existence—or to be expected. Those, then, who would have the national character of Scotland developed, and its spirit manifested, have a plain duty to discharge to themselves and their country before their ideal Caledonia can ever come into tangible existence. Simply as such nationalists they are bound to join those who have undertaken the humane duty of restoring to the people a legal recognition of their right to their native soil. Give the people the nation and they will be national! Otherwise it is only in a few poetical minds that the idea will be preserved—just as any other fancy can be cherished by mere intellectual means. Nationality clinging like ivy to a Wallace Monument, or fostered like an exotic by any other similar contrivance, may be very interesting to lovers of the curious. But growing with an independent people in a free soil all over the country it will be a reality seen by all men and estimated in its cause and consequences as a real blessing.

But all the popular force which can be raised in Scotland is not adequate to the task of placing the national cause on such a sure basis. The isolated people of Scotland have to contend with the landed power of England, Ireland and Scotland—which is the one Anglo-Norman interest. But what is thus true of the people of Scotland is equally true of the Irish and English people who also are the victims of the same system. They are thus, as I have demonstrated, made one in interest—and, therefore, one in duty—in reference to this matter. The only course open for either is to unite with the other in laying thus not merely the foundation of Scottish but also of Irish and English nationality. I feel confident that the people of England are ready to enter into the compact. The Irish are on the point of extending a brotherly hand. Are the Scottish nationalists equally liberal to forgive and forget ancient sores and to rally around the standard of the British people to accomplish a work necessary to their very existence?

1   Daniel O'Connell's campaign for the repeal of the Act of Union had petered out in the 1840s. Revolutionary nationalism of the Young Ireland or republican variety had been crushed, for the time being, in 1848. The Tenants' Rights movement had failed to acquire the momentum needed to bring about land reform.
2   Here Murdoch touches on that perennial Irish dilemma, the conflict between the Catholic church and the more aggressive varieties of Irish nationalism.
3   For O'Connor's land scheme, see Introduction.
4   Bothies were the crudely-built houses or sheds provided by farmers for their unmarried labourers.
5   The writer in question was John Stuart Blackie with whom Murdoch was later to be closely associated.
6   The writer quoted here was Donald MacLeod, the Sutherland stone mason whose pamphlets and letters on the Sutherland clearances, published under the title of *Gloomy Memories*, remain a valuable source of information about these events.
7   The *Northern Ensign* was a Wick newspaper. Harriet Beecher Stowe, author of *Uncle Tom's Cabin*, published a controversial defence of the Sutherland family.
8   For details of evictions in Barra, Mull, Tiree and elsewhere, see Hunter, *Crofting Community*, 73–78.
9   Murdoch here refers to the practice of using cheap Irish labour to undercut wage rates in Great Britain.
10   For a more detailed account of Murdoch's views on this topic, see Introduction.
11   *Ceud mille failte*: a traditional Gaelic greeting; literally, a hundred thousand welcomes.
12   Murdoch here refers to the 'Scotch' land agents and farm managers who were a feature of nineteenth century rural life in both England and Ireland.
13   The movement to provide Scotland with a memorial to Wallace and to the Scottish independence struggle of the years around 1300 drew a fiery attack from *The Times* on December 4, 1856. Wallace, said the paper, was 'the merest myth'. Scotland, it added, was 'manifestly a country in want of a grievance'.
14   Bothwell Bridge and Drumclog were battles fought by the Covenanters in the 1670s. the landowning influence of the Church of Scotland was one of the reasons for the formation,

in 1843, of the breakaway Free Church of Scotland. For Murdoch's views of the relationship between Scottish ministers and lairds, see Introduction.

15 Queen Victoria acquired Balmoral, in Aberdeenshire, in the early 1850s and embarked on a royal cult of kilts and tartan.

An Islay Clearance
1859

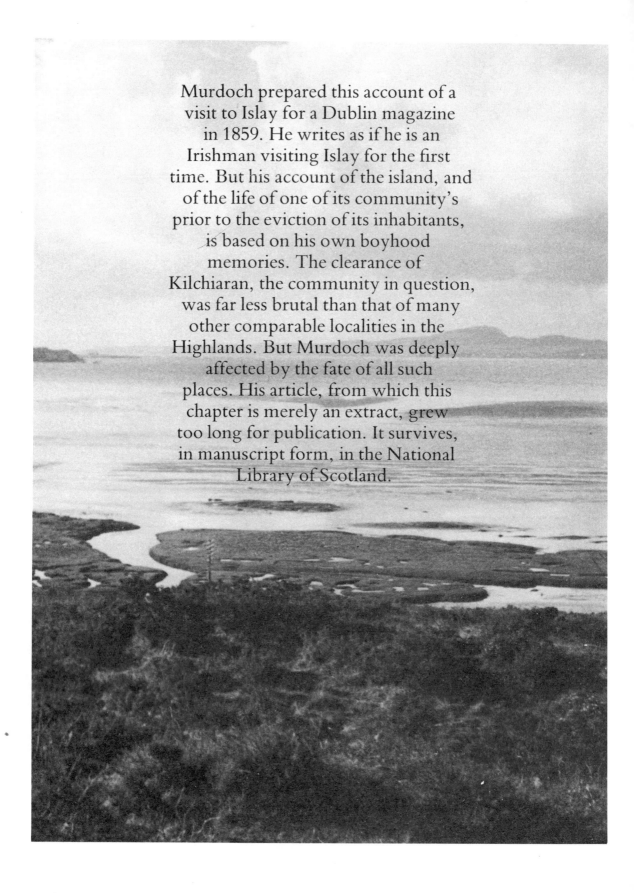

Murdoch prepared this account of a
visit to Islay for a Dublin magazine
in 1859. He writes as if he is an
Irishman visiting Islay for the first
time. But his account of the island, and
of the life of one of its community's
prior to the eviction of its inhabitants,
is based on his own boyhood
memories. The clearance of
Kilchiaran, the community in question,
was far less brutal than that of many
other comparable localities in the
Highlands. But Murdoch was deeply
affected by the fate of all such
places. His article, from which this
chapter is merely an extract, grew
too long for publication. It survives,
in manuscript form, in the National
Library of Scotland.

With all the improvements which have taken place of late years in travelling accommodation, we have become worse, instead of better, acquainted with some of our old friends and neighbours. In the time which we call 'olden', when the clans of Albyn and Innisfail spoke a dialect of the Celtic language which was perfectly and easily intelligible on either coast, the Irish Channel was a ready means of communication at many points where it is now a water of separation.[1] Even down to a couple of generations back, for instance, from Londonderry, from Moville, from Cushendall, from Ballycastle and so forth, on the coast of Ireland, there was constant communication with Islay and Kintyre. And to this day, on the Scottish side of the channel, there are abundant evidences of this intercourse to be seen even in some of the breeds of livestock which bear unmistakeable marks of their Irish descent. Not only so; but after all that emigration has done, both there and here, cousins, second-cousins and so forth—the offspring of alliances formed by the two peoples in the said intercourse—can be traced in Donegal, in Islay, Gigha and Kintyre; although personally they are totally unknown to each other and although political and sectarian ill-feeling is a thousand times stronger between them than it was between their progenitors of a so-called darker age.

With the application of science to the development of improved means of travelling, both by land and sea, we are well pleased. And it is most agreeable to us to witness the efforts now making to develop these still further. But we cannot turn our back completely on the past, nor banish from our mind the somewhat pleasurable ideas with which we associate many of the things of which the present progress seems to be more or less destructive. It was with feelings akin to these that we last summer availed ourselves of improved modern means of travel to visit, by one of the old routes, some of the scenes which we have indicated as being so much more familiar to our forefathers than they are now to us.

For a couple of seasons past the steamer *Islay* has called at Portrush and at Port Ellen, on the coast of Islay, on her way between Oban and Glasgow—thus re-establishing by steam one at least of the old lines of communication between the now partially estranged Scottish and Irish Celts. The *Islay* is a good boat and keeps her visits with as perfect regularity as can be expected from a vessel performing so long a voyage, having such difficult navigation and making so many calls as she is bound to make. Our course from Portrush was north-east and our destination Port Ellen at which we disembarked, leaving the *Islay* to pursue her course northward by Jura, Mull, Morvern and Ardnamurchan for the new key to the Highlands, the rising and beautiful port of Oban.

The chief visible support of Port Ellen would seem to be a distillery which is carried on there by one of the present proprietors of the island. The support of the place is no doubt considerably augmented by the traffic occasioned by the calling of the steamer, the chief of this traffic being with four other distilleries in the neighbourhood. Indeed, it may be said that Islay's chief manufacture and most famous product is whisky—Islay whisky being about as well known as Dublin stout.

In this small island there are at present no fewer than nine or 10 distilleries busily engaged in the manufacture of the mountain dew for the delectation and refreshment of the thirsty Saxons of the Lowlands and of England. A few years ago there were even more, perhaps as many as 15 in all. But the smaller of them have been gradually allowed to fall into decay and there, as in other places, although the taste seems to be in favour of the product of the smaller still, it is only the larger concern which can be worked at a profit. In this respect, as well as in many others, Islay is but a miniature of Ireland.

This island, now so celebrated for its whisky, was once still more so as being the residence of the Lords of the Isles.[2] In all times it has occupied a distinguished place in the estimation of those who have any eye for the beautiful and the useful—and by such it has been denominated the Queen of the Hebrides. And there can be no doubt of its title to this appellation. The climate is mild and humid, as that of Ireland; and although much of the surface is under heather, there is also much very excellent land resting upon a rocky basis of limestone. Black cattle of a very superior description are reared there. Sheep in considerable numbers, too, crop the heather. And for potatoes, oats and barley it is, like the neighbouring little island of Gigha, justly renowned. Altogether it is an island which, under rational management, would support a population of forty thousand souls much better than it does ten thousand. But Islay also has experienced the curse of depopulation which has passed over Ireland.

Remnants of fences there are where there is nothing to be guarded but heather. Rushes and heather have once more overrun the land which was evidently at one time under cultivation. Snipe and sheep now hold almost undisputed possession of what at no very distant period supported whole tribes of men. Here, too, the rage for large farms has done its work. The natives have been turned out.

Kilchoman, as is remarked in Scotland of all the 'kills', consists of the best land in the island.[3] Indeed it is celebrated, with two others, as the best land in the county. Kilchoman in Islay, Kildalloig in Kintyre and Kiloran in Colonsay were pronounced by ancient wisdom as the three best farms in Argyleshire. And tradition has preserved this proof of the sharp eye which the saints, who had the selecting of these locations, had for the good land.

Not only is Kilchoman surrounded immediately by good land under cultivation, but it is backed by an almost unlimited extent of reclaimable bog and mountain with quiet little sheltered and secluded rich spots here and there—as if designed by a wise providence to form the centres from which the operations of reclamation should spread along the glens and over the mountains. These bogs and mountainsides want draining. But that is easily done as there is always a good fall for the water. The mere bog is defective as a soil. But within sight there are actual mountains of shell sand waiting to be conveyed but a very short distance to supply the most of the mineral constituents wanting to make the vegetable bog a productive soil. And there is seaweed rolling in before the prevailing south-westerly winds to keep up the fertility thus obtained.

And not only is there this wide and promising field of labour; there is a willing population to enter upon it if only permitted. But a false economy stands in the way. The people are kept poor, the land waste; and from the community generally is withheld the wealth which this land and this labour are capable of yielding. Nor is Kilchoman at all peculiar in this respect. After exploring many miles in Islay we can declare, from the marks of cultivation with which we met, that in times past nature was taken at her word in this matter and beginnings were made to bring the wastes into subjection to the will and wellbeing of man.

In some places we found the ruins of the humble husbandman's cottage; in others there remained nothing to tell where a human habitation had been but the nettle; whilst ridges, and even fences, could in many places be discerned far away in the interior of wild regions now left to the undisputed dominion of heather and wildfowl. The now prevalent notion that it is only by a system of high and large farming that the most can be made of the soil, and another notion in pursuance of which men are banished to make a solitude for game, have in too many instances in Scotland interfered with the obvious designs of nature. And, as a great and melancholy result, we find the land in a state of wild unproductiveness while the people who ought to be cultivating it are wanderers in strange lands.

Instead of pursuing a south-eastern course from Kilchoman, we turned westward, by a road which crosses the Rinns of Islay diagonally, and made our way towards another of these spots favoured alike by nature and by man— and thus selected by the primitive missionaries as camps for themselves, places of worship for their followers and resting places for the dead. This was Kilchiaran. Here we found a very snug looking farmhouse situated on the bosom of a fertile slope facing the western ocean and curving towards the head of a deep gullet in the rocks below.

On every side there were to be found rich fields, some extending a considerable distance into the interior where they were surrounded by the heathy moorland. About a stone's throw from the dwellinghouse was a suit of outhouses for the accommodation of the stock of an extensive and well laid-out farm. And a little further off still was an old thatched and soot stained house bearing every mark of belonging to another age and another order of things. The old and the new stood side by side in a goodly place where, one would suppose, either could well have thrived. And yet there was no sign of that animation and that prosperity which one is apt to associate with an improved modern Scotch farm steading. The old had lost the life which had at one time pertained to it. And it was hard to say whether the new had ever possessed any life or not. The fine, large farm of Kilchiaran was, in short, without a tenant. And one could imagine the old, begrimed and condemned house of the peasant farmer, who held possession there before the new house was dreamt of, taking to itself some consolation from seeing the more imposing edifice provided for the favoured Saxon now forsaken and yielding to the dissolving elements.

This old house is the only one now remaining of the homes of 25 families which, about 30 years ago, lived on this one farm or townland of Kilchiaran.[4] Of these families, six were those of regular farmers who held the land from the proprietor—the rest being cottiers who had houses, and enjoyed certain privileges, from the chief tenants. And as the constitution of this little community is identical with thousands of others in the Highlands, all of which are now passing away, it may be as well to convey some idea of its elements and arrangements.

The arable land was divided and fenced off into six portions on three sides of the cluster of houses in which the inhabitants were congregated. The fourth side was on the rocks which overhung the ocean. Beyond the bounds of these enclosed farms lay a wide expanse of unreclaimed upland. This formed a common from which young cattle and sheep were able to take a very consider-able amount of their sustenance during more than nine months of the year—some of them, in fact, never being taken home at all from the time of their being let out as year-olds until they were gathered in to be sent, as sturdy, long haired and noble horned West Highland oxen, or heifers, to the great tryst at Falkirk.[5] Of the sheep, the principal portion remained out all the year round also—a few dozen only being allowed to accompany the milch cows on the lea of the home farm and to enjoy the shelter of the house at night. The working horses enjoyed somewhat better care still. But their growing offspring were, as a rule, trained in hardship by being allowed the range of the hill.

The crops may be stated in the rotation in which they prevailed, not only there but elsewhere: oats, sown in the newly broken lea and used chiefly in the form of porridge and cakes by the farmer's household and partly given as a dainty to horses whilst ploughing or engaged in any other regular and hard work; potatoes, manured from the farmyard and from the shore where seaweed and shell sand were to be had in abundance; barley, generally convert-ible into the amount of the rent. Here again oats came into the rotation after which the land was allowed to lie over for a season or two under what nutrient grass and other herbiage it could produce without sown seed. And as the weeding was not attended to with that care befitting the countrymen of Sir John Sinclair, the loss in white crop was in some measure compensated by the natural sowing of grass seed and by the thick sward which soon covered the resting soil.[6] This, with a little flax, completed the variety of crops.

At this time few had attempted the raising of wheat, rye-grass or turnips; and, on the whole, the system of husbandry was far from being what would meet with a commendation from an agriculture committee of the Highland Society.[7] Still, these men lived comfortably; brought up large families in plenty; exercised generous Highland hospitality towards all comers; paid their rents regularly and well and could have found a whole year's rent in advance without selling a head of stock or a sack of grain for the purpose. Every one of them had more than that amount to his credit in the bank at Inveraray.

If they did not pursue a very productive system of farming, neither did they lead a very expensive life. Their means were always above their wants; and, without pinching themselves or making any extra effort at production or economy, they always had wherewith to meet the necessities of a friend in need—and that friend never need have any hesitation in asking for the required aid.

It may be as well to understand a little more fully how a community like this managed to live so well and in such independence—the more especially as we find that, under the order of things which is now coming into operation, the majority of farmers have, to say the least, a pretty hard struggle to make ends meet.

We have already seen that they had their rent paid out of the produce of their barley. Thus the land was safe under their feet and the roof secure over their heads. They had plenty of meal, potatoes, milk, butter, cheese, beef, mutton, eggs, bacon and fowl—all the produce of their own farms—and fish for the catching from the shelves of rock below. Their clothing also was chiefly of home manufacture and the material the produce of the farm. They grew their own flax and steeped, bruised, scutched and even heckled it at home.[8]

Their wives, daughters and servants spun it into thread during the long winter evenings. And a rustic weaver made it into linen, into sheeting, into sacking—or all three according to the requirements of the case. All the wool they required, and something over, grew on their own sheep. That also was washed, carded and spun at home and sent to a neighbouring weaver to be made into cloth of hodden grey, blue plaiding or whatever pattern the gude-wife desired for the comfort and adornment of her household.

It is not necessary to go into particulars for the purpose of showing how, by the exercise of a little taste or skill in mixing and dying, a great variety of useful and even elegant, or at least becoming, articles of both male and female attire could be, and actually was, produced out of these two raw materials, wool and flax—and the greater proportion of the manufacture, too, without the intervention of the circulating medium at all.[9] The weaver was well paid in meal, mutton or beef as in money—and a few days of a horse and cart to draw home his turf, or peat, was to him better than he could procure for any money which his labour would fetch in a regular labour market. The tailor was equally well paid in a similar manner. Indeed, if he insisted upon being paid in cash, it might prove a greater inconvenience to himself than to anyone else; for, besides other considerations, in receiving payment in kind the measure was sure to be 'heaped up and running over'. What came of the bounty of God was given with the liberality which that bounty inspires.

The good old family feeling which naturally existed in active operation among the clans was itself in these days, and in such communities, better than so-called material wealth nowadays. Co-operation enabled them to overcome difficulties and to accomplish ends which the isolated, though extensive, Saxon or Saxonised farmer can only manage at very considerable outlay of money—not always to be had, even by him, in abundance.

At Kilchiaran when the day fixed for the cutting of any man's turf was announced—which generally happened at the time of slack after a good deal of the seed was in the ground—it was not a muster of miserable, unemployed labourers in search of work which was witnessed. All the able-bodied men in the community, and others from neighbouring hamlets, came with their implements to the scene of operations—the principal battalion of them, in all probability, headed by a piper. The work was regarded as a pleasant contribution of good neighbourhood and a day's amusement. Nor, in the midst of this co-operation, was the spirit of competition wanting. There was a happy union of what are now, in improved society, regarded as incompatible principles. While this lighthearted body worked as one for the party whose turf was being cut, there was ample scope for competition among the members as to who should do most and best. At a word, too, the scene of labour was turned into that of sport and the instruments of industry were thrown aside in order that the best leaper, the best runner, the best thrower of the stone might be made manifest on the spot—while work and sport were duly relieved by sallies of wit and staves of song both old and new.

The turf cut, home they hied to the house for which they had thus provided a year's fuel, to be entertained at supper and to conclude the day's 'foregathering' with a dance, the neighbouring damsels being duly invited to participate in the same. In this way the fuel of the little community was, in one, two or three weeks, all cut and the jingle of money perhaps never heard in connection with so important a matter as providing for the cold of a Caledonian winter.

The family feeling came into operation in supplying many other wants, both regular and occasional. One of these was the fulling of the homemade cloth at a time when mills for the purpose were not so numerous as they are now. For this work it was the women who assembled. They were seated in two rows facing each other so as to form opposing pairs. The cloth, properly moistened, was laid along a board on which the two rows of feet met. To a lively description of song, these feet, to the number of a score or more, pounded away at the *clo*.[10] The popularity of this custom may be inferred from the number and prevalence of these 'waulking songs' in the Highlands— to the list of which there is scarce a bard but has made additions.

In this way these simply communities were fed, clothed and warmed. And yet the amount of money used in the whole year by the large family of a comfortable farmer was not equal to what a poor, degraded bothy servant in the Lothians now receives. But who would think of comparing this wretched, hardened outcast, this brutalised creation of a heartless economy, with these old-fashioned farmers? And yet we cannot overlook the fact that the comparison is made and that men have the hardihood to say that it is better for the community at large, and better even for the peasants themselves, to be compelled to give up their lands, their cattle, their homes, their everything and go to be the servants of men who will make more of the land! As we shall see by and bye, Kilchiaran was reduced to the operation of this 'economy'. And with what result we shall see also.

But in describing the old economy of this Highland hamlet we have not yet descended to the sphere of the 19 cottier families who took shelter under the wings of the six farmers. Those who look at this little community through the glass of so-called economic science will see nothing but different degrees of beggary, thieving and starvation. Not so, however, will it be seen by those who know something of what existed even in some of the remote parts of Ireland not many generations back.

The cotts of these cottiers had in some cases been built by the farmers— in others by the occupiers themselves with the permission of those on whose ground they stood. But by whomsoever built, they had never cost anyone much of what he could not well spend. A day of a few men quarried the stones required for one of these houses and this labour was cheerfully given for the asking. Those who had carts lent them and the stones were soon on the spot where they were required. With the assistance of all the hands willing to work in such a case, and with a mason to give a word of direction here and there, the walls were soon erected. And in a week, or two at most, the house was roofed, thatched, floored, inhabited and 'warmed'—no one being the poorer but everyone the richer by the addition of a family to the community and by the increase of goodwill which this co-operation produced among its members.

Whether the house was built by the farmer or by the cottier, the latter was always under obligation to the former and that obligation was rendered most frequently in the form of so much labour in harvest and spring. But it was not for the bare house, or for the ground upon which the house stood, that the cottier was under this obligation. There was grass for a cow and perhaps for a few sheep. There was a ridge in which to sow a certain quantity of flax seed. And the farmer was always glad to give potato ground in return for the benefit of the manure which the cottier would collect for the purpose.

So even in this lower grade absolute want was not by any means to be met with. They had all the potatoes they required. And even if the cow failed to supply them with milk for a part of the year, a child had but to run down to the rocks with a line and catch the fish for dinner while the potatoes were boiling. For clothing, their little stock of flax and wool was available. And it was hard indeed if, during the year, they did not earn more than enough meal to supply them with cakes and porridge. In a great many cases, even these cottiers grew a little corn of their own.

In all such places there was always room for industry to obtain its reward. To a cottier it was an immediate advantage to be allowed to reclaim a bit of ground on the margin of the moor. The first year, by the application of what he could scrape together of seaweed and other manure, he was able to raise an extra quantity of potatoes; the second year he reaped his crop of corn; and in the third the land thus reclaimed was taken in as part of the arable land of the farmer.

This, in fact, is the way in which tens of thousands of acres in the Highlands have been brought into cultivation and in which, in very many instances, cottiers crept by degrees into farms of their own. Instead, for instance, of selling the calf when it was a year-old, they managed to get grass for it until it attained to maturity. So also with a lot of sheep. And then when a small farm was to be let, the poor man, with a little assistance readily rendered, was established. And from all we could gather of what was done, and of what might have been done had the people of Kilchiaran been allowed to pursue their own quiet way, even under additional rent, the arable farm would have expanded to six times its present size and, instead of merely a caretaker and two or three poor labourers, it would be supporting a comfortable, independent and happy population of at least 250 souls.

But by false and foolish counsel the proprietor was induced to break up this prosperous little community.[11] A Fifeshire farmer, supposed to be wealthy, came to the country to look for a farm. Kilchiaran was the one he coveted. The landlord, desirous of introducing the light of Lowland farming among his people, agreed to let the stranger have the land—even before the expiration of the leases by which the natives held it. He offered these natives farms elsewhere—an offer which some accepted. But whether they accepted or not, they were all turned out and dispersed and the Fifeshire man installed— not exactly in their place but in the new house and steading which were prepared for him.

Some of the old tenants went to law with the landlord and were ruined. Some went to America. One man, whom we met on our tour, is a miserable pauper in the country. And one, in his extremity, stole a few turnips from a field belonging to the proprietor, was imprisoned for the felony and died of disgrace and a broken heart. As a natural consequence, the humble cottiers were scattered to the four winds of heaven. And not one stone remains upon another to tell where their cosy hearths once blazed—excepting what we saw in the one old sooty house of which mention has already been made.

But although these poor people were thus made to suffer, and a local wrong perpetrated, it will no doubt be said now, as it was then, that the change was one of those rendered necessary by the progress of society—and could not fail to be productive of good to the community at large. Saxon energy, skill and capital were to have greatly increased the produce of the farm. Thus an immediate addition was to have been made to the nation's stock of food. An example of good husbandry was to be set to all who saw, or heard of, what was doing by the Lowland gentleman. General improvement was to be spread and increasing rents would flow into the exchequer of the proprietor.

That it was with a view to some remote good of this kind that the wrong was done cannot be doubted—for, at the outset, the new tenant paid no advance of rent. On the contrary, he paid nearly a third less than his predecessors were prepared to pay under new leases which were to have commenced in three years. And the costly dwelling and outhouses were all built at the expense of the landlord. So that, by all accounts, there was an immediate loss on the transaction, independently of the lawsuit and other matters with the outgoing tenants, of something little short of two thousand pounds.

And yet all this money was thrown away. No sooner did the man from Fife take possession, with his new stock and implements, than he set about laying out the land according to his own Lowland notions. But instead of exciting the veneration of his neighbours, who were to have learned improved methods of husbandry from him, he but provoked their ridicule and supplied them with new arguments against innovation. As a school of agriculture, the new Kilchiaran was a failure. The surrounding people knew the capabilities of the soil. They knew what would ripen in the climate and also what could be disposed of at a profit in the market. All this knowledge they saw utterly disregarded and condemned—and a system, found serviceable on the east coast, stupidly attempted to be carried out on the west.

Even as a private speculation, the failure was just as complete. The prognostications of the natives proved true. The Lowland farmer could not take a living for his one single self and his few servants out of what had so well supported the scores which preceded him. In three or four years he threw the farm, the new house and the costly steading on the landlord's hands and left the place forever.

A curse seems to have hung over it ever since. It is now more than 30 years since the deed of wrong was perpetrated. And from that day to this, no one—landlord or tenant—has been able to make anything of it. One or two Lowland tenants have since made an attempt to turn the place to account—but with even worse results than those which attended the first man's essay and with still additional losses to the landlord who, not to speak of the increased rent which he might naturally have expected, lost all the capital which he sank in the new buildings.

But these results surprised no one who was at all imbued with the spirit of the ancient polity of the native Celtic people. The power of the landlord was unjustly exercised to gratify the covetousness of the stranger. Both sowed iniquity and they reaped simply the fruit of their own doings. In short, the case of Kilchiaran is but one among thousands which can be quoted by the thoughtful Highlander to show that it is not only wrong to take the land from under another man's feet, but that the wrong cannot be perpetrated without bringing its own visible punishment.

1   Albyn and Innisfail are poetic names for Scotland and Ireland.
2   See Introduction.

3　Kilchoman is in the westernmost part of Islay. The prefix *Kil* in any placename indicates the presence, in any early Christian times, of the cell or church of a Celtic monk.

4　Kilchiaran, like other Highland townships before the clearances, had a number of tenants and a larger number of subtenants. Murdoch says there were six tenants in the 1820s. A rental of 1817 indicates that there were then nine. I am indebted for this information to Gilbert Clark, Port Charlotte. The distinctive circular steading built in the 1820s, when Kilchiaran was cleared, still survives.

5　Falkirk was the scene, each autumn, of the sales at which Highland cattle were marketed to southern dealers and farmers.

6　Sinclair was a Caithness landowner and noted agricultural improver of the period around 1800.

7　The Highland and Agricultural Society was founded in Edinburgh in 1784 and was concerned primarily with agricultural improvement.

8　These are technical terms for the various processes concerned with the production of linen.

9　The circulating medium, money.

10　*Clo*, cloth.

11　The proprietor was Walter Frederick Campbell.

Ireland, London and Shetland
1853-1866

Murdoch's autobiography resumes.
After a further period in Dublin and
other parts of Ireland, he was
promoted and posted eventually to
Shetland. There he maintained his
involvement in journalism and this
chapter contains selections from his
newspaper articles on Shetland
issues.

For a few days I remained in the lodgings to which James Craddock took me on my arrival in Dublin. But having an introduction from Mr Burrell in Campbeltown to the widow of an excise officer who got scalded to death in one of the distilleries, I went and stayed with her in Dalymount Terrace on the way to Glasnevin. The widow was a fine woman of the name of Grazilier, with a very promising only daughter, and I could not have been better placed—although the house was very pinched. The daughter, Elizabeth, was at milinery or dressmaking in the city and was the picture of health and youth and activity.

In the course of some time, Mrs Grazilier moved to Portland Place, still on the north side of the city—being on the bank of the Royal Canal with the North Circular Road just a little street or so behind. Although thus on the outer rim of the city, we were not far from the centre—for the reason that, just in this section, building was backward owing to some mismanagement of the Mountjoy estates. While in other sections of the outer rim of the town, building went on; here everything was at a standstill. There were mud cabins within a stone's throw of Mountjoy Square and Eccles Street, two leading places.

The Mountjoy stagnation, however, had given us the advantage of being with our faces to the country. And still we were not far from the GPO in Sackville Street—the finest street in Europe. We could be in the country in 10 minutes at the most; in about four minutes in Cavendish Row; and in Sackville Street in 10 or 12. These were all good parts of the city and occupied at that time by some of the leading citizens.

But it was away in the very opposite direction, south and west, that fashion—if not civilisation—travelled. There were such first class places as Merrion Square, Kildare Street, Dawson Street, St Stephen's Green and Harcourt Road. And beyond the South Circular Road and the Grand Canal were the great and fashionable outlets of Rathmines, Ranelagh and Pembroke Street. And, in the course of time, what used to be the classic Donnybrook became quite the abode of the wealthy.[1]

In the business regions, the lower bridge, then called Carlisle Bridge, was in the centre. From the north end you looked up Sackville Street. Unfortunately, the view was broken somewhat by Nelson's monument—against the presence of which I always protested. Looking east you took in Eden Quay and the Custom House. And westward was Ormond Quay and the Four Courts. These, with Earl Street and Mary Street, branching off Sackville Street, and some others off the quays mentioned, are all places of business of every kind.

Then, if you go along the same bridge to the other end, you look eastward along Sir John Rogerson's Quay and westward along the south bank of the Liffey till you reach Merchants Quay opposite the Four Courts. You can look southward from that point by two good streets, Westmoreland and D'Olier Streets. By the former you can go on to College Green.

The sight from College Green is very animating, I consider. Standing with your back to the college entrance, you look westward—taking in, on the right, the corinthian outline of the Parliament House; taking in also a very fine building belonging to one of the insurance companies, jewellers shops, drapers and so forth. This is perhaps the least uniform succession of buildings in any street I know. But the very variety in plan of so many good, solid and large buildings produces a very fine effect.

One of my outlets from the city was by the northern road leading through the ancient village of Swords. Along this road I had a number of dealers and retailers to visit—and quite a considerable number of mills and kilns. On this northern road I went out through the suburbs of Drumcondra, Belvidere, Santry, Turnipin, Cloghran and on to Balbriggan. Swords is an old, decaying town—but with excellent land on each side of it. And the crops, the cattle and the pigs were all that could be desired.

From Swords, I took a turn westwards, taking in some large mills at Brackenstown before making my way home through Finglas. This was a long journey. But for a long time I had it over by noon—going away at five in the morning and getting home early so as to catch the medical classes.

Everywhere the country was fine and the splendid hawthorn hedges con-tributed much to the beauty and richness of its appearance. But these hedges many a time proved a great hindrance to me. When I knew that I was, by the roads, going far out of the direct course, I tried a short cut over the fields. But the hedges, with their terrible ditches, were a great consumption of time. When, after a severe scramble and some tearing and scratching, you got through the hedge, you were merely at the top of a great fence—with a deep ditch before you, lined with briars, brambles and other underwood. And besides these, the ditch sometimes had a considerable quantity of water.

Before the famine of 1846 this rich country was minutely divided among a tilling class of small tenants. At the time of which I speak, it was all, or nearly so, in large grazings—much of it in the hands of the great cattle dealers in Dublin. But the ruins of houses and fences remained to show how little care had been bestowed by the government on the population.

One of my leading duties over all this north side of the county of Dublin was visiting mills and kilns to see that they were not being used for drying malt. There was nothing of the kind being done and, in so far as the direct interests of the revenue were concerned, the inspection was a sheer waste of time and energy. But I did not waste *my* energy. In the course of my visits, I collected statistics of the yield of meal and flour given by the grain of different periods. I had, to a certain extent, exhausted the *Agricultural Returns* as to the extent of land under different crops at different periods and also as to the arable produce. I now had a clear record of the progress, or rather the retrogression, of agriculture in the country. But this I was able to make still clearer when I added the records of the millers. In every case I found that the yield of meal was much less than say, 20 and 30 years earlier.

I exhausted the mills on the north side of Dublin at this time and, some years later, those in the counties of Waterford, Tipperary, Kerry and Limerick. But so indifferent were the newspapers to such matters that I never made the use of these statistics which I ought.

I should add that I afterwards pursued the same inquiry in the Scottish counties of Inverness, Ross and Cromarty and Nairn. In this connection, the testimony of Mr Munro, the miller at Milton Tarbat, Ross-shire, is particularly valuable. I had obtained from him the particulars regarding the decline in the yield of meal by the grain—this agreeing with what I had found everywhere else. Just as the land was made into large farms, so the produce per acre was becoming less. When done, he said: 'Do you know, I find the

grain of the crofters yields more meal in the mill than that of the large farms.'
And more than 10 years later, at Benderloch in Argyll, I was repeating this
when the miller of the district spoke up—saying that he found the same thing.

This showed a curious kind of progress: reduction in the population; even
a greater proportionate reduction in the number in the occupation of land;
reduction in the area under crops; and reduction, finally, in the produce per
acre of the land under tillage.

I attended so many of the medical classes in Dublin that, while learning
some of the details of the constituents of drugs and of the human body, I came
to the conclusion that present medical science is an accumulation of crude
opinions—and medical practice very much a matter of experiment.

I had, however, a spell of hydropathy. I got a bad cold and, having to get
a certificate in order to seek leave, I went to a Dr Gordon, a friend of Dr
Charles Cameron. He told me I had pleurisy. So rather than allow that ailment
to hang about me, I went to the establishment at St Anne's Hall, Blarney,
near Cork, and was there some three months under the cure of Dr Richard
Barker, the first man in Ireland to take the water cure and the first man in
either Ireland or Great Britain to adopt the turkish bath.

I considered it an acquisition to have become acquainted with Dr Barker.
He was a quiet-going man who went about among his large houseful of
patients in a dreamy sort of way—taking in what people said without medical
pedantry or hospital superintendance. He, of course, prescribed, suggested
and advised. But, in reality, he left people largely to their own cures. He had
well provided tables. But he recommended abstinence from animal food and
supported the recommendation by living on plants and grains and fruits.

He was himself a trophy of the water cure. When in the prime of his
manhood, as to age, he was given up as beyond recovery. His lungs were
only remaining in fragments and every change of temperature or of situation
laid him up with fresh congestion or inflamation. However, one time he was
taken suddenly thus in Dublin, he determined to give up such applications
as were prescribed at the time. And shortly afterwards the attack was subdued.
From that day he foreswore drugs and bleeding and blisters and became a
strong man—although the missing portions of his lungs were never reproduced.

Dr Barker was medical man under the Board of Governors at the time of
the potato famine and the cholera.[2] In this capacity he had a field of operations
which afforded him wonderful experience and many facts with which to
support the system of treatment which he had adopted. Indeed he said that
no other system would have done any appreciable good. He had hundreds
of poor people in his hands at the same time for cholera and was kept going
without halt from village to village and from house to house. He could
not wait with one—and scores dying on every side. When he found a man
prostrate, and to all appearances in the grips of death, he took a blanket out
of his dog cart, dipped it well in water, rolled the patient up in it and left him
lying there with a bucket or can or flagon of water to drink when he got well
enough to take it.

In this rough and ready way, Dr Barker put scores of them through his
hands and had very few deaths. The persons so treated got well so quickly
that, on his passing next day, they were going about their business with rich
blessings on the head of the good doctor who had saved them from death.

It was here at St Ann's Hall that I first became acquainted with Dr John Gray of the *Freeman's Journal*. Mrs Gray and Edmond, their son, were there.[3] She suffered much from noises in her ears. By and bye, the doctor came and so did their other son, young John, together with the boy's tutor, Michael MacNamara. Mr MacNamara formed a sort of liking for me and, in this way, I became more intimate with the Grays than I might otherwise have been. Dr Gray was a very pleasant, as well as a very able, man and Mrs Gray a fine companionable woman. By the bye, both his father and her father had been in the excise.

I had come to Dublin to the First Ride, succeeding that very decent Irish gentleman, James Craddock. And I had for my supervisor a very gentlemanly little man belonging originally to Kerry, Henry Pomphrett. It was in this station that I did most of the Dublin agitational work. One of the effects of the agitation was a disposition at headquarters to treat the service in a better spirit generally. So my Ride was raised to the rank of a Division and I was appointed officer of the station—which came to be called Dublin Twentieth Division—on July 1, 1856.

To qualify for supervisor, by having some knowledge of distillation and other spirit duties, I got appointed to the Marrowbone Lane Distillery. After less than a year here, I got appointed to Drimnagh where I had very little to do among three paper mills and some grain mills and kilns. This was quite a small spot, two or three miles out of Dublin and on the bank of the Royal Canal.

But the very day I removed to Drimnagh, where we had a very poor shell of a house, a Bill was brought into Parliament to repeal the duty on paper— and I was once more off my moorings. I was not long in suspense, however. Before my duties at Drimnagh were ended I had an order to Waterford First Division. So to Waterford I went. And having there no entanglements with societies such as fell off me when I left Dublin, I had nothing to hinder me from preparing for my examination for promotion. I began with arithmetic and went on through book-keeping, the excise instructions, Acts of Parliament and general orders. I even did a good deal of correspondence with some friends also approaching to be examined—in order to perfect myself in reporting cases to the Board.

Meantime, I was still writing regularly for the *Agricultural Review*—and was paid as regularly. I had much intercourse with Joseph Fisher of *The Waterford Mail*, a public-spirited man of old Quaker stock and an expert among statistics. I also wrote a little in his paper. But in Waterford I never allowed myself to get involved in exterior work as I had done in Dublin.

We got settled in a good little house with garden at St John's Hall and I found Henry Rundle, collector, John Blair, chief clerk, and Richard Coogan, supervisor, very friendly. Mr Rundle, was a blunt Englishman, Mr Coogan a pawky Irishman and Mr Blair, although very Irish in his character, was nearly a Scotsman. He was overflowing with fun, wit and humour.

My intercourse with the Waterford traders was also harmonious. There were merchants who had spirits in the warehouses and with them I was done about twelve or one in the day. There was a malthouse, a kiln and a tobacco factory to visit—and my work was complete. Never again had I so easy a station and I was to be far from satisfied that I was doing well in leaving.

Waterford is the great market town for parts of Waterford County, Kilkenny, Tipperary and Wexford—and is resorted to by large numbers of splendid men and women. Corn, cattle, swine, turkeys, geese and horses find a market here. And for butter it is second only to Cork—if it is not equal to that beautiful city on the River Lee. The men and women were large—as became a people fed on the produce of such lands. And at that time the language spoken was Gaelic. On a market day it was so general that I heard nothing else.

Waterford shared in the revival and development which resulted from the establishment of independence in Ireland in 1782.[4] It has more than one excellent approach by land on good roads; and the fine trees which overhang these roads add much to the amenities of the place. There is a quay about a mile long on the Waterford side of the River Suir—and some shipping accommodation on the Wexford side. There is a great export trade with England and very superior steamers to carry it on. There are also large curing establishments—insomuch that the most of the finer class of pigs are killed on the spot and only the larger and the coarser are exported alive.

This pig rearing and breeding was no doubt due to an immense improvement which had taken place in recent years. This was initiated and pushed on by a Mr Joyce, an English tenant of the Abbey farm on the Wexford side of the river. He imported a fine Berkshire sow and bred litter after litter until he was largely instrumental in displacing the older breed in all the country round with a stock of swine which sent into the town many thousands a year—as uniform in their perfection as if they had been cast in one beautiful mould. And Joyce himself made his fortune and was a power in the land.

This pig feeding drew large imports of Indian corn to the port and the great mills which, in more populous times ground wheat, were now chiefly at work grinding this imported food for swine. But I may add that the 'yellow meal' became a considerable article of human diet—also greatly, it was acknowledged, to the bodily good of the population. I was assured that numbers who previously suffered from stomach and liver complaints recovered their digestion and appetites and became well and strong. The great round iron pot, with its contents of yellow meal, was hardly ever from the fire. It was thus always ready for use. And good it was with sweet milk. I have often regretted that this wholesome and cheap article did not become accepted by the Highlanders as it did by the Irish.

Here at St John's Hall, Waterford, was our eldest son born whom we called John. He and his two sisters, Frances and Jessie, with their mother, were left there when, in the early days of June 1862 I received orders to proceed to Somerset House for examination with a view to promotion to the rank of supervisor. I set out by steamer and in due time took train through Wales from Milford Haven.

I was fortunate enough to be one of four in a compartment, the others being, I concluded, Tipperary farmers. They soon took me into partnership over abundance of beef, fowl, bread and other eatables calculated to make travellers comfortable. Every care was taken, however, by overcrowding to the windows, to allow no more partners into our compartment. The Tipperary men were most hearty companions and did all they could to make me feel as hearty as they did themselves.

The travelling was rather slow and when we reached Lanfagan we came to a stop caused by damage to an axle. Down we came out and sauntered about until the train was ready to start. But our sanctity was here broken in upon. And although the Tipperary men were all that could be wished for, I was, on the whole, pleased to have incursions made upon us every now and again by lively Welshmen—the Welsh being so full of their language, their history and their music.

Englishmen take their own superiority so much for granted that they do not feel the need of asserting it. Scotsmen have their own quiet way of maintaining their own proper level. Highlanders generally are not so instrusive as to think of getting up any demonstrations of their nationality. Irishmen, as a rule, if they do obtrude their nationality, do it very modestly and with a view to gratifying those whom they address. Welshmen, however, seem to feel themselves bound to assert the riches of their intellectual possessions. And to me it has always been a decided treat to fall in with the patriotic Cymric. They seem brimful of facts and arguments in support of their own claims. A run through Wales, whether north or south, gives a useful delving to the mind of a Highlander. And I shall never forget the bright examples of rare enthusiasm which I have witnessed in places in which I have had the privilege of meeting with the active-minded Welsh.[5]

In due course our train took us to Paddington in perfect safety and a cab took me to the Strand where I meant to lodge in Sam's Coffee House near Somerset House. But the second London Exhibition was on and Sam's was full. I had been studying Bradshaw on the train, however, and was not so much put about as a stranger on his first visit to London might be supposed to be. I turned up one of the streets which strike out northward from the Strand and made for Roberts Temperance Hotel, Holborn. But there was no room. In like manner I tried several other places—all to no effect. I then knocked at Anderson's Caledonian Temperance Hotel. This also was full to overflowing. But Mr Anderson, who was an old temperance lecturer and Scottish poet, came out with me to the head of the street and placed me in the hands of Mrs Leader, a nice, kind Essex woman, with whom I made my headquarters for months after.

Next day I joined the muster of candidates for promotion. We went upstairs in Somerset House and were for several days under the eye of a watchman in order that no advantage should be taken of one another's assistance. All memoranda were debarred. Every sum, every answer, every word must be done from the unaided internal resources of the essayist. It is of no general interest how these examinations are framed and conducted. I passed, while some who were better qualified were sent back.

This, however, may interest my friends: although I had been a disturber of the order of things, I did not find any hostility towards me in this great red tape institution. On the whole, a good many of the red-tapists themselves were rather favourable to my success and believed that I had all the qualifications required—howsoever I might show in a formal examination. There were one or two slips in my performance—in book-keeping, I think. As I was receiving my sentence, however, I remember the chief of the department saying to me: 'We know you can do better.'

After some few days, I was ordered to Guildford, some 30 or 40 miles into Surrey, to officiate for Mr Rockford Connor, one of the nicest men ever in the service. This was one of my good fortunes; for in those days there seemed to be no idea at Somerset House that a man fresh from the duties of a division officer needed any training, direction or advice. He was sent out with all the responsibilities of a supervisor—with never a lesson as to what his duties were. But Mr Connor was a gentleman in the highest sense and did all he could to make the business easy for the novice. Even the forms in every possible case were ready made out for me—so that I had nothing to do but fill them up.

Guildford is on the River Wye and is the county town of Surrey. My duties took me into Hampshire; also to Farnham, where William Cobbet was born; to Aldershot of the great camp and to Godalming, a great cricketing district.[6] The country about is very fine and very varied—from light and heavy loam to thin sandhills covered with heather. But my time at Guildford was short and soon I was back in Somerset House.

My most important action in the capital was really outside the department. I had introductions to several persons connected with the press in London, among them Mr Charles Cooper of *The Morning Star*, since of *The Scotsman*. And at the time I was going to London, A M Sullican encouraged the editor of *The Universal News* with the intimation that I was going to the great city and would be a help to him. I think the help was mutual. I received pecuniary help while much in need of it. And I wrote a good deal for the paper—giving matter in reference to Ireland which was hardly known. At this time also I wrote London Letters to *The Nation* and to the *Waterford Mail*.

I saw Cooper and, I think, Justin McCarthy in the office of *The Star*.[7] However, I never wrote to it but once—although there was never a paper in London that I would have liked better to write in. It says little for the character of English politics that such a paper could not live. No, it was too good to live in the atmosphere of a country gone over essentially to mammon and to the demon of war.

Mr Rockford Connor, on a visit to London, took me to see a friend of his, a Mr Haynes. We had a long and pleasant chat with Mr Haynes—and when leaving we were to meet again so interested did we become. To make sure of our meeting again, he asked for my address. When I wrote it and handed him the paper, he exclaimed: 'Good God, is this Finlagan?' He had not realised he was talking with the writer on the Sutherland Clearances in the *Mark Lane Express* of which he was one of the editors. Indeed, it was with him I had communicated all the time.

Mr Haynes was overjoyed to meet with one who had made so good an impression as I had done with these articles. He introduced me to Mr Tuxford, one of the proprietors of the paper. From him I experienced many kind attentions and afterwards wrote for him from Shetland. I remember that when I thanked Mr Tuxford for inserting my vindication of the Sutherland people, he said no thanks were due. He could not refuse insertion to an exposure of so cruel a procedure as that of the Sutherland managers.

Also in London I soon came to know Mr John Macqueen, Lincoln's Inn Fields, one of the Corribrough family and cousin to my own mother. He was kind and attentive to me and introduced me to different persons of position besides giving me some monetary help when we were going away to Shetland. He got me passes to the Houses of Lords and Commons which were so effective that I was able to get such passes for myself and others afterwards merely by going to some of the clerks there.

But the introduction which I valued most was to my own cousin, the daughter of my mother's brother, Donald or John MacPherson, and wife of Dr Clements living at Teddington, near Twickenham, Richmond. Her mother was living with her—a fine, active-minded Englishwoman who was proud to have had a good Highland husband. My cousin was an uncommonly fine woman—full of information, well-cultured and of a refined manner. She played better than but few women whom I have ever met.

Among the men whom I met occasionally was James Logan, historian of the Scottish Gael and fellow writer with MacIain on the Highland clans.[8] He was then old. But he was active-minded and knew a great many of the London Highlanders including Cameron Macphee, Colin Chisholm, MacIntyre North and many others whom I met. I found that when young he had had his skull driven in—above the left temple, I think—and had had the brain covered with a plate of silver. This, I thought, accounted for some of the excitability which he sometimes showed—and for his inability to resist the effects of spirits when he took them. He was a great authority among Scots and most willing he was to oblige. I found him of use in connection with the British Museum and other repositories of documents of authority.

After Guildford I remained in the chief office at Somerset House for some months. But in December 1862 I was sent to Clonmel to officiate for Mr Richard Hutchins, supervisor there. This was the capital of Tipperary and in the heart of a rich country. It was somewhat convenient for me, too—as my family were still in Waterford.

In the neighbourhood of Clonmel is Marlfield where St Patrick's Well flows out of a great opening several feet wide and one and a half deep in the limestone rock in such quantity as to supply the wants of a cornmill and a large distillery. Besides its quantity of water, it was supposed to possess healing virtues and offerings were hung up on the couple of trees which grew on its banks.

The land all about is a very good, strong and productive soil. And the people who grew on it, as well as the crops, were stalwart. The people of Tipperary have always been considered the most troublesome in Ireland—being largely the descendants, it is said, of Cromwell's disbanded troops from England. That much at anyrate of England's troubles in Ireland may be traced to her own sowing. Men may go to Ireland full of English feelings. But in the course of a generation or two, they become, like the Fitzgeralds of old, more Irish than the Irish themselves. As Whiteside said long afterwards, the Protestant descendants of the English settlers were among the most successful of Irish rebels.[9]

I had work enough in Clonmel District—long journeys and no means with which to pay for conveyances. Things have been improved now for examiners and supervisors—and even for officers. But the changes had only been promised then.

I left Clonmel on April 3, 1863. I had a few days with my family at Tramore, near Waterford, where the fresh and strong breezes off the Atlantic make themselves felt. Then I made back, by Dublin, for Somerset House. I need not say much about the time spent in London from April to September—when I took charge of the Tralee District in the county of Kerry. When leaving the chief office, I remember Mr Carling, who was one of the grudging old supervisors general at Somerset House, saying to me: 'You are going to see the Lakes of Killarney at the public expense.' As will be seen, however, I was to do a very laborious and expensive part of the public duty at my private expense.

I got to Tralee and found that Mr Hart, the supervisor, had been out of business a fortnight. That was one thing. Then, as I was adjusting my mind to the regular work, he said: 'You will have to take the stock all over the county and that will cost you £10. Besides the taking of them is behind.'

I felt that I was in a fix. When he told me, in regard to the expenses, that I would not get any of them from the Board of Inland Revenue, I said: 'I think I *will* get them.'

'No,' he said, 'several persons have tried and they have never been paid.'

This was very hard. But I said to myself: 'I will do the business as if it were my own and I will then make a bold attempt to be repaid.'

I set out next day for Killarney and took the stock there with the assistance of the officer. The day after, I went by the Bianconi car over Mangerton for Kenmare where I arrived as wet as if I had been dragged through a river. I did my business and got bills here and elsewhere for my outlays. After a sort of drying, I set out, on an outside single car, at six pm for Cahersiveen away on Valencia Bay. I was not long on this journey, much of it along the shore of the great bay called Kenmare River, when I discovered that the horse was blind and the driver well on with drink! So, although overpowered nearly with sleep, I kept awake.

Well on in the night we reached Sneem and halted at an inn. I was put into a little stall in which drams were drunk by visitors—a cold, damp place. However, I got up and, looking about, I saw a bright light escaping towards me from below a door. I knocked and was greeted, on the opening of the door, by as fine a peat fire in the middle of the floor as I think I ever saw—and the best sight one could meet with in the circumstances. I was not slow to accept the invitation to sit down and enjoy the warmth.

We soon got into conversation and, these being a Gaelic-speaking people, we drew all the closer from my being of the same speech. I broke ground by asking the meaning of Sneem. I had caught sight of the rocky, knotted bed of the river as the moon shone on it. And when they had no solution ready I asked them the Gaelic for a knot. The answer was what I had anticipated, *snaidhm.* I concluded that the river was so called on account of what I had noticed. Other topics followed and we got on as thick as brother's bairns— they telling me many things about the country and the people.

We left the Sneem peat fire after due rest had been allowed the horse. And in the morning I went to bed in the hotel and shooting lodge at Waterville— away up in a fine open country where there was a wide view of land and ocean. There is good shooting there and even a lake for fishing. But at that season I had the hotel to myself. After rest and refreshment I went on next day to Cahersiveen, one of the poorest collections of Irish habitations I ever saw.

And yet I retain a distinct recollection of the fine style of Mrs Fitzgerald and Miss Fitzgerald of the inn or hotel—and of how delightfully sweet was their speech. I have noticed this in different parts of the county of Kerry and can hardly imagine a better style of speech—so musical, so chaste and conveying so much the idea of a kindly politeness. If one could establish all over the kingdom one style, one accent, one tone, I would vote for the speech in which the aroma of the heather and a whisper from the stream mingle to sing several thoughts into the souls of men as is done, in many cases which I have heard, in Kerry.

Of the Lakes of Killarney no one can give an idea of them. In suitable weather—with their accompaniments of woods, rocks and variegated clouds—they are ravishing. But in inharmonious weather there is no beauty to be seen excepting what has nothing to do with the lakes—namely, the mountains and the distant peaks of Macgillycuddy's Reeks.

Of course, Kerry is mostly *ciar* in hue—although it is said the meaning is *Ciar Righ*, the dun King. It is remarkable that the hue of the people's complexion is in harmony with that of the country—as if the shadow of the mountains were photographed into the skin. Another thing, the people generally are of low stature. But they are remarkably compact, erect and active—with well-developed legs and firm step. Their training favours agility. In keeping with the rest, the women carry all their burdens on the tops of their heads.

But I must resume my stamp inspecting tour. On I went by Milltown, Castleisland, Killorglin and back to Tralee. But I still had to visit the far-projecting promontory of Dingle. All the way from Tralee to Brandon, on the coast, is very rough. I had a 26 mile journey under a continuous pour of rain on the outside car. But when I got there I was well pleased with the picturesque spot whence I looked out over the Atlantic and down upon the white sands of *Ban Traigh*, now called Ventry. I had a pleasant night there and came back next day to follow up by going on to Listowel, Abbeyfeale and Tarbert on the Shannon—where a small neck of land goes out and gives the meaning we have in Scotland for the word.[10]

And now for the tussle with the Board of Inland Revenue. I made out my account for £8 15s 4d. This was one pound five shillings less that was said by Mr Hart—perhaps because of my abstinence from strong drink. I said very little by way of preface, simply that the application was, I knew, unusual—but not more so than the circumstances in which it was made. It was accompanied by quite a bunch of little bills. I had kept all such—excepting for railway fares and one tea I remember not asking a bill for at Killorglin. I put in even that account, though; and I sent the whole to Somerset House.

The thing was a matter of some wonder and speculation there—as so many previous bills on the same account had been wrecked by the functionaries. It took the gentleman to whom the papers had been referred some two months going back and fore to the supervisors general—among whom was Mr Carling aforesaid. But the last official letter which reached me at Tralee contained the Board's order to pay me every penny—with the further order to relieve the supervisor of that duty in the future.

It was now near Christmas and the New Year and I hastened off to Bingham in Nottinghamshire where my family were staying with my brother David. And an awkward journey it was, the different trains connected so badly. At Crewe I had a very long delay. But even that had its variety. Not far off in the station I caught sight of a little man muffled to the nose and the upper part of his face out of sight under a slouch hat. By and bye, I heard him utter the Scotticism: 'I'll be into *The Advertiser* tomorrow.' And I said to myself, although the speaker was put further out of ken by hoarseness: 'That is Willie Clark.' So I drew nearer to him—though he moved off.

By and bye, a large bundle of papers which he had under his arm, as if offering them for sale, disappeared. And he kept moving off until I saw that he was likely to be away altogether. So I pushed on and got before him just as he was getting out of the building. At first he pretended not to know me. But, as usual, he was up to the occasion and gave me to understand that he was conducting *The Crewe Advertiser* and would be glad of any contribution from my 'able pen'. The little dodger was still from hand to mouth as a principal and still at his tricks. But, for all his wiles, he was still a newsboy.

At Nottingham I should like to have seen more of the town and to have strolled through Sherwood Forest to tread the footsteps of Robin Hood. At Bingham I had a sight of the rich lands which abound there. And I was assured that the crops were in keeping—as I saw the cows, the pigs and the turkeys to be. But I had no time to explore and I was back in Somerset House to 'enter on' the day after Christmas.

I was for a few days at Chelmsford in Essex, but had no time to see or hear much. And by minute of March 16, 1864, I was appointed supervisor in Shetland. From that time until April 4, when I went away, I did very little examining. There was a tartar of a supervisor general, William Irvine, over us at the time. Noticing how little progress I was making, he said: 'You will not have much examining to do in Shetland. I think they have made a wise selection.' I certainly did not like going so far away. But my stay in Shetland was no blank leaf in my life.

On the way to Shetland we had the company of Mr John Robertson, shopkeeper in Lerwick and curer in Skerries, and I well remember him telling me that among his goods for sale at one time were spirits.[11] One night, however, he said to his wife: 'I have been thinking that it is not in me, as a Christian, to sell such an article. But I do not see how we can get on without it. Our returns are so small.'

'Well,' she said, 'that is not the question. Is it according to God's word? If it is not, your duty is to drop it and leave the issue in his hands.'

'We acted on that sense of duty and truth,' said Mr Robertson. 'We did sell what we had in stock. After that, when it was asked for, we simply said we had none. When the time for renewing the license came, we took no action. The whole thing seemed to melt away and at the end of the year, instead of falling off, we were £200 better than before. And God has prospered us ever since.'

To which I add that one of the last things I did in Lerwick was to move Mr Robertson's election to be a magistrate. And to his enterprise soon after is due the beginning of the vast improvements which are now to be seen in Lerwick.

But to go back to our arrival. We landed in Lerwick on a wet April morning from the steamer, per a small boat, on the strand—and crept as well as we could into Commercial Street, the one narrow street in the town. And yet when I was there some years later, there was quay accommodation for three large steamers, with several hotels to hold the visitors, streets on every side and a townhouse worthy of a city crowning all on top of the hill.

It would hardly be right to omit mention of my connection with *The People's Journal* while I was in Shetland. Soon after I went there, I wrote to the editor—offering to supply paragraphs of news, where there was news, as well as comments or 'leaderettes.' It was agreed and the work went on.

And besides doing much to promote the improvements required, I understand that I raised the circulation.

In my comments for the paper I went in for the telegraph being extended to Lerwick; a proper pier; water from the Sandy Loch; a weekly steamer to the North Isles instead of the sailing packets; a new town to the west of the old in Lerwick; a proper revenue office in Shetland: all of which have been accomplished facts for years. And I kept poking at improved husbandry—especially deeper digging and the preservation of fish bones and other offal for the ground.

As I have said, I ran John Robertson, on my own nomination, as magistrate. And I was glad to hear that he went at the required pier at his own risk. The new Lerwick I take some credit for. And the credit I won in *The People's Journal* holds good in that office to this day. The proprietors sent me *The Dundee Advertiser* for more than 20 years as a compliment and made me a present of a splendid edition of Shakespeare for what I had done for them in Shetland.

The People's Journal, January 20, 1866. Repeatedly have I urged that there should be a factory in Shetland for the making of native wool into cloth. I do not know the extent to which the thing is done. But I know that from all parts of Shetland wool is sent south to be made into wearing apparel for men and women. There is thus, clearly, the raw material on the spot. And, as clearly, there is demand for it and for the articles which can be manufactured from it. I think there can be no doubt that there is water power to drive a mill. But, even if not, there is an almost inexhaustible supply of peat which could be made use of to generate the requisite steam power.

Another suggestion I wish to offer in connection with the woollen business. Shetland is famed for its fine soft wool—adapted for shawls, veils, gloves and the finer descriptions of underclothing. In attempting to improve the breeds of cattle and sheep, or to replace the native breeds by larger breeds capable of carrying more meat, the idea of preserving and improving that particular breed which bears this soft wool should be allowed a prominent place in our minds. I know that one of these sheep cuts a sorry figure beside a Cheviot or a Southdown—both as regards wool and weight. But let the wool and the mutton find their proper level in the market—and to the fine knitters the fine wool should be vastly more valuable than the coarser sorts.

Then take into consideration the cost of feeding the native breed, on the one hand, and the larger breeds, on the other. I am not at all sure that the absolute superiority lies with the latter. Devote a given extent of land to each and let each have the full benefit of the best modes of feeding. Have a regular market for the fine wool—and not allow it to go at the same price as the coarse. Then see which lot draws the largest amount of money, directly and indirectly, for the capital laid out. When I speak of the indirect receipts, I have in view the very great importance of the fine wool to the domestic manufacturer of Shetland. If the fine wool-bearing sheep are allowed to be extirpated, the finer sorts of the Shetland hosiery will be knocked on the head. And not only will Shetland suffer, but the wearers of the articles in question will have to do without them.

The People's Journal, March 17, 1866. The Shetland Agricultural Society's show of produce was held on Tuesday, February 27, in the Subscription Rooms, Lerwick. There were very good samples of grain, turnips, cabbage and even of flax. But the day was so very unfavourable that the exhibition could have no great effect on the general production of the country in future years. And even among those who were present, and exhibited, there was considerable dissatisfaction with the result as regards the awards. But there is no reason to despair on these accounts. No matter how imperfect the decisions of the judges may be, a good show of superior produce will do something to dispel the delusion that Shetland is incapable of yielding good crops. But in order for the full lesson to be given, there must be much more than an exhibition.

There must be an intelligible account of all connected with the production: the nature, condition, situation and aspect of the soil; the mode and time of tillage; the quantity and quality of the manure; the seed and the time of sowing; and the subsequent treatment and the time of ripening. And then the samples exhibited should be selected so as to show the general results. A man may force a drill of turnips at the expense of an acre. Much the same may be said of every other crop brought to a show. The Shetland Society should institute prizes for the best managed farms and the tidiest cottages. And while doing this and other things to improve the skill and habits of the Shetland farmers, something would require to be done to remove the impression among tenants that good produce is a snare—that he who improves his land merely offers his landlord an excuse for raising his rent.

The People's Journal, August 11, 1866. It is really distressing to witness the straits to which poor people are reduced in Lerwick for want of water. The town pump is besieged from morning to night. It is no uncommon thing to see 20 women about it—some standing close around the iron tube; one trying to persuade the liquid far away down in the bowels of the earth to come up; while others sit by, with their knitting, hoping that perhaps in the course of the day their turn will come to exercise their powers of persuasion.

Then there may be a hundred buckets or more standing about—left there by persons who had not the patience to wait. Others—old women and young, boys and girls—are seen at all hours wandering about in quest of any dribble which may be found in an unfrequented corner or a suburban well. Drains are being improved in the town. But there is no water to carry off the refuse which is thrown into them. So, in addition to the more direct personal injuries which this want of water is sure to inflict, these drains are almost certain to be little better than tanks of fermenting filth.

And yet, as we have repeatedly mentioned, there is an abundant supply of water within a mile and a half of the town. Let us again urge upon the chief inhabitants the course which they ought to adopt. It is true the evil presses upon the poor, but what can they do in the matter? Besides, the evil effects of last year's scarcity of water were not confined to the poor. They found their way into some of the best families in the place—some of which are now mourning the loss of their dear ones in consequence.

The right way, as we think, is to call a meeting of the inhabitants and there and then appoint a provisional committee to collect information, and report within a given time, on the best plan for bringing water into the town from the Sandy Loch or other source. If the chief inhabitants will not move, any two or three can draw up a requisition to the chief magistrate, get it signed and make the other arrangements for the public meeting. One person holding back is no reason why another should do so. It is rather a reason why he should step forth.

The People's Journal, September 1, 1886. Some short time ago, we made reference to the changes which were about to take place on an extensive property in Shetland—the Annsbrae and Garth estates. The subject has come before us repeatedly since and in so important a light that we deem it our duty to devote a little special attention to it. The first point which presses itself on our attention is the behaviour of the managing party in this matter. We are not going to call the right of the landlord or his factor in question—although we may, in passing, say that the best foundation on which a landlord or a factor can rest his claims is that supplied by a prosperous and contented tenantry working in love and understanding with those above them. We will assume even that the landlord and his factor, in this case, desire to place their claims upon such a foundation—and that the new management is intended to promote the good of the tenantry and the interest of the landlord.

But taking into consideration what we mentioned particularly at the close of our last observations on this subject, the tenacity with which the Shetland peasantry adhere to old practices and their distrust of all innovations, we cannot refrain from saying that the first intimation which the people receive of the coming change should not be in the form of an abrupt proposal to conform or surrender within a few weeks or months.

As the matter appears at present, most persons will conclude that the whole plan is a plausible project for getting the tenants to eject themselves. And indeed so much is it the fashion now to prefer land without people, it is not unreasonable to suppose that this uncharitable supposition is, after all, the truth of the matter. If it be, we will venture to assure the perpetrators of this plot against so many of the Queen's subjects that they will not go unpunished. God gave the earth to be inhabited, to be subdued by human industry, to be rendered fertile as a garden and to support bountifully the largest number of those bearing his image. And so surely as anyone steps in between God and the carrying out of those His most obvious designs, so will characteristic punishment overtake the transgressor.

We have been told that threats of violence have been scattered far and wide through Shetland against the new factor—that his life is not safe among the people and that Shetland will soon be another Ireland. We have said a word to the factor and the landlord. Let us say another to the tenants. This idea of Shetland becoming a second Ireland was, as explained to us, that not only would the people be ejected, but they would take the law in their own hand and have life for life. Now this connection of the matter with Ireland is most instructive. And to those who make the connection it ought to be a solemn warning.

Granting that, in individual cases, Irish landlords have been deterred from executing their threats by a terror of the blunderbuss, any such advantage to the people has been 10 times over counterbalanced by the effective odium which the shedding of blood has fastened upon Ireland as a nation. Those of the Irish who took the law thus in their own hand, while thinking they were serving their country and their race, were in reality putting a powerful weapon into the hand of their enemies.

And thus, while Poland and Italy and Hungary, and even the slave states of America, when they sought to be a separate nation, could command a large amount of public sympathy, Ireland, whose cause is surely as good as that of any of those nations, is never able to elect any sympathy, any countenance, any support, any aid when she would attempt to redress her wrongs. In this case the punishment is perhaps much heavier than the offence. But that only makes the application stronger to the case in hand. Every Irish landlord shot has counted as 10 against the nation and every assassin has counted as 20 to the infamy of the nation—because, no doubt, the assassinated were of a powerful class who could command every defaming and damning power in the land.

So let the Shetland peasantry take warning. Let them withdraw their threatenings against the Garth and Annsbrae factor and banish vengeance, as they would the very fiend, from their bosoms. Whatever be the provocation, to raise their hand against their fellow man is a sin against God. And in taking vengeance out of His hand, they are also placing themselves beyond His protection and laying themselves open to the legal power which their enemies may be only too anxious to bring against them. Shetland is very little known at present in the south. It will be a sad thing if it becomes known with blood on its skirts. Hitherto it has been remarkable for its purity in this respect. But one drop of blood spilt, as threatened, will a hundred times outweigh the ages of innocence which it has enjoyed. And from an unknown state Shetland will emerge into infamy and contempt.

I cannot bid adieu to Shetland without some account of my latest adventure there. For much of my sojourn in Shetland it had not occurred to me that I had anything to do with the lonely Fair Isle—about midway between Orkney and Shetland. Now I was to voyage to it.

I had already been to Foula—far out to the west, some 18 miles by sea from Walls—and, on that occasion, all had gone well with me. The island is not bad, its soil being fair. And it is of interest as the home now of one of these great birds which are said to be a match for the eagle and are, on that account, valued as a protection to sheep—the skua I think they call it. The fishing is good. But landing is only possible at one narrow bight on the east side—and that is inaccessible with rough weather.

Some years before 1866, when I went there, my pleasant friend Mr Robert Sinclair, draper, Lerwick, had some exciting experiences of the danger of the island. It was in October and he was going there in a boat belonging to the island which had been sent for him to teach a music class. When they were about half way out, the wind from the east rose and with it the sea. And as they neared Foula, the situation became one of extreme anxiety to the mariners. There was no turning. There was no entering of the bight possible. And the rocks were bare on either side.

Looking ahead, they saw that there was a crowd on the sloping rock, which formed a natural slipway, as if anxiously on the look-out for them. No consultation with the men on shore was possible. However, the mariners confidently relied on help from them. They set full sail and, under the utmost speed, let the boat rush in on the rock. And, as the mariners had anticipated, the men on shore, so many on each side, caught the boat as she beached and ran in with her—adding their own force to that of the wind and landing her, with her crew, high and dry in perfect safety. This was all well for them. But it was not until the next April that their friends on the mainland of Shetland received tidings of how they had escaped from the dangers of the storm.

I had no such experiences of Foula. I landed and went over every croft on the island, taking its dimensions and the crops and stock on each towards making up the *Agricultural Returns* for that year—the first year of their being collected in Great Britain. And I got back in safety.

To Skerries I had been a year or two previously on the ordinary business of the department. The only thing adventurous connected with this expedition was my wife being with me in a small smack for carrying fish and curing materials. The accommodation was anything but comfortable or nice. Everything was rough and looked anything but clean. Indeed decent John Robertson, to whom the boat and the curing station of Skerries belonged, rather advised her not to go. And she long retained a lively recollection of the voyage. The cooking and serving of the food by the poor, honest but rough men; the wiping of the cups with their fingers; the tea tenacious with strength; and the smothering hole in which we were stowed away along with a little old-fashioned stove which puffed smoke and ashes back upon us: these were not conditions calculated to send the mind back with pleasure to the expedition.

The nearest approach to an adventure after this was a visit to the Flugga lighthouse. Although built upon the hard rock, such is the force with which the waves of the North Sea dash against it that the lighthouse is liable to frequent shocks. And these perturbations tell so on the attendants that they are frequently shifted on account of the nervous state into which both men and women fall after some time on what may be called the last joint in the long tail of the British Isles.

As for sailing among the islands, that was a matter of course. I would set out in one of the seven packets which started for the North Isles every Tuesday with the goods which came into Lerwick on Sunday by the weekly steamer. Thus I perhaps landed at Symbister in the island of Whalsay—then on to Fetlar, one of the smaller isles but the best of the whole as far as it went. It was said to be the granary of Shetland as it grew more and better grain than any of the rest. It was also noted for a breed of horses a good deal larger than the native ponies. They had been bred by Sir Arthur Nicolson between a Shetland sire, I think, and an Arabian dam.[12] They were quite sizeable and carried a man quite off the ground.

On the west side of this line of sailing was the island of Yell—nearly all bog and so called, I understood, on account of its barrenness—the word Yell being akin to the word 'yeld' applied in Scotland to cattle not in calf. Shetland is, as a rule, devoid of beauty. But I have opened my eyes of a morning in Mid Yell Voe, after sailing into it at night, and seen it quite beautiful.

From island to island I have gone thus, landing on one side and then walking to the other. Indeed sailing was far from pleasant to me and I preferred walking even when I could command a packet. Scores of times I have been sick and helpless in island boats.

Shetland is remarkable for the absence of public houses. Yet I never had any difficulty in obtaining lodgings. In some places, such as at Hillswick and Reawick, I dared not think of paying. In these places my hosts were pleased to have a stranger and I always found them nice and kind and willing to impart information. Let me add here that nowhere have I known education so sedulously promoted. And never have I known any people who possessed the gift of good penmanship like the youth of these islands.

I now return to my expedition to Fair Isle. After losing a whole day waiting for a breath of wind, I set out in a small smack, the *North Star*, belonging to a man of the name of Tait at Firth, Dunrossness. It was one o'clock of the second day ere we got out of Lerwick Bay. It was dark ere we got south of Sumburgh Head. And it was five in the morning of the next day when we got into the small shallow, rocky creek on the south shore of the lonely Fair Isle.

I got ashore, had breakfast and proceeded to carry out my survey. I inspected every holding and made my record of every holder and of every acre of the different descriptions of crop which he had sown—as I did of every head of cattle and sheep and pigs which he possessed. The work was very interesting to me and, although it was laborious and even intricate in some places where the surface was greatly broken by rocks which cropped up in so many forms and in so many places, I took a pleasure in it. It helped me to see further into the conditions in which the poor people lived.

By five o'clock in the evening my work was done and I was thinking of spending the night on the island. But as I was having something to eat in the house of the Free Church missionary, one of the men came from the boat asking me to hasten on board, that we must clear out of the port at once or else the bottom would be knocked out of the *North Star* against the sunken rocks—the wind had so risen. This was a disappointment to me as I did not wish to spend a second night at sea and I desired to have more time with the people of this strange island.

However, I got on board and we got out of the wretched port not a moment before time, the sea was becoming so wild under the rapid rising of the wind from the east-north-east. I felt the incongruity of having to leave a port and go outside to face the storm—so different from what would happen anywhere else. However, out we came and so violently had the wind and sea got up that a large ship sailing to the west was forced to lie to in the lea of the island. We, however, cleared out to the east and stood for the mainland of Shetland in the teeth of the wind and in the face of a roaring, surging sea. As it happened, the tide as well as the wind was against us and, although we kept her bow in the right direction, the *North Star* was making no way. Even tacking we made little progress.

After a wearisome time battling thus, we held a council. And I went back to my resting place below thinking that we were to take advantage of wind and tide and make for Orkney rather than be out in the stormy ocean all night. When I inquired some time later, however, I found that Tait, the young skipper, could not find it in his heart to lose so much way as going to Orkney involved—and that he was still beating northward as well as he could.

I was down below lying as flat as the motion of the vessel would allow—for even in smoother water I was a bad sailor. Thus I was an object of pity. Every time I raised my head my stomach asserted its nauseous dominion over my whole body. And so the little vessel rolled and tossed and jibed. Sometimes she seemed to jump from the crest of a mountain wave and come down with a thud as if on the solid bed of the sea—leaving the seasick victim to imagine that the next moment the cold seawater would be rushing through the broken sides of the shattered ship. Again and again did this distressful experience succeed other sensations little less distressful. But the brave little craft held on, pounding away, seeming to shake her head and fling out her mane in defiance of all the elements.

She went far away east in an attempt to get even the smallest bit of a hold of the wind. Then to the west again a similiar attempt was made. But so far as could be felt on board, we were making no way. Nor was it likely we should so long as we had wind and tide to contend with. Then the tide changed. Now we had but the one force to contend with, we thought. Then a new force sprang up in the turmoil caused by the opposition of wind and tide. The vessel tossed still more and her rolling was even more disagreeable. However, we did make some way. At dawn of day Sumburgh Head was looming ahead of us and, after some hours, we were alongside when on the larboard tack. Still it was nine o'clock in the day when we made the bay of Firth where we got into shelter—all of us, master, men and passenger, glad to land and seek some rest.

The brave young skipper was fain to go to bed at once. And I cannot tell how thankful I was to feel the solid earth once more under my feet. So thankful was I to be off the sea that, although the *North Star* was to be at my disposal in the course of a couple of hours to carry me the 21 miles to Lerwick, I ordered a horse and, after some breakfast, rode on—determined, if possible, to have no more of the North Sea excepting what I should navigate in getting to Aberdeen where I must land on my way to Inverness.

I may add that, though I had been appointed to Inverness on my own application, I had had some doubts and regrets over the matter. I was leaving as I was about to reap the crops of a croft on which I had expended a good deal of money and care. I had treated it well and everything promised well; potatoes excellent; turnips good; oats beyond common; cabbage, carrots and parsnips all good. We would thus have had to buy very little of our staple food. And so I had a clear idea that we could live cheaper in Shetland than in Inverness. But all I got out of that bit of ground, in which I had taken a loving interest, was one meal of potatoes and one or two cabbages. However, the voyage to and from Fair Isle put an end to all doubts and I was truly thankful that my seafaring days in Shetland were within a month of being at an end.

1   Donnybrook was once famed for its rowdy fair and so became synonymous with uproar and disorder.
2   Board of Governors, the poor law authorities.
3   Sir John Gray was owner and editor of *Freeman's Journal*. His son Edmond became a prominent nationalist politician in the 1870s and 1880s.
4   Ireland obtained its own legislature under the leadership of Henry Grattan in 1782. Although regarded with great respect by nineteenth century nationalists, Grattan's parliament had, in reality, only nominal independance.
5   The Welsh *Eisteddfod* was reported regularly in *The Highlander* and the Welsh held up as an example to Gaelic speakers. See, for example, *Highlander*, Nov 25, 1876.
6   Cobbett, the early nineteenth century radical and propagandist, held views on agrarian issues that were not dissimilar to those of Murdoch.
7   McCarthy, who edited *The Morning Star* in the mid-1860's, became a prominent Irish nationalist politician in the 1880s and 1890s.
8   Logan, born in Aberdeen in 1794, had published *The Scottish Gael* in 1831. The injury to which Murdoch refers had been received at a hammer-throwing contest.

9   James Whiteside was the lawyer who defended Daniel O'Connell in 1843 and who afterwards became Lord Chief Justice of Ireland.

10 The word denotes an isthmus, as in Tarbert, Harris.

11 Robertson was a prominent Lerwick councillor and magistrate who, as Murdoch remarks, took a leading part in the development of the town.

12 Nicolson was then owner of Fetlar.

Campaigning in the Highlands
1867-1879

Murdoch returned from Shetland to Inverness where he was to remain for 15 years. There, on retiring from the excise, he founded *The Highlander* and began a new career as a newspaper editor and political campaigner. This chapter draws on Murdoch's autobiography and on his *Highlander* editorials.

About the middle of August 1866 we took our departure—wife, Frances, Jessie, John, Ronald and Alexander Sullivan whom we somehow always have called Charlie. And after a night's rest in Aberdeen we arrived in the capital of the Highlands. I had never been to Inverness since I was a small child incapable of taking in any of its features. But I was very much surprised, on seeing the place with man's eyes, that my father and mother had not dinned into my head the many features of beauty which give to the situation its supremacy over every other town known to them. I was greatly pleased with the change from the poor Shetland Isles. It was early autumn, too, when all is at its best, when men and money are flying about and all the energy of town and county is in full activity. And soon came the Northern Meeting with the games, the balls and the mustering of the grandees of the north together with their visitors and their sporting tenants and friends.

The official duties were very much more onerous, and the expense in discharging them greater, than in Shetland. But I never regretted coming to Inverness. Besides its many natural attractions, the country possessed those of the many relatives who lived within a few miles. To me the change was as from a strange country to the land of my own people. And I soon made friends and took a great interest in what pertained to the capabilities and improvement of the country.

I was ushered in among the total abstainers in Inverness. There was some extra work in hand at the time through the starting of the Free Templars.[1] This was the organisation which first met me and I joined it and worked with it. But I put my hand to the work in every connection and both in town and country. I joined the Literary Institute and read some papers on 'Why is there a Land Question?' Today it seems strange how little the question was understood. I dare say there are some who will look back with wonder at their own obtuseness only 26, 27 or 28 years ago—seeing how events have come forward to prove the incredible. What a time it takes to waken up the bulk of mankind to anything but the necessities and expediences of getting on in the world!

In Inverness there was a deal of that sort of conservatism which consists of concurring in what goes on. The Liberal Party was about as conservative as the Tory Party when anything was proposed which required going to the root of the evil to be rid of. All the papers in Inverness were Liberal nominally; but not one of them dared to stir beyond the customary pace. The *Inverness Courier* was the consistent supporter of the large farm system which had done so much to impoverish the Highlands and it swore by the landlords as a class. So I did not expect to find scope for my views in that quarter. Still I got considerable masses of information on the state and requirements of Ireland into it! The most of this was in the shape of resumés and portions of papers read before the Social Science Congresses. Then when I propounded a scheme for making the Longman into a promenade, and having sea bathing at the door of the Inverness people, the *Courier* favoured what I said and even indicated a willingness to subscribe money towards promoting the two objects.[2]

I have no hesitation in saying that in the Highlands the *Inverness Courier* was grossly out of place and used its influence to promote a policy which was inimical to the country and to the people. It published what the editor, Robert Carruthers, thought pleased and promoted the selfish interests of the landlords; and it was hand in glove with the big farm holders. It published most libellous articles against the Highlanders and when refutations were sent they were suppressed or mangled. It upheld the Sutherland policy of consolidation and eviction all along. And even so lately as 1883 when Tom Sellar wrote a defence of his father Patrick, the *Courier* seized on the poor people—although the son's defence mostly amounted to an assertion that he cound find nothing in his father's papers to bear out the accusations against him. He did go beyond that to say that Donald MacLeod wrote only from hearsay, having been out of the country at the time of which he wrote. But the *Courier* was too ready in taking up this allegation; for ere the Royal Commission was out of Bettyhill in 1883 I myself had the succinct testimony of Robert Campbell of Ard-an-casgaigh to the effect that Donald was on the ground and part of the time in Patrick Sellar's own employment! The Campbell family and the MacLeod family lived beside each other in Rossal, one of the branches of Strathnaver. They were removed at the same time to the same place—until another removal separated them.[3]

We first took up abode in what was known as 'The Old Athenaeum' in the High Street where our next baby was born and died. We then went to Barnhill. After a year in Barnhill we removed to Drummond New Road where we had a house called Rosebank together with an acre of ground from John Noble, the bookseller. The land there was so divided that a third was taken up with the house, the garden and a nice green lawn with some ornamental trees. When we got there I made about an equal division of the rest, putting a third under potatoes and turnips and leaving the other third as pasture.

I now had an excellent opportunity of proving some of my notions. I got a cask set up in a back corner of the garden, saying to the girl that I would give her something if she would pour all the slop she could into it—kitchen, bedrooms, washing house and so forth. The ground was very poor—hardly anything but gravel. However, I prepared the garden for seed and plants and put them down without any manure. This was a daring innovation. But the cask was there and nearly always full. With an old saucepan to which I added a long handle I baled the stuff into pails and carried it carefully to the ground. To cabbage plants I applied it by dibbling a big hole near each plant and filling it—instantly covering all up to prevent evaporation. With onions and other plants in rows, I drew a trench all the way along, filled it with the liquid manure and covered it up. So with potatoes, turnips, etc, even before they showed above the earth. This ladle feeding went on all the season and the plants were receiving day by day—or rather early and late each day—as they were able to suck up of matter which was in the best possible state of preparation for them.

Nor did these draughts half exhaust the available liquid manure. I drew upon it also for the lawn, always taking care to follow with clean water. For this, for the pasture behind and even for the garden, I procured a long india rubber pipe with a rose by means of which the grass was instantly washed clean with pure water after the foul application from the cask. I did not attempt the bit of pasture with the liquid manure; but I gave it a sprinkling of guano and sprayed it with my clean water tube. By the time the lawn was well grown, the cow had eaten the pasture bare. She was then kept in and the lawn mown for her and by the time it was exhausted, which was about a fortnight, the grass was up again and she was let out. Three or four times in the season these changes were made; and with the addition of the bottom leaves from the cabbages the cow was kept in good milking condition.

The potatoes grew apace, tops and tubers. They were not only large and numerous, they were excellent food. Stupidly, I do not remember the kind. The cabbages showed the greatest capacity for their food supply and also showed how worthy they were of the good nourishment. They grew enormously and had to have some of then removed to make room for the rest. At their greatest expansion they covered an area of four feet in diameter! Nor was this all. They were so rich and tender and that in a season during which there was not a cabbage in the neighbourhood the size of my two hands— the season was so dry. I sent out to several of my neighbours presents of these giant plants and they caused quite an astonishment—their own were so small and sapless.

To all beginners with crofts or with gardens I commend the above to their adoption. No amount of solid manure, at whatever cost, would have yielded results equal to those I obtained from the rich liquid. Indeed with many plants and in many soils plenty water, pure from the burn, will do wonders by helping the nutriment which they might otherwise miss. Instead of the roots hunting about, the liquid circulates among them carrying the nutriment to them. Merely putting hard, tenacious matter in a dry state into the ground is leaving matters of very great importance to the chapter of accident. This ought not to be.

Rosebank was a very nice place and I regret that we ever left it. But I got word of Bruichnain, halfway between Clachnaharry and Bunchrew, and that it could be had at very little more than a nominal rent. The house at Bruichnain was very poor. There was a dirty outside sort of a kitchen; then a sort of half kitchen, half room with a bedstead and space into which we put a very good little American range. From this apartment we went into a little hall out of which we went out out by the front door on to a gravel walk outside. On the other side was a sort of parlour with a front window, looking out to the Beauly Firth, and an end window in the far corner looking out and down into a wooded glen or dingle. From the little hall there was a crooked sort of stair by which we ascended to three little rooms. But there was not a place in good repair and when we entered we found a colony of bees between the ceiling and the outer roof. I was too busy to attend to these interesting colonists and lost an opportunity of turning bees to proper account. I regret it now. But, as I have said, I was very busy.

The situation of the house is perhaps the best of all. You turn up to the left as you come along the road from Clachnaharry, cross the railway and go up a steep, curved road to an old ice-house on the left; then turn to the right and go on to a well rounded approach to the front door on which a carriage could turn easily and gracefully. From this you looked down several rounded terraces from which magnificent plane, ash and chestnut trees stretched upward to reach the open sunlight above. To the right, towards the road by which we came up, were trees of various kinds and sizes. To the left, away down into the dingle, were many more, with various kinds of brushwood—brambles, hazel, blackthorn—and some tall, straight larches and a few silver birches with their shivery leaves glistening in the sunlight.

These almost natural surroundings were the charm of the place. So quiet and sheltered were they that we felt that the house was only a place in which to sleep and eat. The children—Francis, Jessie, John, Ronald, Charlie and Mary—were hardly ever in the house, wet or dry, summer or winter, excepting to their meals. The wind might blow outside to 'drive the horns off the cows'. But once one got into these grounds it was perfectly calm. Even the rain seldom made any way among the trees. So complete was the shelter that none of the children ever thought of coming into the house. If there was a wider opening here or there, by which a few drops made their way, there were many spots perfectly secure. Many a time I have come in wet and windbeaten—after doing battle with the elements and while still hearing the sound overhead of the wind among the treetops—to find myself in what seemed a charmed region. The children, I hold, got so much of the out-of-doors essence of life in this delightful place that they have benefited from it ever since.

And yet we had delightful glimpses of the Beauly Firth. It is seldom rough; and sometimes we saw a vessel making its way to the head of navigation or downwards towards Kessock Ferry.[4] Beyond the Firth were the variegated landscapes, green and brown and gray, of the Black Isle with Redcastle to the left a little and Charlestown and North Kessock towards the right.

The great drawback was the danger to the children that the trains might catch them. Morning and evening, going to and coming from school, this was always a terror to their mother. And it was a drawback with the men who brought us coals to come up the steep road. I do not think that ever a coalman came to us with a second load! Poor Angus Chisholm, who at that time had the farm of Phopachy, was the only person who ventured several times to send a splendid horse with loads of turnips to us. Turnips, straw and hay were needed, for we had a cow and also a pony. For the former there was grazing among the trees and Francis and Jessie milked her.

Of this small farming we had many disappointing and often instructive experiences. In the course of our stay we had one little Shetland cow which came to grief somehow—got her bones broken. Then we had two Ayrshires in succession; but if there had been a dairy near I do not know that we would not have done as well without them. The hens—of which we had a good stock—and some ducks were a gain. They foraged much for themselves among the trees.

Our experience with ponies was not very satisfactory. The first, which came from Uist through the laborious kindness of Mr Alexander Carmichael, became vicious and could not be kept among the children.[5] We got another which, although very strong, was wearisomeness to the driver. He was so lazy he was not fit for the trap. So we parted with him and heard that, as a crofter's horse in cart or in plough, he did very well with my old friend John Campbell, Englishton Muir, who, after using him for years, sold him to advantage.

To the rest, there is still to be added the good garden behind the house in which I sowed, planted and weeded to a degree which excites my wonder now. A great part of the work connected with it was keeping the hedges on every side tight against rabbits and hares which abounded in the grounds about.

As I have conveyed, the place was delightful. But it had the drawback of having an old and partly decayed house, and I remember that the corner window in which I sat and did most of my writing was in a wall which was actually crumbling with damp behind the old paper—which could not hide the defect. I had suffered, even in bright Drummond, from rheumatism and was very much disabled many a time. I did not think of this when going for economy at Bruichnain; but ere long the muscles told of the evil action of the damp and the ailment increased until I got alarmed by signs of it travelling towards the heart. One of the results was that, after laying up for some time, I sought retirement and superannuation; and, on the certificate of Dr Duncan Mackay, obtained both.

All this time I wrote largely in the cause of the Land for the People and always had talks and consultation with friends interested in this matter. Among these were Mr John Barclay, a well matured and wide read economist, and Mr William Campbell of the East Coast Railway. With John Noble I had a good deal of radical talk and with Bailie Alexander MacBean and his sons Donald and William all of whom felt the want of the Highland element in the local papers. William Mackenzie, now of the Crofters Commission, gave an open ear and a willing heart to the idea of a Highland paper and came with me often to Bruichnain. Mr William MacGregor of the Caledonian Bank had a strong feeling in favour of a Highland organ. Dr Mackenzie of Eileanach, that fine old gentleman, wanted a paper which would go in for smallholdings and minute husbandry. Charles Fraser Mackintosh in his first speech to the Inverness Gaelic Society showed that he wanted the Highland spirit to have vent.[6]

I think the first person to offer money to start a paper was Bailie MacBean. Soon after him came Mr Matthew Elliot and John Macdonald, Mr Gordon, Mr Alexander Maclennan and Mr Alexander MacPhail; and when the proposal took shape Dr Mackenzie and Fraser Mackintosh showed their interest in the shape of £100 each, letting the shares be in my name.

Things came on by degrees until a meeting was held and a prospectus discussed. The one I had drawn up was under the name of *The Chieftain*. It was Mr Henry Munro, who put £10 into the concern, who suggested *The Highlander*—and it was at once adopted. Mr Roderick Scott was drawn into the enterprise, terms of association towards tha formation of a limited liability company were drawn up and printed; and as soon as forms of application for shares were ready I went out to canvass.

Meantime there was a rumour of an excise presentation to me on my retirement. This gave the bank courage to trust me with money before shares were paid in. And Glasgow, Edinburgh, Greenock and Dundee responded—as did men in London and other places, with Mr John Mackay, then of Shrewsbury, and his brothers in Wales and even in California and Ceylon being the most liberal.[7] Mr John Mackay went into the matter with great force, coming all the way to attend meetings in Inverness and going out to canvass among likely men far and wide. I went myself to London but what I found there was a desire that I should start the paper among themselves. However, it was not a paper for Highlanders in the cities I had in view, although their assistance should be cultivated, but a paper in the Highlands—by Highlanders and for them—in which Highlanders at home could express themselves as they had never had an opportunity of doing before. So in the Highlands, and not in the first city or even in the second, should it be carried on. And in the Highlands we set about the business.

An office was taken in a small place close to the Castle Wynd in what was then the Commercial Hotel, and Hugh Fraser, a man of much experience and real ability, was engaged. Then Bailie MacBean's son, Alexander, an excellent tradesman, was engaged and sent to Glasgow and Edingurgh to provide plant. After a good deal of reconnoitring, a printing office, long the paint shop of Mr Tough, was taken in Church Street. But it proved too small and, before the machine was set up, we had to break through a wall at the back. As we found out in the end, Alex MacBean had bought the machine without seeing it and when it came he was at his wits end to get it together. We had the matter set, and the hour of publication on, and the machine still in a state of disorganisation. It never did work rightly and every now and again the whole ponderous affair stopped altogether and hours were lost every week in consequence. However, the paper was got out and the demand, even in the town, was such that it could not be supplied.

The Highlander, May 16, 1873. We this day place in the hands of Highlanders a journal which they can call their own. This we do with the distinct view of stimulating them to develop their own industrial resources and of encouraging them to assert their nationality and maintain that position in the country to which their numbers, their traditions and their character entitle them. It is a good and righteous thing for our people to cherish a measure of pride in the stock from which they have sprung and to feel as if the eyes of their forefathers are upon them, restraining them from everything which might sully their good name and inciting them to deeds worthy of their lineage.

The particular type of humanity to which we belong is itself worthy of being preserved and developed. Instead of affecting to surrender the type of humanity which we have received, we are bound to hand it down with all the fullness of development of which it is capable. That is what intelligent men in other lands demand of us. They deprecate a tame uniformity, the result of one race giving in to another. They wish to see both the Celt and the Saxon thriving; and if they can grow side by side, two good varieties of one species, each gaining and rejoicing in the growth of the other, so much the better. But it cannot be so if the one race denies this liberty to the other, or if the other shrinks from maintaining its own distinctive character and position.

There are sentiments and tendencies of thought; there are fragments of an ancient polity—traditions of the older time—hanging about us, which it were well to cherish if only to help save ourselves and others from the hardening effects of too eager a pursuit of gain. We venture even to think that some of those lingering memories go to fit us for making contributions of considerable value to that national public opinion which is necessary to the satisfactory solution of some of the gravest social problems of the day.

It will thus be seen that, whilst we desire to be thoroughly practical, we do not ignore what is called 'sentiment'; that we prefer to carry sentiment along with us in whatever we would do for the good of the country. The discovery has not been left for us to make that too many of these schemes which were laid down for the alleged improvement of the Highlander were carried out in utter disregard of some of the people's best sentiments and in opposition to ideas which are now beginning to be pretty generally respected. Contemning the sentiments of our people was very nearly akin to despising themselves, and that very naturally led to the very general practice of under-valuing even the material wealth which lay around us.

There are our rivers, our lochs, our moors. Are they for no better purposes than sport while our people are half idle in their bothies and the nation wants food from the land? In regard to those things there is a change coming over the public mind. And we are not unprepared to hear London journalists and Edinburgh reviewers, one of these days, giving forth as the deductions of modern science some of these old-fashioned notions which they cast back in our teeth some years ago as the mere 'sentimentalities of Highland enthusiasts'.

One thing, then, is clear: a certain tide of evil influences which has been wasting our country has began to ebb. In the course upon which we are entering we shall have to do battle, no doubt. But it will only be with ignorance and prejudice, passion and greed. The growing intelligence of the age is along with us. And it is for us to take it at the flood.

The Highlander, July 12, 1873. We have been particularly careful so far not to allow any cause which we have espoused, or which we may yet espouse, to be injured by rash or exaggerated statements. We are well aware that by raising our voice to a high pitch, by screaming forth our opinions on certain questions, we might have commanded greater sympathy in some certain quarters. But we should, at the very outset, have closed against ourselves, in all time coming, the ears of those classes from whom it is of the utmost importance to gain a hearing. We determined that we should make a reputation for sober, earnest truthfulness, and for consideration for others. At the same time, there could be no mistake that we were on the side of the Highland people against all comers—and thus we should be sure of a patient and respectful hearing when we did speak.

It has been a misfortune that so many of those writers who have taken up the cause of the people, whether in town or country, have written in a manner to afford their opponents at least some pretext for saying that they—the writers in question—were guilty of exaggeration and were unworthy of being heard. We know that this opinion is a gross exaggeration. But like many other exaggerations, it can be passed to good account by discriminating men; and we are quite justified in learning caution, if nothing else, from it. In making these remarks, we have the LAND QUESTION before us particularly. We had it before us, as the most important which we could well touch, ere *The Highlander* saw the light, and we have had it before us ever since.

We are conscious of the importance and dignity of taking up a leading position in regard to so vital a matter, and the more we have felt this, the more determined we have been to watch our step, and move only so far as we had solid ground under our feet.

One thing we have kept before our mind, and that is to avoid the appearance of making *The Highlander* a mere grievance-monger. We were well aware of the fact that there is a great grievance in this country arising out of the relation in which the people stand to the soil. And in so far as mere facts and principles are concerned, we could any day make out a strong argumentative case in favour of a scheme by which a revolution might be wrought in the country. But in a case like this, it is not an argument put into a leading article, or into a nutshell, and swallowed up all at once, that is required. This sort of thing is all very well in its own way. But we must have facts, if possible, in their proper relations. And we must have 'line upon line, precept upon precept, here a little and there a little', until the leader or the advocate is, so to speak, reinforced from every side, and his arguments sustained and illustrated, at the same time that the public mind is kept constantly awake on the subject.

Turning from this column to those columns in which the provinces find utterance, we think two things will strike the reader. The first of these is the sober, cautious, and matter-of-fact way in which our correspondents express themselves. There is no straining after effect, no exaggeration, no fierce denunciation of alleged evil-doers. Facts are stated, suggestions are offered, claims are put forth, principles are laid down and left to work out their logical results in the public mind. One marked result can now be gathered within the compass of *The Highlander* itself. From one end of the country to the other, there are complaints in regard to the land. There is not a district in which the evils of a defective land system are not complained of. From within a short distance of the Pentland Firth a voice reaches us that the people have been swept off the land and that the soil is not made to yield its proper increase. From the straths of Sutherland, from the mountainsides of Ross-shire, and from the glens of Inverness-shire, Argyleshire and Perthshire much the same sound reaches us; from Kintail, Lochalsh and Lochcarron; from Glenelg, Lochaber and Badenoch; from Strathspey, Strathdearn and Strathnairn; from the islands of Uist, Barra, Skye, Raasay, Mull, Islay and Arran there is a wonderful concord of testimonies to the effect that wrong has been done to the people, and loss inflicted on the nation as a whole, by the manner in which the land is administered.

So that without any straining after effect, and without anything to excite distrust as to the correctness of our own or our contributors' statements, we may say that there is within the limits of *The Highlander* itself a positive demonstration that our country, from one end to the other, is labouring under the malign influences of a vicious land system.

With this cloud of witnesses bearing such testimony, we are justified now, we think, in speaking out without fear of being charged with exaggeration or straining after effect. In fact, with such backing as we now have, it must be plain that we could not, even if we were willing, evade the solemn duty of raising our voice in an unequivocal manner on the subject; and this we mean to do.

From the first, my aim was to have a high-toned journal and to let Highlanders feel as much as possible that it was an exponent of their views, feelings and hopes. So we gave every encouragement to native talent. We put the Gaelic article in the forefront; and we called up a band of young writers from different quarters who supplied news and ideas above news.

At Braes in Skye was John George Sutherland from Rogart. He was teacher there and he took up the cause of the people with zeal and did what he could to cultivate their spirit as well as to obtain justice for them. He wrote on local and on general subjects and did it with originality and vigour. He gave a long series of papers on Rogart, its hamlets and its people. And he arranged for me to lecture in Portree on the occasion of my first visit to Skye.

There were several other writers in Skye who helped to keep up in their respective localities an interest in the paper and to make it worthy of support as representing the Highlands in all parts. In Sutherland, in Lewis, in the Uists, in Kintyre and in Islay we had staunch supports. In Edinburgh we had James

MacPherson, a zealous and well-read correspondent who supplied much solid matter. In Glasgow we had John Pinkerton, a Bowmore lad, first; then Nigel MacNeill and John Whyte as correspondents; then Charlie MacKinnon Ramsay who was a very excellent reporter and did all for nothing excepting one pound which was sent him at the time of liquidation.

Among my prominent contributors was Dr Charles Cameron of Dublin whom I had known well as Professor of Chemistry to the Dublin Chemical Society and who gave a long series of illustrated articles on the utilizing of peat. A zealous friend and supporter was Alexander Carmichael, then in the excise and on duty in Uist and Benbecula. He not only wrote but got some men of means to take shares. He was my host and guide when I went that way and he has been a sterling friend ever since.

But good though these and many others were I had to work hard at home and abroad. I have travelled Glasgow, going up stairs and down, into dwelling houses, warehouses, shops and factories during the day and evening collecting accounts and at night attending meetings and perhaps speaking—and after all that I had to make out reports and send on the money to pay wages next day. Many a time I was so tired that I had to give up and take a little sleep with my head on the table to regain strength enough for the work. To fit me for the night's work, after the day's fatigue, I have taken a warm bath and a cold thereafter, as a refresher, and rested, say at a soiree, nibbling fruit. I have to record here that on many occasions I have been helped in the kindest manner by John Whyte—and by Henry, John's younger brother.[8] But the toil of trudging streets and stairs for the subscriptions, often several times for the same account, was terribly exhausting. Add to which that I was seldom exempt from the fear that the whole concern was being sold up for debt any hour the agent of the creditor might think proper.

When I started I thought I would have nothing to do but the work of the editor in the office—with time for reading, reflection, composition and the working out of great and beneficent ideas. But it was a common thing for me to set out on Thursday night—when the forms were laid ready for the machine to roll off its sheets—and to take the night train to Edinburgh or Glasgow, Perth or Dundee, to collect money to pay wages on Saturday. The night journey by the Highland Line was one of the most dreary. All night on the way to Glasgow or Edinburgh—with only an occasional nap to prepare for the toils of the morrow! We were having accounts accumulating in our favour over a wide area if we could get them in. That, however, was a very difficult matter. I was the only hand to collect them. But if I gathered little money, I gathered much information and became a known power in the country.

Simon Finlayson, one of our correspondents, arranged for me to lecture in Stornoway, Mr Kenneth MacKenzie, bank agent, to preside. Simon wired for the subject and the answer we sent was 'Highland Remedies for Highland Wrongs'. But when I got there, Mr MacKenzie was afraid and I consented to give 'The Heroes of Ossian'. This was my first visit to Lewis and from there I went to South Uist by the steamer and landed at Lochboisdale. There were a good many people there waiting for arrivals by the steamer and a good many no doubt from idle curiosity. I took advantage of the gathering and spoke to them; and when concluding I intimated that I would be there the next evening and for them to come and bring more with them. But they did not come. They did not want, or they were afraid, to listen. That was one lesson.

I went south a bit and then north as far as Creagorry in Benbecula and had the privilege of being entertained there by my old friend Alexander Carmichael. At a place called Garrynamonie, a dog came yelping out at me followed by an old man who called to it, 'Come in here.' In Gaelic I asked him if it was English he spoke to the dog. 'Oh,' said he, 'Is that English?' That was simple enough and might be taken as evidence of extreme ignorance. But when I got into conversation with him I found him not only intelligent but eloquent. He had been a tenant in Heisker, away out in the west, where people lived in peace and plenty—everything they required growing under their own eyes. But in the course of time they were dispersed hither and thither. What struck me most were the rich descriptions he gave of the island and of the comfort and character of the people. I was sorry afterwards I had not taken note of his descriptions and I asked Mr Carmichael to get for me at his leisure a full account. His answer, though good, was discouraging: 'If I attempted to take down every eloquent speech that came my way I would never be done.'

As I went along I saw some of the wretchedness of the people: the poor land they held and in such small quantities while there were so many large and good farms. Then their husbandry was slovenly, their houses uncomfortable and as for their crops, they could be nothing but poor on such land. In several houses I saw a portrait of Mr John Gordon, the landlord, and it so impressed me in his favour that I felt things were not the outcome of his desire.[9] So I resolved to write to him. I gave a sketch of what I saw and begged him to come down at once and see for himself what he and his agents were responsible for. I was told that he had not been there for 10 or 12 years.

With Mr and Mrs Carmichael I had the best of entertainment, physically and mentally. He was full of Gaelic lore and busy gathering more. For this work, indeed, he had gone there and remained—to the loss of promotion in the excise in which he was much esteemed. He had been in Dublin, where I first met him on his arrival with credentials from Archie Sinclair the First, and after that among my friends in Islay. His first station was in Cornwall where he found much to interest him. But he came to the Long Island as the great repository of Celtic traditional lore and he worked the mine as no man ever did before.[10] Not only that but he made friends wherever he went. And unconsciously I reaped a good deal of the result. Wearing the kilt, as we both did, I was many a time taken for him as I approached; and I found that the good impression thus made often stood to me after the discovery was made that I was quite another person.

All this time the poor people in South Uist were in such a state of slavish fear that I never got a meeting—although I often tried and visited the island repeatedly. The first break in this ice of repression was effected rather curiously. On one occasion I had ranged from Barra to Carnan but could not get a dozen men to listen. Just as I was nearing the ford at Carnan to cross into Benbecula, a subscriber to *The Highlander* told me that, down at Iochdar, there was a gathering of people repairing a fold and that if I went I could address them. I took the hint, put off my shoes and stockings and hurried down through pools and over streams and leaped in among them. They could not well run away from their work and there they were at my disposal.

150

I asked them who acted as foreman over them. 'Oh, no one.' But after a number of remarks I got them to elect a foreman and let him act as chairman; and a very intelligent man Lachlan MacDonald was. I then asked who ordered them to gather to the work. 'The constable,' they said.

'And who gave orders to him?'

'The ground officer.'

'And who appoints the ground officer?'

'The factor.'

'And who selects the constable?'

'The ground officer.'

'Dear me,' I said. 'Don't you have any say in the selection or appointment?'

'Oh no.'

'And what is wrong?'

They gave the chief place in their wrongs to the taking of the land from them and making it into big farms; and to the sending in among them of poor people cleared out of other places to make other farms larger or to make new ones. In some cases they specified that even the cattle of the factor's friends were put in among their cattle on their reduced pasture. And they had no redress.

'And now,' I said, 'what have you done to put things right?'

'Nothing.'

'Have you complained to the factor?'

'No, we dare not do that.'

'Why not?'

'He would drive us away off the estate.'

'You have a good, kindly landlady. Have you laid your case before her? I am sure she would listen to you willingly.'[11]

'No, we have not. We dare not do the like of that.'

'Well, now, I am here to ascertain your grievances and there are thousands elsewhere who are willing to help you. But the first thing they will ask is: "What have they done to help themselves?" And I must say nothing and my hands fall at my sides before them. I am helpless.'

So I told them that their first step was to let Mrs Gordon know their grievances. 'Will you sign a petition to her if I prepare it for you?'

'Yes, we will.'

I went on: 'I will write in Gaelic that you may know exactly what is being said and I will place it in English alongside so that Ranald MacDonald, the factor, shall not have to translate it for her and put his own private interpretations into it. I will write it and leave it ready for you to sign on Monday.'

'Ah, but,' said someone among them, 'they will not sign when the time comes!'

I happened to have a large sheet of brown paper in my pocket at the head of which I wrote a pledge in Gaelic for them to sign—promising to sign the petition when ready. To this I got 53 signatures.

I had to leave early on the Monday. But I left the petition with Father John MacColl, their priest. In course of time it was sent on; and after a good deal of waiting an answer came conveying, I was told, the intimation that they were allowed to elect their own constables! There was not much in this. But there was a good deal in an effort being made by themselves and there was something in no one being punished for the daring deed. That was the first meeting ever held in the island towards anything being done in the interest of the people by themselves—and their own share in it was very small! I took care, in the course of it, that I was not teaching them; not telling them what to do; not putting grievances into their heads; not exciting their discontent. I was being instructed by themselves and if I went away defectively informed that was their fault. Small though these proceedings were they were the breaking of the first link in their chains. From that day no school was large enough to hold the meetings which followed an intimation that I or any other land reformer was to address them.

Meantime, I was finding that one of the best things for myself and the poor people was that the low finances of *The Highlander* necessitated my going out among the people to collect subscriptions and to make use of opportunities to address them. And I may add that I did not address them exclusively on the land question. I often spoke on 'The Stuff We Are Made Of' and told them of the constituents of the body and how to keep it in vigour; sometimes on temperance; and, in the larger townships and villages, on some Gaelic literary subject so as to encourage the people to set a higher value on things pertaining to their country and particularly to their race, lore and language. This last has always been a leading object with me. Even if I had the power to put each family in the best possible position by means of rich grants of money under an Act of the legislature I do not think I would be doing half the good that I was doing in developing their own capabilities and stirring them up to work out their own salvation.

The Highlander, August 22, 1879. 'What is the use of trying to preserve the Gaelic language? It will be dead at any rate in another generation.' A statement to this effect meets us in quarters sometimes assumed to be high; although we can testify that never have these prophets been so much out of accord with the real intelligence of the age. We can assure those who are in a hurry to bury Gaelic out of their sight that, so far from being the advance guards of intelligence, they are really the laggards behind. Whilst the Celtic chair movement has been sowing good seed in the minds of Scotsmen and the Irish Societies have been establishing classes and issuing class-books in tens of thousands, while the various Highland Societies have been rekindling Celtic enthusiasm and the long disenfranchised Highlanders at home have been enjoying some of the advantages of an organ of their own, those who are in such haste to have Gaelic removed out of their way are going about the world with their heads down and their eyes intent upon gain.[12] They think that the chief thing in this life is to pile up money and that the language for money-making is English; so they go in for English and have no patience with those who would devote any thought to what tends to raise their fellows above the same level. If we interrogate those prophets we find that, as a rule, they really know nothing of what they pronounce upon so decidedly. It would seem that Gaelic differs from everything else in this respect, that the less one knows of it the more competent, or at least the more confident, he is in pronouncing upon it. One learned Teuton gave expression boldly to the idea that a knowledge of Gaelic was in itself a proof of one's ignorance. But this, and a number of other exhibitions of overbearing conceit on the part of the opponents of the Gael, would never find expression if the Gael showed that respect for himself, and for the things which pertain to him, which we hold to be his own due.

'But what is the use of preserving or cultivating the language?' One might almost assume that there was no need to answer such a question. As long as the language does live and is a medium of communication, instruction and worship among hundreds of thousands of Scotsmen, it is surely worthy of fair and liberal treatment—in their province at any rate. So long as history, farming, fishing, not to speak of religion, can be taught more successfully to a people in Gaelic than in English there is use in preserving and cultivating it. So long as our rivers, our mountains, our towns, our castles are to a large extent named in Gaelic, the language is worthy of being studied and cultivated and spoken. So long as there are proverbs and songs and tales afloat in that language, which have not been preserved in type, Gaelic is as deserving of being as carefully cultivated as any branch of science or art. And yet these are only the veriest superficialities of the subject.

We go in for the preservation and cultivation of the language for the sake of the people whose mental treasury and repository of culture it is. We enter the hut of an old man, in South Uist say, and we get into conversation with him. We look about and we see that the walls are rough and bare and the *cabair* all varnished with the black deposit of the smoke.[13] The furniture is almost beneath the application of the term. But we get into conversation with *Tormoid Ban*; he describes the landscapes of the small western isle in which he lived the most of his prime, the society of which he was a member; and we become somehow electrified with the ideas which are brought before us by the magic of the classic language in which he conveys his thoughts; and the hut itself acquires an interest which many a good, large and well-furnished house could never suggest.[14]

We proceed from these things to the lore of which the old man gives us specimens—some of which may be found in the *Book of the Dean of Lismore* and in *Leabhar na Feinne*.[15] Even in the prose stories there are passages which for force and melody, and richness of colouring, cannot be equalled in any language. There are, for example, the wonderfully rich and suggestive passages in which the sons of Uisneach are each described; the comparisons called forth by the beauty of Deirdre; the scenes described in stories in which the brooks, the trees, the birds, the setting sun and the rising stars are all called in and fixed in a picture which cannot be effaced as long as the mind lasts.[16]

The walls around may be poor and rough. But the walls of Norman's mind are hung up with pictures which are not equalled by those of the laird in his castle. Why, the language were worth preserving, and worthy of being learned by strangers, for the sake of these pictures alone. Abolish the language and all this beauty, and all this historic thought which it adorns, are lost to the race and the poor Highlander sinks to the level of the mere English hind who has no though above his bacon, his bread and his beer.[17] Abolish the language, and even erect white cottages with blue slates and good furniture for those who come after the Gaelic-speaking Gael, and there will be a hard, sordid, barren atmosphere within and without compared with what would be there if the people and their language were preserved and cultivated as they ought to be.

But even this does not reach the depths of the matter. Wise men recognise that there is an education of the race going on and that the grandchildren are educated in the grandparents. It is thus, for example, that the thoughts and words and deeds of the wise and brave and generous men who have gone before go to nerve and stir their descendants to equal, if not to greater, deeds. Who will not acknowledge that the prowess of Fionn and Osgar and Diarmaid, and the grand hospitality and ready forgiveness which accompanied their bravery, have had much to do with the development of that Highland bravery, gallantry and chivalry which have shed lustre not only on the race but on the nation![18] Napoleon understood this sort of thing when he carried about with him a translation of the poems of Ossian.[19] But abolish the classic, the brave, the generous and the beautiful world in which the cultured Gael lives thus and you sink him into the hopeless and spiritless condition of a man who has lost his history, his kith and his kin, who has only found that he never had anything worth preserving or worth struggling for, and that the sooner he leaves the scene the better for the poor carcase which remains!

And to the extent that the work of disparaging Gaelic and Gaelic lore has succeeded, Highlanders have actually sunk in this direction and we meet numbers—alas!—who are more afraid of rabbits than the rabbits are of them; and who have neither the faith, the hope nor the sentiment to make an effort for themselves or to preserve the good name which has been handed down to them. If the greatest enemy of the Highlanders had aimed at the most successful plan of making them offer themselves up as a sacrifice to the greed and ambition of others, he could hardly have devised a more successful one than that of taking the chief mental inheritance from them and making them feel that they were no better than the empty and broken shell from which a worthless kernel had been taken and thrown away.

The language and what it contains are worthy of being preserved for the sake of the people whose they are. And it is not as a matter of mere sentiment we advocate this preservation, although we hold that sentiment itself is a commodity without which a man is little better than a brute. We advocate it also as we would education, history, chemistry, agriculture, the fisheries—all as so many potent agencies in improving ever the physical condition of our poor misrepresented people. The sentiment, the taste, the memories, the emulation, the self-respect and the race-respect which the preservation and cultivation of our language and lore promote in our people are like fresh currents of life let into their veins, fresh vigour into their nerves and more stability into their bones—and going to fit them better for all the duties devolving upon them as individuals and as clansmen.

The Highlander, June 6, 1879. We lay it down as a canon that if our people are to be prosperous, comfortable and independent, they must respect themselves and they must set the full value on what belongs to them. This does not imply that they are to go about boasting of what they can do, and of what their forefathers did, and then expect that others are to put all right for them what they should do for themselves. This rather is the outcome of the depreciatory and depressing teaching against which we have been writing for years. Our proprietors and factors, our ministers and teachers, in too many instances, were for many years doing all in their power to make the people feel that really Highlanders were of no value at home; that they were all very well to draw water and hew wood for the money-makers of the south; but as landholders they were positively in the way of the men who were deserving. Their language, their literature, their customs, their traditions were of no value; and the sooner and the more completely they were forgotten the better for those whose interests alone were to be considered.

It were easy enough to reason our way through every step from these sentiments as causes—to the dirty huts in Skye, to the backward husbandry in Mull and to the neglected fishings on the coasts of the Hebrides. The world is only a larger school; and if you are continually dunning it into the head of a boy that he is a dunce and incapable of learning, you are doing the most likely thing to make him of no use. Indeed one of the best testimonies to the superior qualities of Highlanders is the fact that they have escaped deterioration so well as they have done. Notwithstanding all that has been done to crush faith and hope and enterprise out of them, they have done some work these 20 years. They have improved in husbandry and in cleanliness; and they have launched out on the ocean as fishermen to a very creditable degree in the circumstances.

But our contention is that if they had been taught the manly self-respect to which we have referred, and had the value of their own belongings and surroundings been duly recognised by their teachers, then there would have been ten times the progress made. This is one of our standing arguments in favour of the teaching of Gaelic in Highland schools. A few weeks ago, we pointed to the folly of allowing children to grow up with only one language when it was as easy to learn two as one. The argument made use of this week addresses itself strongly to those who think only of the material progress of the people.

The teaching of Gaelic, the preservation of Gaelic lore, the cherishing of Highland sentiment—these are valuable in themselves as so many additional furnishings of the mind and, as we well know, they nerve men and women for something for which there would otherwise be no heart. There is nothing which the very existence of *The Highlander* makes more apparent than that sentiment is a potent factor for material work. No doubt there are many who think that it would be far better to force the people to adopt improved husbandry, and the like, than to try to keep Ossian and Fingal and Cuchullain alive in their minds.[20] As we have abundantly shown, we very much value agricultural improvement. But the least sentimental will allow that improvement will be much more effective and more congenial when it comes as an intelligent result of high and generous thought and feeling.

If a young man, for example, sits out at the end of his father's cottage with a dirty cap on his head, a cutty pipe in his mouth and his two hands in his trousers pocket—what is the use? Climate, land and fate are against him— so says the factor. And he sits and smokes, knowing nothing of the past and having no hope of the future. The factor comes round and says to him, you dirty, lazy fellow, go and dig that ground, build yon wall and remove that water or else I'll send the whole of you out of the place. No one expects much out of this sort of thing, even when the inanimate sod of a man goes to work.

But imagine the young man who has been taught to value his language, his traditions, his race, his circumstances. He looks about him and he thinks of the credit of himself, of his family and of those who went before him. He says to himself, 'I am surely capable of something better than this. I see what my forefathers did in battle. I see that this land around me is capable of being made something of. I shall not put discredit on my race or on my country by leaving it no better than I found it.'

Follow this idea up with the practical instruction which ought to be in every youth's hands in his own language and you will have a transformation which will astonish those who do not know the power of sentiment. We refer here to what we have so often mentioned, a small class book in Gaelic on Agriculture and Domestic Economy—something which ought to be used in every Highland school. We need not enlarge on this: the wonder is that school boards have not seen to it before now.[21] The two things would act and react on one another. The practical use of the language would commend it; and the love of language and people and country would act upon the enterprise.

There is thus a system of life in the Highlands which is incomplete, which is to a large extent a failure, just because the language and the sentiment have been neglected. If you are to have a full-grown Highlander, you must cultivate his mind in accordance with the genius God gave him. And if you are to have the Highlands turned to the best account, you must have it done by men who can see before them, and behind, and who can find motives for action in things finer and nobler, though not so tangible, as bread and beef. If you are to have them cultivating land and growing bread and beef, you must cultivate themselves as men and not leave them on a mere level with the cattle and the implements among which they work.

I must go back to the office of *The Highlander* and add some items about our volunteer staff. Of course we wished the possessions and capabilities of the Gael to have due prominence. Among the very able contributors who soon turned up was Mr Farqhar Maclennan, Dornie, Lochalsh. Even after his location at Hawkesbay, New Zealand, he continued to send poems in his most excellent penmanship. The late Dr Garbett, Beauly, and Police Constable A W MacLennan, a Black Isle man, became liberal contributors. I may mention John MacGillivray, also in the police, who wrote a good deal of verse as well as prose, and well he wrote both.

We had Mr Livingstone, teacher, Fort William, for a while. But he was thirled to the *Courier* and was not a zealous Highlander. By and bye, Mr Skinner, teacher in Oban, took the matter up and did better. We had a good district in Easdale among the slate workers.[22] We generally had a young correspondent in Lewis; but he, as a rule, went away south as he acquired the use of the pen. In Shieldaig, Lochcarron, Christopher MacKenzie did some awkward writing, but we put it into shape when we got it. In Gairloch we had some teachers who wrote for us and, at Dornoch, Mr Bridgeford was a good steady informant especially when anything horticultural was to be reported. Simon Finlayson—who travelled for John MacSymon, grocer, and Robert Simpson and Sons, drapers—wrote particularly in connection with temperance and evangelistic meetings. It was he who sent the brief but pithy report of the Uig flood for which Captain Fraser took action against us for libel.[23]

Captain William Fraser bought from the trustees of the then Lord Macdonald the splendid estate of Kilmuir in the north end of Skye. It was said that the price was £82,000 and that he hoped to sell for £200,000. It was a splendid estate for crops, cattle, sheep and shooting. The soil was good and the region embraced the fine farms of Monkstadt, Scudaburgh, Duntulm,

Kingsburgh and Cuidrach. The estate is almost the only one in the Highlands on which crofters have good land—but at that time dreadfully over-rented. Captain Fraser had had to bond it; and to meet interest and principal he raised the rents three different times under the business management of Alexander MacDonald, solicitor and banker, Portree.[24]

I had inquired pretty minutely into the state of matters and reported as mildly as I could—for I often met the proprietor who was a reader of *The Highlander* and professed to take a Highlander's interest in all the paper dealt with. There was great discontent among the people. They tried to see him. But he never came—or, if he did, he speedily went away again. And the factor would hardly condescend to reason with them.

But the flood came in rushing streams from the mountains, along the tops of which lightning shot in great darts of fire, until the two rivers which entered Uig Bay at two different places came together in one overwhelming body. And it was not merely that the masses of water, and the force of their action, was out of common; but the freaks of rivers and streamlets were extraordinary. The south river rose and carried away about two-thirds of the old burying ground, tumbling coffins, bones and even undecayed bodies about and sending them down into the sea. And by some strange directing side force this stream was sent out of its way so far that it reached Captain Fraser's new mansion house and deposited in the dining room the coffin and the dead body of Captain Fraser's latest evicted crofter!

Nor was this the end. The flood continued to rise—for the clouds above roared, as if in labour, to send down desolating torrents to carry bridges, fences, roads, trees and all before them. There was a well grown plantation and a considerable extent of pleasure ground affording shelter and ornament to the mansion house; but all was either swept away or covered over with the scoopings out of the face of the mountains. When all this was well forward the poor manager, Mr Ferguson, ventured over to see how matters stood in and about his master's house. While he was inside, the river made another bound upward and onward and swept house, greenhouses, stables and every trace of buildings and improvements away. So complete was the destruction that when I went back a short time afterwards I could not tell where house or garden had been.

Mr Finlayson sent on a short paragraph stating what had happened and mentioning that the whole had come, according to local opinion, as a judgement for Captain Fraser's cruelty to his tenants—and that the very dead had been called from their graves to reprove the people for submitting to his treatment of them. It was also reported that the people regretted that it was not the landlord rather than the manager who had been carried away by the flood. The result was the prosecution of *The Highlander*.

I do not think Captain Fraser was so furious himself. But others were glad to hound him on; and there were others even than landlords and their factors who did not relish a revival of manly Highland feeling in the country—and the sooner the organ of that feeling was crushed the better.

Captain Fraser's factor, valuators and others were brought forward to prove that we had injured the sale of the estate. And I noticed that Sheriff Blair was very hard on us, just as if it were a matter of course that we were a gang of evil-doers who delighted in making mischief between men and masters, between landlords and tenants. The belief was that so clear was his mind on this point that he had his judgement written out the day before the trial as he was going off in the evening on private leave. He heard the witnesses for the prosecution. We called no witnesses. All that was done in that way was to call me to be cross-questioned; and I told a simple story which showed that I was only labouring by means of the paper to bring out the state of matters in the country and let all improve and benefit under an order of things which resulted from the spread of light. Alexander MacKenzie of *The Celtic Magazine,* who professed to know, said that I earned £50 that day by my appearance in court; that the damages given in the prepared interlocutor were £100 but that Blair reduced it after the hearing to £50.[25]

Another thing, from that day forward Sheriff Blair was quite altered in his manner towards me and was really pleasant and friendly and even interested in our success. Indeed he suffered more than anyone in the case. The sheriff was held up to the greatest ridicule in *The Scotsman* immediately after the affair. *The Scotsman* began: 'Prisoner at the bar, I fine you half a crown and may the Lord have mercy on your soul!' And it went on to comment on the high-flown terms in which the sheriff spoke of the offence charged against us—until I was sorry for the sheriff myself and was thankful he was away long enough for the risibility of Inverness to subside.

But *The Highlander* was under the penalty and the costs; and how were we to meet them? In an office in which we were always pressed for money to pay expenses it was not easy to save money to meet a big extra account. But friends far and near in a small way helped us. There was a concert got up in Glasgow to make a little money for us. Individuals sent in donations. And I was putting by what I could towards meeting a charge of £84.6s—to which damages and costs came.

On the last day of grace, when the money must be paid or the plant and place surrendered to the auctioneer under a decree of court, we were sitting in the little office in Church Street—the gentlemen present being Matthew Elliot, Alexander MacLennan, John Macdonald and Dr MacKenzie, the chairman. All put together, we had in hand £69.5s to meet wages on the morrow and pay the damages. Our silence was disturbed by the knock of a small boy with a note from Mr Charles Innes, saying: 'I have a telegram in which you are interested. When you have time, look in.' I put it into my pocket, intending to 'look in' when I was free.

'Oh,' said the active-minded Mr MacLennan, 'you should go now. Who knows but it is the money!'

And when I went it was: 'If Murdoch is pressed today, stand to him and hold me responsible for fifty pounds.'[26] I took £25 so as to have some money to meet office demands. And to the astonishment and disappointment of Mr Burns, the law agent, who fully expected that we should have to surrender, I handed him the full amount awarded his client. We crowed a little over our enemies and we even gave *The Scotsman* leader on the sheriff's deliverance. On the whole we were the better of what we had passed through.

It will be concluded that the life of the editor of *The Highlander* was a laborious and a most trying one. It was all that. And many a night, even after going to bed worn out with fatigue, I have been unable to sleep with the anxiety. I have tossed and suffered such a degree of positive agony that the perspiration rolled off me in streams. And in the morning I had to face the work and the fight without one wink of sleep to help to fit me for the business. I was not even in the comparatively easy position of a man endeavouring to keep a business going. I was engaged in a mission for the deliverance of a whole people out of a bondage as hard as that of the Hebrews of Egypt. And if *The Highlander* came to grief, the pioneer in the cause of the Highland people was dead and they were worse than ever. I was engaged in the cause of a race of people who had no one else of their own to speak for them and particularly no organ through which they could speak for themselves. And what business had I to undertake such a work? Should I not have left it to someone able and instructed in the mechanical part of the business and who could cope, at anyrate, with the troubles of a printing office? But there was one thing: I had not the disappointment of failing in an attempt to make wealth for myself. That was not what I set to work for.

On the other hand, I had glimpses of satisfaction in coming in contact with so many who had exalted aims in life and who were inspired by the motive of promoting the good of their fellows. And among the poor people whom I was labouring to elevate there were numbers of bright, pure, noble minds whence emanated influences which had a life-giving effect and which went to create a feeling that life was worth living. And there was a certain soothing effect in the wonderfully poetic narrations of old lore in the humblest cottages. What mental pictures were drawn and hung up within my memory!

Another thing: I had always cherished a poetic and exalted idea of everything Highland. The word itself was beautiful in my eyes, as were the mountains and glens with their woods, waterfalls and overhanging clouds. Then the poetic mind of the Highland people had made for them a world of their own which the mere Saxon could not realize or imagine. No picture was so acceptable to me as that of a small, kindly, enlightened Highland family in its cottage beside the burn with its hazel, its blackthorn, its birch, its bramble, its primrose and its meadowsweet in the light of the sun and in the shelter of a cosy glen! Every way you take it, the idea of the Highlands is elevating. And to suit all I donned the Highland dress to be all the more really Highland.

But no poetry in dress or in sentiment was proof against the want of money enough to carry on our ambitious enterprise. We were in the agonies of impecuniosity. This necessitated my being often away when I was much needed at home. And it is remarkable that all the time, whether at home or abroad, I do not think that half a dozen leading articles were from anyone but myself. Even the news, particularly when I was away, was largely from my pen. I was always opening up fresh ground—making myself known in, and acquainted with, fresh localities—and getting the people everywhere interested in their own paper. And really we had a large circulation, although I am sorry to say that the payments were slow and the income small in proportion to the papers issued. And it would have been smaller but for my going out after it.

I remember one morning we were sorely pressed for the wages and to pay for paper and postage; and I went to the canal basin on the strength of the hope that Mr MacKintosh would be there at the early hour of starting and he would frank me to Fort William. All I had was five-pence. Mr MacKintosh did tell the clerk not to charge me. But by the time we were at Fort Augustus I was feeling the need for food, and, although there were women there with bread and milk, I was afraid to ask for any lest the charge would be what I feared—six-pence. So I did not ask. But the women, being perhaps as poor as myself, were importunate in pressing sales. To their pressure and to my own feelings I yielded and got a good meal; and, as fortune favoured me, I had only three-pence to pay. That I felt to be a narrow escape. I got along without any further charge to Fort William where I soon collected, I think, £10 and was able to post that amount home that night. And what a relief that was!

I had next to go all the way to Arisaig, a pretty country once you are there. This was one of Clanranald's centres of power and not far off at Dorlin is *Caisteal Tioram*, the scrap of the old estate which is still held by the family. There is a Macdonald family at Bunacaimb in Arisaig most of whom are superior pipers. It was even said that one of the sisters played well. George and Angus and Colin are prize players; and Colin is a good Land Leaguer.

South of Arisaig is Moidart, much broken into by the sea and diversified with bog and rock. As I am in this part of the world I may make my way past Acharacle, on the Ardnamurchan estate, and on to Loch Sunart and Strontian. Along Loch Sunart the country is varied and lovely with high rocks, beautiful creeks and fantastically rooted trees among the rocks. There are some, but not many, good farms. There might, however, be good crofts or small farms; there are so many nice, sunny and sheltered spots with suitable bits for cultivation. But as in so many other places there is no encouragement given to human beings.

All this country belonged at one time to the Riddells. But Sir Thomas, whom I found there, had only a remnant of the once great estate. As I went towards Strontian, I met with a good many of the people about and heard some of their complaints. I even held a meeting under a splendid elm tree which sheltered us well from the rain—and here I heard more. So on the morrow I paid a visit to Sir Thomas. I told him that I had heard what his tenants said and that I considered it a duty to him and to myself to let him, if he thought proper, tell his side of the story.

'Oh, you mean to interview me?'

'Well,' I said, 'if you choose to put it so there is no harm. But I have told you my real object. I do not wish to go away with only one side of a case when I have access to an authority on the other side.'

'Well,' said he, 'and what do they complain of?'

'At present they are overflowing with complaints to the effect that you have done them out of their legal and moral right to choose their school board,' I said.

'Well, have they not got a school board as good as they could have chosen themselves?'

'That is not the point,' I said. 'They had the right to make their own choice and they feel that they have been deprived of that right in an unworthy manner.'

'I maintain that they have no cause of complaint.'

'You will not satisfy them that they have not every cause to complain. They were ready to go to the poll with men of their own choosing to look after the education of their own children—for which they are paying. As the time for nomination neared, you wrote to them to make no nomination until they heard from you; and when they heard from you there was no time to make their nomination.'

'They did send in nominations.'

'Yes, but they were too late; at least the returning officer, who happens to be your factor, sent back their papers saying they were too late.'

'You make a great noise over a small matter.'

'It may be small in one sense; but it is large against you; and it goes to convince them that you have no confidence in straightforward legal proceedings.'

And so forth. But from being somewhat mighty at the outset he became more modest. And after some talk on other points I left him with the conviction in my mind that he was the last of his race hastening to the end of his tether. He had no faith in law or in principles of right and wrong; and he must manipulate everything lest the people about him should do anything for themselves. He managed to have his local manager inspector of poor; his coachman was postmaster; and his coachman's wife was postmistress!

Here in Strontian is one of my model crofters; for I have always made a point of finding out and proclaiming the humble husbandmen who work their land well. I do not say that Alexander MacPherson at Ariundle could not have done better in some respects; but certainly not much in the circumstances. He had only three acres; but he kept two cows and thus he got beyond Jesse Collings' and Joe Chamberlain's model even away among these Highland hills.[27]

The Highlander, August 1, 1879. Our main purpose here is to show that the crofter system is not so hopeless, abject and unworthy as some would have us believe. We are not going to insist upon the possibility of having good crofts here because there are well-managed peasant properties in Flanders, Saxony and Switzerland. We have cases enough in the Highlands to show that there is no reason to despair of the crofters. The first case which we shall quote is that of a mason of the name of MacRae at Bernisdale in Skye who has seven acres for which he pays £8 of rent. He trenches all his ground 18 inches deep and manures it well. He keeps three cows and 16 sheep but no horse. And besides a good lot of potatoes—and, of course, lots of straw and unthreshed corn which he gave to the cattle—he had 16 bolls of oats last year out of which he had 14 bolls of meal. He is just now engaged upon an improved dwelling for himself, having proved that the land is worth having and worth working well. But he earns a good deal by his trade as a mason.

The next case is on the same estate of Skeabost and is much more to the point—as Calum MacDonald looks nowhere else for a morsel of his support. He is not at all a strong man. He has had no help. And he has had a large share of sickness in his family. He, however, believes in his occupation. He was willing to pay extra for a lease; and, seeing him an industrious man, the proprietor gave him a lease, making no addition to the rent. He has six acres at £5.2s. and pays 14s.6d. for the outlay in improving his house. When he entered upon the holding he paid £13 for 16 sheep. He keeps two cows with their young, sows 4½ bolls of oats and six or seven barrels of potatoes. He makes seven or eight bolls of meal and sells about £4 worth of hay. The most of his tillage is done with the *cas-chrom*—than which, he says, there is no better instrument.[28] And he generally gets about two days ploughing done for pay in the year as he does not keep a horse to eat its own head off.

In these cases the landlord encourages the crofters to do well for themselves and they are given to understand that they have a right to hold up their heads as men and be as independent of the laird as he is of them.

We pass over a number of cases which might be mentioned in a variety of moods and tones till we reach Loch Roag on the Dunvegan estate. The land on each side of this little arm of the sea is very much what is generally found in the hands of crofters on large estates which have been laid out in large farms. It is in small scraps among hills and rocks.

Some 26 years ago, Mr John MacKinnon, a shoemaker, set up a small hut surrounded by peat banks and gravel holes. By degree the thatch gave way to felt. In the course of time slates succeeded. By the time that was done he ambitioned a better house and, having 16 of a family, he required to enlarge. So he set to, without feu or lease, and built a good two-storey house. He was cautioned not to do so; that he might be removed and all that sort of thing. But let the consequences be what they might, he held that it was his duty to press on and only stop when he was compelled. He has gone on and has never yet been stopped. He has now a good croft—drained, trenched, and under crop in regular rotation. And long before there was ryegrass anywhere this season in Skye to cover the ground, his was waving on the breeze. Turnips, potatoes, oats, cabbages and other useful crops grow with him to his entire satisfaction. And after all his labour and outlay, the only difference he would make if he had the thing to go over again, would be to have the work completed much sooner and reap the full fruits so much earlier.

Mr MacKinnon's doings have told on numbers of the crofters about. One of his ideas is that bad houses have a demoralising effect on the people. They cannot see to read; they roam about in an aimless, idle way, open to temptations which would never reach them if they had nice, comfortable and well-lighted homes to stay in. Mr Hugh Chisholm, Vatten, on the opposite side of the loch, and Messrs Murdo MacRae, Kensalroag and Malcolm MacRae, Roskhill, deserve to be mentioned here for their taste and enterprise in regard to houses, crofts and gardens—because they go to show what can be done even without encouragement and without the protection of a lease.

We might quote several cases on the Sleat estate of Lord MacDonald. But we shall make a bound to the mainland and take a case in which there has been no encouragement given and none expected. And what Mr Alexander MacPherson, shoemaker, Ariundle, Strontian, does may perfectly well be done in most cases. He has only of arable land what takes five or six bushels of oats and about eight barrels of potatoes. The yield of the potatoes is about 70 barrels. For this land and a superior house and garden he pays £10 of rent; and £7 10s outside for the grass for three cows which he keeps. He and his two sons delve all the ground, knowing that in several respects the spade is superior to the plough. He makes no meal. He says that he finds it wiser to give the corn in the sheaf to the cows; otherwise he could not be sure of each having a calf every year. The potatoes and the milk are thus the produce which reaches the family.

He has a beautifully kept garden with plenty fruit and flowers besides potatoes and other vegetables which he uses abundantly in the house. All the dirty water, every scrap of refuse and all the weeds are carefully preserved in a dung pit where they are thoroughly rotted to serve as manure. He has ryegrass growing in hard spots where there are only a few inches of soil on the top of the granite and, what with the spent liquids about the house, that grass is ready to lodge it is so rich and heavy. The corn in like manner, and the potatoes, are made to grow uniformly over land the granite skeleton of which can easily be traced in the heights and hollows which abound. By the use of the spade he keeps the soil from slipping gradually to the foot of the hill. He takes care that the rocks which come so near the surface are kept covered with earth; and at the ends of the drills of potatoes there are no blanks such as would certainly occur if horses and a plough were allowed to go ram-stam among them.

As we have seen, Mr MacPherson does everything to a nicety and with due regard to cause and effect. His stock, which embraces the cows, a well-selected pig and hens, are kept in clean, tidy houses—the very position of the houses being fixed with a view to the improvement of the croft. Mr MacPherson cultivates a spirit of manly independence and self-reliance and respect in his sons; and, while they can do so much better than their neighbours are doing, they are not so conceited as to think the country is not good enough for them.

The above are samples of the 'poetry', shall we say, of the Highland crofter system. And they are examples which could be followed in ninety-nine cases out of a hundred, particularly with the proprietor's encouragement. They could be largely followed, as we have seen, in spite of some discouragement. And we have no doubt that they will be followed by a good many of the crofters whatever the proprietors may do. We have some hope also that the crisis which has overtaken sheep farming will lead proprietors to try and do something to make it more easy for men to acquire and cultivate crofts than heretofore.[29] Meantime, crofting is not so hopeless as the exterminators thought they had proved it to be.

It will be admitted that this travelling of the country, mixing with the people of all grades, was a good education for me. Although sometimes it was hard work, and the gatherings of money small to a mortifying degree, I confess that I would not for a great deal have missed that education. I feel sure that, although at the time it was harassing, it has done much to make my life good and long. I flatter myself, too, that my oral teaching was of great use in inspiring the people with the moral courage which was so distasteful to Sir Thomas Riddell.

But I must return to the affairs of *The Highlander*—although I have little to tell but incidents showing that our straits were increasing. Creditors were becoming more urgent and, I fear, our debtors were not becoming correspondingly thoughtful and punctual with their payments. Our subscribers were not as sensitive as they ought to have been to send on the money without our having to go for it; and agents were very heedless as to our necessities. I remember going to one Grant, a merchant at Shieldaig, Applecross, and presenting an account—for £4.00 I think. Meantime, a commercial traveller came in and carried away, as Grant confessed, all the money in the shop. And although I was there in such desperate need, I had just to go empty handed.

No doubt we were engaged in a labour of love and were not disposed to be hard. And our customers seemed to act as if they had to do, not with a struggling concern, but with a rich fountain of benevolence and power. And so they never exerted themselves. Indeed many seemed to think that, being a company, it was quite right to leave us to our resources and even to bleed us. And so we always had of money due to us what would well serve our purpose if we had it in hand. Even now, after so many years, I calculate that to myself alone, for the time I held and worked *The Highlander*, the people who were receiving it owe me £500 for which I have the accounts written.

As October 1878 approached its end, the directors reluctantly resolved to give up the struggle and consented to liquidation. Everything was done within the time to have the plant and paper sold as a going concern. On November 2, an attempt was made. But no offer was received for it as a whole and the sale was put off for a fortnight. Meantime, the concern was kept going, two successive papers being issued. But when the next weekend arrived there was again no bid for the concern as a whole. There being now room for the alternative of selling piecemeal, this was done; and a considerable number of articles were sold off. I felt as if the last blow had been given to *The Highlander* and to me as its editor—or very nearly so.

Still, much of the plant was there. And although the prospect of pushing on seemed very dark, I did not, over the Sunday and the Monday, allow my mind to be fully occupied by the dark mass of total failure. I was cogitating and putting together in my mind as to what might be said in another issue. I was not very bold, I think; I should rather say that I was tenacious. I would not admit defeat and on the Tuesday I came down to the office and met one of the boys who went with a good will to gather the rest and as many of the men who could be got. And one of them sprang forward with a little poster about the size of his hand inscribed with a call to the staff to rally, that *The Highlander* was still alive and would beat the *Advertiser* all to sticks.

While the staff was getting underway I went out among the shopkeepers telling them that I was going to bring out another issue. Would they give me a prepaid advertisement? In a short time I was back with over £7.00. No so bad! The paper came out. It was only about half its former size. But we offered it at half its former price. And scarcely was the mutilated sheet in the hands of the readers when money began to come in—in shillings, in crowns and even in pounds. One decent woman in Easdale, Mrs MacLean, seized a sheet of paper and went out amoung the slate workers there, calling out: 'The *Highlander* is in distress, you must come to the rescue!' And in a few days we had her sheet with a total of 17s 4¼d to help us out of the ditch. Sums came from all parts of the country—some, I know, as high as £6.00. And before the rest of the plant was sold we had £120 and more in the bank and were able to buy the articles which remained. So we pushed on.

1 Free Templars, a temperance organisation.
2 The Longman is an area of land to the east of Inverness.
3 Patrick Sellar had been responsible for some of the more notorious clearances in Sutherland in the early nineteenth century. His son's publication was *The Sutherland Evictions of 1814*, London, 1883. For Donald MacLeod, see Chapter 4, note 6. For the Royal Commission in question, see Introduction.
4 The head of navigation, the northern end of the Caledonian Canal at Clachnaharry.
5 Carmichael, an excise officer and folklore collector, was a close friend of Murdoch. See Introduction.
6 MacKenzie was the uncle of Sir Kenneth MacKenzie who served on the Napier Commission. Fraser Mackintosh was to become a leading Highland MP. See Introduction.
7 For MacKay, see Introduction.
8 John Whyte took charge of *The Highlander* during Murdoch's absence in America in 1879-80. Henry, his brother, wrote Gaelic poems and translations under the name *Fionn*.

9 John Gordon's father had been responsible for some of the more notorious clearances of the 1840s and 1850s. For a more detailed account of Murdoch's dealings with the Uist estate management, see Chapter 9.

10 The Long Island, the Outer Hebrides.

11 This was Emily Gordon, widow of John Gordon referred to in note 9 above. She later remarried and became Lady Emily Gordon Cathcart. See also, Chapter 9.

12 For the Celtic chair movement and other manifestations of Gaelic revivalism, see Introduction.

13 *Cabair*, roof timbers.

14 *Tormoid Ban*, literally, fair-haired Norman. This was almost certainly the man referred to above.

15 The *Book of the Dean of Lismore* is an early sixteenth century anthology of poetry and related material. *Leabhar na Feinne* was compiled by John Francis Campbell. See Introduction.

16 Deirdre was a fenian heroine.

17 Hind, farm labourer.

18 Fionn, Osgar and Diarmaid were fenian warriors.

19 Napoleon is said to have carried on his campaigns a copy of the influential but controversial 'translations' of 'Ossianic' and other traditional Gaelic verse made by James MacPherson in the eighteenth century.

20 Ossian, Fingal and Cuchullain were fenian heroes.

21 School boards, the locally elected bodies in charge of educational provision after the Education (Scotland) Act of 1872.

22 Easdale was a slate quarrying centre.

23 For details of the Fraser libel case, see Introduction.

24 MacDonald, factor to several proprietors, was known to crofters as 'the uncrowned king of Skye'.

25 MacKenzie was a prominent Highland writer and historian. Murdoch, incidentally, disliked him intensely.

26 The telegram's sender was Murdoch's ever faithful backer, John MacKay.

27 Chamberlain and Collings were leading Liberal land reformers of the early 1880s. By way of summarising his case for creating more smallholdings, Collings coined the phrase, to which Murdoch here refers, 'three acres and a cow'.

28 *Cas-chrom*, foot plough.

29 The collapse of wool prices in the 1870s brought an end to the sheep farming boom which had followed the clearances.

A Highlander in the United
States and Canada
1879-1880

Murdoch spent the winter of 1879–80
in North America. His account of
his travels there forms the last section
of his autobiography. That account
is considerably augmented here by
selections from articles which
appeared at the time in *The
Highlander*.

In 1879, some time after I took up *The Highlander*, subsequent to the winding up of the company, I was on the tramp in the Hebrides—collecting money, pushing for subscribers and dunning debtors. I had been in the Long Island and went by boat to Skye and travelled southward. And I finished with exactly 100 new subscribers, the last taken on the steamer before landing.

When I got back, things were not in a very flourishing state. But I had encouraging letters from England, Ireland and America besides what I had from different parts of Scotland. And I had a good friend in Glasgow, Mr George Alexander of the Gorbals Brass Foundry—an intense Scotsman, with perhaps Highland blood in his veins, who took a great interest in the paper on account of its upholding of the rights and ideas of the Scots as a race. At that critical time with us, he wrote to John MacKay, our great and ungrudging friend, to see what could be done to make my position in the paper what it ought to be. And shortly after that he offered me £50 as a loan to enable me to go to Canada in quest of help among the Highlanders there.

The proposal was accepted. I made such arrangements as I could to allow of my being away some months. Among these were several bills which friends signed for me to be available in the event of money being short in the office. And with rather a faint heart, I set out in September from Glasgow on the liner *The State of Indiana*.

We enter the bay of New York, leaving Long Island, with its own great city of Brooklyn to the right and Staten Island and New Jersey to the left. These may be regarded as the natural breakwaters by which the great city is guarded from the Atlantic waves. One is reminded of Dublin Bay, in moving in, more than of any other entrance to a large town that I know of in the Old World. But the resemblance does not hold good in many particulars. Clontarf and Dalymount are poor affairs to compare with Brooklyn; and Kingstown, Monkstown and Ringsend come sadly short of the magnitude and variety of the streets and institutions of New Jersey.

We are detained a long time making declarations as to our luggage. This over, we are taken by a tender to the shore where all our goods are spread out in a great, wide, covered wharf; and then comes the opening and searching of boxes, trunks and cases. The thing is done quietly, methodically and with great civility; and although it takes a great deal of time, no one can find fault with the manner in which the officers go about their business. There is no sign of a desire to detect people in fraud. The duty has to be done and the functionaries do it as pleasantly as they can.

I have often commented upon the fact that our false policies at home send away our best men. One cannot judge very well of the character of the men whom he sees bustling about at a landing like this. But I must say that so far as mass of body and brain is concerned, America has managed to have it waiting for us here. The men are tall, spanking fellows; and the easy manner in which they go about their business indicates that they are conscious of their ability to do their work without any effort.

While I am waiting at the wharf for some of my fellow travellers to get through the hands of the customs gentlemen, I am accosted in the most unmistakeable Islay Gaelic: 'The kilt will do very well in this weather!' And most pleasant it was to hear the accents of the Queen of the Hebrides away here. The last of Scotland I saw was Islay. And the first spontaneous salute in America was from an Islayman of the name of MacFadyen from Port Charlotte.

At last we make our way out of the wharf. The horses, I perceive, are nothing to our Clydesdale animals either in weight or condition. But they are admirable as having a good combination of strength and action. They cannot possibly carry the loads which the Scotch or English dray horses carry. But they will double their speed. I noticed that the horses here have remarkably good feet. The Clydesdale's weakness is in the hoofs. But these New York beasts have a perfect hoof. And they require it; for the roads and streets are not nearly in such good condition as they are in the old country.

The architecture and the business of the streets through which we pass remind one more of London than of Glasgow. Buildings have been thrown up in a hurry. There is no massive solidity of architecture. But there is business, business, business. By and bye, we are in the great artery of New York. But we can hardly think that this is Broadway at all. It is better entitled to be called Longway, being nearly six miles in length, or as long as from Inverness to Dores. But it is no wider than Buchanan Street in Glasgow and, of course, nothing approaching the width of Sackville Street in Dublin. It must have contrasted only with some old, narrow streets which gave way when business demanded more room outside and in.

Already I have dipped into a good many places and I am rather impressed with the number of persons who know about *The Highlander*. I find friends in *The Herald* office and in *The Scottish-American* office and in the *Irish World* there is a long and highly gratifying welcome to the editor of *The Highlander* on the occasion of his visit. Patrick Ford of the *Irish World*, by whom I was well received, at once wired to Dr William Carroll, Philadelphia, that I was there.[1] And almost by return the doctor was up and waiting for me in Marchants Hotel not far from the New Jersey ferry. I had had some correspondence with the doctor and he had always showed a disposition to help with *The Highlander*. Now that I was in America, I was his guest; and he invited me to accompany him to Philadelphia.

Dr Carroll is a stout, strong and active man with broad shoulders, strong limbs, a large flow of brown hair worn somewhat long, strong beard but whiskers shaven. His forehead is broad and prominent and his features marked. His nose was not what would be called classic; it was inclined to be round and the beard left the lips to be guessed at. Altogether he was then, I should say, about 45 years of age and five feet ten in height.

Of Dr Carroll's mental dimensions it is not easy to speak. He was always busy with something besides his profession and seemed to have the confidence of others. He had the power to influence those with whom he came in contact. He took a wide view of public affairs and seemed to be influenced by the idea that he was in the world to be of use to his fellow men, the Irish and the Americans having the chief claim upon him. Along with the Irish came the Highlanders, on account of their race and language, and I, being engaged in promoting the interests of the Celtic people, came in for a particular share of his interest. *The Highlander* came thus within the purview of his concerns and he thought of how he could help it to live and to be of use to the Celtic people. I think that in a letter which I had had from him he gave me a hint that there was some money which could be had to help the cause—although he did not say where it was nor to whom it belonged.

However, he brought three other gentlemen to me in the hotel and told me that they had resolved to let me have $3000 for *The Highlander*. They would let me have $2000 then and the rest later. They paid me down the first instalment and, some months later, the balance was given me by the late John Breslin.[2] They did not say how they had got the money and I did not ask. I was too thankful to get it to raise any questions about it, and, in all my subsequent intercourse with Dr Carroll, I never asked him about it. But I will state here that the friends of O'Donovan Rossa thought the gift to me was out of funds which in some way had been under the management of O'Donovan and that these funds had been placed for greater safety in the hands of my friends.[3]

The O'Donovan party became dissatisfied that I was doing no O'Donovan work with the money. This was the more provoking to them, and to him, in that I had written to the British press that O'Donovan was not the power among the Irish-Americans that he would have people think. This brought me into his bad books so far that he urged all Irish-Americans to boycott me. Altogether I was in bad bread with that faction and the fact came out in some of their debates—in which it was declared that I was doing nothing for their cause. Of course, if I had been making use of the money in dynamite and all that, I would have been a 'white haired boy' with them. But I was not. I was anathema.

A particular sequel to this is worth mentioning. Some of the debates of the O'Donovan Rossa party came into the hands of a writer in *The Scotsman* and straightway—on their complaint that I was not using dynamite—he charged me, in December 1882, with being engaged in this country in blowing up bridges and mansions, at the instance of Rossa and his fellow writers. Although I wrote to *The Scotsman* again and again, not a word was ever inserted in that paper and, so far as it was concerned, I was left under the stigma and was misjudged accordingly—as I found in Assynt and the Reay country when I went in 1883 to prepare the crofters for Lord Napier's Royal Commission. The only approach to a vindication that I ever got was through Sir Kenneth MacKenzie, on that Commission, asking me about the accusations and affording me the opportunity to say that there was never any connection, understanding or co-operation between the O'Donovan Rossa party and myself.[4] This was reported. But *The Scotsman* never withdrew its accusations nor in any way made amends for its foul attack upon me.

In two hours I came a distance of 90 miles from New York to Philadelphia and more than ever do I wonder at the backwardness of the folks at home in regard to railway carriages. I cannot understand why directors spend so much money on stations and offices for mere purposes of ornament and why they are so slow to adopt the improvements which have been so readily made in this country. We walked in at the end of the carriage, which is 50 feet long, and walked out at the other end when we reached Philadelphia—after sitting as comfortably as if we had been in a drawingroom.

The run was through a flat country, partly cultivated and partly under trees. There are no forests; just enough of wood to make the landscape pleasant. Fields of Indian corn, buckwheat, cabbages and grass are the agricultural features with, of course, cattle which all seem to be red with a few white streaks. The houses are all built of wood although most of them are three storeys high. There are whole villages of these wooden houses; and the towns of Elizabeth, Newark and Clinton, through which we passed, are largely of the same material. In Elizabeth I did not see a house of brick or stone although there is plenty of clay for brick and although brick and pottery are manufactured at Clinton.

The people about have not got out of the fashion of the early settlers in regard to house-building. Everywhere I see signs of the feeling that they can live very well without building houses and laying roads that will last for ever. They go in for making all these things serve them—not allowing the means of life and comfort to become their superiors as is too often the case.

The land all along from New York is a red clay very like what abounds in the Kilmuir estate in Skye. The husbandry is nothing noticeable. Everything looks rough and abundant and ready. There is plenty land and all is fertile. They put in the seed and in a short time they reap. They do not require to slave at it; and our necessities in the old land make a good market for their produce. The folly and waste and cruelty of the old country are telling to the advantage of the new.

Although I had no intention of visiting Philadelphia, I now feel that it would have been a great mistake not to have come. It is difficult to know what to begin with and, even when I do begin, I know that I have only the faintest view of things. I shall, however, make a bound to the top of the Girard College, an institution set up by an eminent merchant of this city for the education of orphan boys. At the present time there are 800 of them—fed, housed, clothed and educated with all the care which is usually bestowed upon the sons of well-to-do citizens. The building looks to me as if it covers considerably over an acre of ground.

But what makes me mention this institution first is this: I made my way to the top of it. The roof is covered with great slabs of marble. On these I stood, as on the top of Tomnahurich at home, and looked eastward to the River Delaware and westward to the River Schuylkill. After London and Manchester and Glasgow and Dublin, what strikes one is the absence of huge masses of building. The city is typical of the American democracy which ensures a wide and much more equal distribution of property than with us. No mansions of dukes and marquises and earls: these props of British society do not exist. And not only does the city get on without them; it would gladly shake off the imitations which speculation has enabled some Americans to get up.

In the matter of grand mansions public opinion is so strong that the man who would command respect must avoid ostentation. He who makes such a display comes at once under the brand of 'shoddy'. There are masses of wealth, no doubt. But there is a wholesome opinion abroad which does something to check corruption. The fathers of this city were careful on that point. The Swedes, the Quakers and the Irish have all kept a wholesome check upon the development of purse pride and upon the abuses which grow and flourish under the shadow of great accumulations of property.

All this is seem from this eminence. The streets run north and south and east and west—at right angles. There is at present in course of erection, in Penn Square, an immense city hall—the design, by the bye, of a Scotsman. Your Inverness Town Hall, which has cost so much labour and thought, is a toy to stand on a bracket within that of Philadelphia. But again the houses of the private citizens are just two, three and four storey erections with no great disparities between the regions of the rich and the haunts of the labouring classes. And rich and poor, from the way in which the town is laid out, have the benefit of fresh air to an extent which none of the old world cities can command.

The brick houses in this city are slight. But they are so well planned and executed that they are very comfortable and healthful. There is not a cottage or tenement in Philadelphia without its bath, for example. What a world of health and taste there is in that one thing! I go in for a wooden or a brick house with a bath in preference to a granite house with its large drawingroom and no bath. I find my own idea amply confirmed—that it would be better for us at home to be content with far less costly houses in the matter of hewn stone and rich adornments inside for the sake of being our own house-owners and having those healthful conveniences which we too often sacrifice to pride and vanity.

Then along the Philadelphia streets are rows of trees, mostly maple, which give a fresh rural aspect and feel to them. Look east or west, north or south, and it is through an avenue of trees. Then almost every street has its tramway cars and both shade and expedition are secured in moving along. There is a great deal of travelling by these cars. Fine, long, easy cars they are, like those of Glasgow.

The great fact here is that property, convenience, comfort and means of healthful enjoyment are well distributed; and the benefits enjoyed are due as much to the forethought of the men who laid the foundations of society as to the extent and fertility of the land on every side. At the first, and at different times since, great precautions were taken to save the city and the state from the corruption which is sure to follow such vast accumulations of property as exist in the old country. It is not a transfer of our people to this country that we need; it is a wise administration of what we have at home. With that we can have health and strength and morals—and a reasonable amount of wealth on which to live and help one another and to serve God.

That is my impression so far. I may change my opinion as I go along. I am open to conviction; and if I see that it is our duty to flee from the rot of the British Isles, I shall say so with all sincerity. I must admit, however, that with all its great advantages of climate, extent, soil and mineral resources, one cannot escape the thought that this continent is the great home of the races who are to rule the world in the time to come.

The good Doctor Carroll entertained me for a fortnight at his home at 617 Sixteenth Street, Philadelphia. The doctor then came with me to New York where I got the remainder of the money. This I sent home to the office, keeping only what was necessary to cover my travelling expenses. And from New York I sailed on one of those palace steamers which carry businessmen and pleasure-seekers up the River Hudson to Albany.

I fear any attempt of mine to describe the 'Rhine of America' would be a failure. To some of my readers I shall convey a very good idea when I ask them to imagine the two sides of Loch Sunart, from the mouth to Strontian, sprinkled with villas, with villages, towns, churches, cities and forts. Let them imagine still further the *Iona*, with two most elegant decks above the present structure, and she sailing up Loch Sunart in place of the patient, plodding *Plover* which has done her duty so well and so long. America boasts very justly of its Rhine, the Hudson. But we may boast in the same strain of Loch

Sunart, although one can hardly remember any habitations on its shores besides Glenborrodale, Salen, Laudale and Strontian.

The trip up the Hudson is one of the great treats. The wonder to the slow-going Briton is the extent to which the whole of these fine 'Highlands' has been taken possession of by builders and laid out in such a manner as to have one of the happiest combinations imaginable of rural and city life. But one is disappointed with the want of originality and of poetry in the names which have been given to the places along the romantic river. The Yankees seem to have been in too great haste in fixing the names of their towns. It looks as if the naming had been left to stableboys. Cozzen's Landing and West Point Landing—the latter being the name of the finest elevation on the river—are good, or rather bad, examples. I am pleased with the native names which have been retained in Ontario, Toronto, Ottawa, Simco and some others and would have kept more of them if I had had the choosing. I should have been better pleased if the United States had been known by a native Indian musical name; and as a native name was not chosen, I would have preferred Columbia to America.

But there was compensation at West Point Landing for the want of names. Here the steamer which landed the passengers from ours bore her name, *The Highlander*, boldly on her front and was to me, of course, a greeting warm and grateful—far beyond what it could be to anyone else on board. I hastened to throw a copy of *The Highlander* to its namesake, but was too late and so missed an exchange of cards.

From Albany I pushed on, taking the train to Rochester. At Rochester I was soon introduced to a good Highlander and a brave Skyeman, Mr Angus MacDonald. I could not have been more fortunate. Mr MacDonald seemed to know everyone both at home in Skye and in Canada and in the States. And what is more, he gave me his aid in the most friendly manner. Mr MacDonald is agent at Rochester for the Anchor Line of steamers and I can assure both the company and intending passengers that a better man could not be found to fill the post. He soon introduced me to several other Highlanders including Mr Alexander Stewart from Skye, Messrs Gordon and Angus from Inverness and Mr Cameron from Fort William—all of whom I was glad to find doing well.

From Rochester I made for Buffalo where I found myself at once in the hands of Mr Donald MacLeod from Stornoway, Mr Allan MacDonald from Croy near Inverness and Mr James Mann from the smithy at Inshes above Inverness. The message which I have from some in Buffalo is that if people would work hard at home, steer clear of drink there and be content with moderate living, they might get on as well as men do in the States—that is, in dealing and manufacturing. But everywhere the immigrant nearly shudders when he thinks of the land laws:'The idea of my being at the beck of a landlord in Scotland after my experience here! No, no; it won't do. Here if I work hard and mind my character, I may have a farm of my own, improve it, keep it or leave it to my children.'

I should not omit to mention the warm and deep interest which was taken by several Irishmen here in the cause and fate of *The Highlander*. They were quick to give us credit among British papers for being at all times disposed to do the Irish some measure of justice. They were grateful for that small mercy and ready to serve me to the extent of their ability. That is something for me to be grateful for. They will find that their goodness has not been thrown away upon me.

From Buffalo to the Falls of Niagara is only a run of less than two hours. I had several views of the great cataracts. The first sight was not up to the expectation. Everyone seems to form an exaggerated idea of the extent of the falls and so is disappointed when he sees the reality. But then another view raises the sight again and you come away duly impressed with the grandeur of the display.

The river is divided by several islands something like what takes place on the Ness. They break the stream into several as at Inverness. The islands are connected by bridges and laid out with walks and seats and summerhouses. On one of the islands is a large paper mill. On others there are mansions, lawns and so forth. I had the benefit of the electric light when viewing the grand scene at night. There is talk of the whole of the grounds about the falls being bought from the Porter family and laid out as in international park open to the public. I have no doubt the thing will be done. The idea of public parks has a great hold on the minds of the States and Canada.

All western New York, on the American side, and along from the falls to Hamilton round the head of Lake Ontario and on by Oakville to Toronto, forms a grand fruit-bearing region. Apples, pears, peaches and grapes grow in the most luxuriant abundance—insomuch that, in many cases, the fruit is never lifted off the ground but left for the hogs to gather for themselves.

The Central Fair was held at Hamilton when I reached. The sheep were enormous; the pigs were very excellent; there were some good serviceable horses, middling cows and splendid fruit, butter and cheese. There was a section for the exhibition of the farm and other produce of Manitoba. This was the chief attraction of the show. Manitoba is just now the Eldorado of Canada; and judging by the potatoes, mangels, turnips, oats, wheat and Indian corn which have been produced, there is no reason to question the great expectations entertained in regard to it.

A few miles out of Hamilton, at Oakville, I came upon Mr John MacCorkindale, at one time of Cluanach near Mulindry in Islay—also a veteran Highlander from Skye of the name of MacNeill. Both have been in the habit of luxuriating in *The Highlander*—sent to the latter by a nephew in London. So I was at once taken possession of and treated both by Mr and Mrs MacCorkindale—who is also of Islay stock—as Islay people know so well how to do with strangers.

From Oakville I took the train for Toronto and there made for the house of William George Murdoch, barrister and son of my brother George. He and his wife received me kindly and treated me in the best manner possible. She was a beautiful, dark-eyed and dark-haired young woman; and a picture of her on exhibition had created a sensation. She was presented in so captivating a light that the whole was called 'Beware'!

One of the leading Highlanders in Toronto was Mr Hugh Miller, druggist, King Street, a cousin of the famous Hugh of Cromarty.[5] To him every Highlander was supposed to gravitate. I found Mr Miller all that could be expected and he was glad to receive me as being from Inverness where he served his time in the drug business. He was an active and true friend to me all my time there, taking an energetic part in getting up a meeting for me to address.

The resolution I had come to was that I should call upon this universally recognised, though uncrowned, chief and say to him that I called as a piece of loyalty to so good a Highlander, but that I did not mean to avail myself of his attentions as I was sure he would be in almost constant requisition. This I did; but it was all nonsense. 'No, no,' said he, 'you must make every possible use of me as it is a duty and a pleasure for me to promote your views.' And I had not only his word and his time, but his personal attentions and exertions. And every day there was some new hint, some new move and some message for, or from, some other good man who desired to serve *The Highlander*. *The Globe* somehow got a budget of facts about me and, giving it to the world, I was soon recognised in the streets—and it would do many a one at home good to know what magic there is in the tartan.

Well may the rich province of Ontario be proud of its capital, Toronto. The inhabitants do not profess to be rich as the men of Lombard Street, London, or of Ingram Street, Glasgow. But they have the riches of that manly independence which thrives on a free soil. It would do the hearts of our people at home good to see the healthy democracy which thrives here in the common-sense foundation of almost every family in the country owning its own farm. That is the great fact of this country. And to those who experience the effect of that fact, the system which we have so long tolerated in the old country appears as absurd as it is hateful. Invernessmen, Islaymen, Skyemen and Irishmen whom I have met with here laugh with scorn at the wretched system of landlordism and flunkeyism which has grown up in the land of their birth. And several of them who have been home to see their friends declared that they would never cross the Atlantic again—so disgusted were they with the despicable subserviency of the rank and file of our people to the privileged classes above them. Here good natured people laugh with derision at the wretched pretensions of those who lord it over the people in the old country. One of the surest ways of incurring contempt in this country is to affect aristocratic airs.

Scotchmen, and particularly Highlanders, have got quite the upper hand in this province. Perhaps the finest business house in Toronto is that of Messrs John MacDonald and Co, Front Street and Wellington Street. This John is a Stratherrick boy and still a young man—fit for any work which bears the true moral stamp. He might have been at the head of a large section in politics. But he is chary of pitch and he sticks more to moral and religious work. He has made an enormous business in 'dry goods'—as the drapery business is called in the States and Canada—and built a house which towers above the rest of this foremost of wholesale streets.

On the same street are Gordon and MacKay, MacLean and Co, Galbraith and Co, James Campbell and Son, MacIntyre and Co, whilst in other streets we have the Mathesons, MacKintoshs, Murrays, MacDonalds, MacPhersons, MacGregors, MacMillans, Morrisons and MacMasters— all pillars in the commercial fabric of the commonwealth. Then in municipal and provincial politics and government we have the MacDonalds and Mowatts and Morrisons and MacKenzies, whilst MacDonald and MacKenzie are the chiefs in the Dominion arena of politics. And of those whom I have mentioned there is hardly one who does not speak and love Gaelic.

What a galaxy of light and power our country lost when it cast out the stocks from which these men have sprung! A free land system in the old country would have ensured that these men, or men like them, would be at the head of the nation in place of the imbecile members of worn-out families who have no claim to rule but what they derive from their material possessions. We have lost the direct use of their power. But we shall have that power indirectly, I hope. Some of these men will send home waves of sympathy and encouragement to help those who are labouring for the emancipation of the serfs in the Old Country and we shall by-and-bye have something in politics analogous to what we have already in that influx of food which is undermining a vicious system of rural economy.[6]

I sailed the entire length of Lake Ontario and more from Toronto to the Highland town of Cornwall on the River St Lawrence. My sail was under the command of Captain Sinclair of the *Corsican*. Many a one in Islay and elsewhere will be glad to hear of one of the Sinclairs of Mulindry. The captain is the second son of *Baldi Breac*, the first Islayman I ever knew. He is a cousin of the late Archibald Sinclair, printer, Glasgow. Of course we had several yarns about Islay and turned over a large number of names and events; but it was sadly mixed with melancholy.

Cornwall is the capital of the country of Stormount and in some respects the capital of Dundas and Glengarry. It is the most Highland place I have been in yet. The second and third generation speak Gaelic; but the young who are now growing up are not likely to know any. Almost everyone I have seen is of Knoydart stock. Nearly all are MacDonalds—MacDonalds right and left. And the most of those are Roman Catholics as their fathers before them were.

There is excellent land here and there is much wealth in the hands of the people. Excellent crops are raised without much expense and there are both the River St Lawrence and the Grand Trunk Railway to carry the produce to market. There is not nearly so much fruit grown here as to the west and south of Toronto and, altogether, there is not the same bright appearance of enterprise that one sees near Hamilton. The people are less ambitious to push on. They are more amenable to the idea that having food and raiment they should be therewith content.

Still, here as elsewhere there is a rising among the people for the far North West and there are numbers of farms to be sold. There is an idea, which is very commendable, that the fathers should plant themselves where there will by plenty of room for their sons to settle near them. Accordingly, the man of 100 acres here is for selling out and going where he can get 600 acres—so that he may have 100 each for himself and his five sons. This idea has taken possession of thousands—aye, tens of thousands—in the Province of Ontario alone; and they are on the look out for immigrants to buy their present possessions.

This I take to be the best opening for the great majority of immigrants. By looking out, as they may easily do, they can get a farm of 100 acres, with dwelling houses and outhouses ready to hand, instead of going to the bush or to the prairie and roughing it for several years. If 100 acres are too many— and the belief is gaining ground even in this country that farmers can have too much land—two families can buy 100 acres between them if it so happens that they do not fall in with lots small enough to suit their minds and views.

I am quite satisfied that large numbers will be out here next year—to be followed by many others as soon as they can get out of the entanglements of Old World leases. The idea of owning one's farm will grow even in the

M

minds of the immigrants; and they will not be long in this country when they will wonder that they have been so long satisfied with paying rent for the land of another.

I must mention here that in times past there were fearful hardships endured by immigrants. Striking out into the forest and there cutting their way to a bit of ground in which to sow a few bushels of grain and plant a few potatoes; living somehow until the crops grew; aye, living a life which is now almost incredible. All this sort of thing has come to an end. And besides that, there are farms to be had in these settled parts of the country. Then there are the vast prairies of Manitoba, ready for the plough; and everything is being done to facilitate the settlement of that country. There will be no more of those terrible hardships. Indeed, this generation of Canadians has, to a large extent, given up the work of clearing land. You see great patches along the roadside, all the way from Niagara round the head of Lake Ontario and on to Montreal, in which the work of clearing the land has been given up—the young Canadians thinking it too hard work, and quite uncalled for, when land free of trees can be had for nothing. Besides this, there is an idea growing up that there has been too much clearing; that there should have been great belts of wood reserved for shelter, for the regulating of the temperature and for the supply of fuel in the time to come.

I next took the steamer *Bohemian* to Montreal and found myself in a strange surrounding. The vessel was crowded with people, the great majority of them speaking French. Numbers could speak nothing but French although born and bred in the neighbourhood. Some spoke French, Gaelic and English. The French are much more tenacious of their language than the Highlanders are; and I am told that in some places east of Montreal there are MacLeods, MacDonalds, MacLeans and MacKays who speak nothing but French. It is very strange.

The French have got a wonderful hold away in this quarter. And there is a growing feeling, among others, that the French are going to 'overrun' the whole of this region; and this they regard as a bad prospect. As a rule, they say, the French are a backward race. They have not the enterprise of the Scotch. They are content to plod and potter along in a small way, saving money rather than making more. And where other settlers come to grief from their overleaping the mark, the French creep in and buy the farms thus for sale. In this way they act the part of the tortoise in the race with the hare. I do no more here than repeat what I have heard said of the French. I have not had time or opportunity to sift this matter for myself.

I was struck at once by the solid and elegent architecture of Montreal, as I had been by the fine and varied scenery of the St Lawrence. This river, which for purposes of communication is a continuation of Lake Ontario, forms an important section of the great waterway by the Welland Canal into Lake Erie, then by the St Clair River into Lake Huron and thence again into Lake Superior and eastward from that into Georgian Bay. These waters are of immense help in developing a country whose chief exports—timber, corn and cattle—are heavy and bulky and for which, all the world over, water continues to afford the cheapest way.

At Montreal I was taken in hand by a Mr Murray who kindly drove me about with horse and conveyance, taking me not only all through the city but quite out and around it. There was also a bookseller of the name of Watson whose place formed a sort of centre for me. I also saw a Mr MacKay, one of the great Montreal merchants, originally from Sutherland. He, like others, subscribed for *The Highlander*—but took no shares. Thus, although the trip was no great gain, it was not a loss.

From Montreal I made for Glengarry, landing by the Great Trunk Railway at Lancaster. Then I made for the more central town of Alexandria. Everywhere here Gaelic is spoken and spoken with such a flavour that you would hardly think that many of the speakers could speak anything else. Indeed in new Glengarry, I am quite satisfied, Gaelic is spoken in greater purity and majesty than it is in old Glengarry or Knoydart—whence so many of the new Glengarry folk's progenitors came.

I have not time or space for a description of the country here. I must say this, however, that while there are considerable patches of bush and of half-cleared land, striking north for 100 miles from Lake Ontario and the River St Lawrence, the country is much more thickly inhabited than the Lothians are in Scotland. And as for travelling for hours or even days nearly as you can in Sutherland, without meeting with a farmhouse, you are never out of sight of them here. At Alexandria, as at Lancaster and Cornwall, the MacDonalds and MacLennans and MacPhersons and MacRaes abound.

Almost due north from Toronto, some eight miles, lies Lake Simco. All around this Lake you will find dense settlements of Highlanders—just as if the erstwhile denizens of the Herbrides carried with them their love of water and desired to gratify it by keeping near the waters of even a minor fresh water lake. Scarcely hoping to visit so many, I made a dash for Nottaswaga and there held a most hearty meeting. The night turned out windy and dark and the numbers present were not great. But they were alive to the value of each man being the owner of the land he cultivated and so had no hesitation in passing a strong resolution against the feudal system in Great Britain and Ireland.

There was a considerable fall of snow during the night I spent in Nottaswaga. But when I got down again towards Lake Ontario there was only a slight covering—barely what satisfied the Canadian taste for snow. A winter without snow is a failure in that country. For one thing, the roads are so bad that rain soon has them all mud, and if there is frost without snow, the masses of mud become great hard lumps over which one travels as if it were over heaps of stones. It was now past the middle of December and there has been very little snow—so little there were lamentations that there was to be no real winter, no proper travelling, no sleighing.

On my return, however, this time from the skirts of Georgian Bay, a great branch of Lake Huron, even Toronto had got on its buffalo coat and rigged its sleighs, and the cabs and street cars were all gliding along as quietly as cats, but for the tingling of their bells. I had often heard of the Canadian winters; but I do not know that I ever took the idea in rightly until I was in the midst of them. And from what everyone said about the intensity of the cold which they always anticipated, I could not enter into these delights in anticipation—excepting in regard to improved locomotion. I did many a time wish for snow enough to make the roads passable. But I did *not* wish for the keen, penetrating cold which I understood to be inevitable.

I must honestly say, though, that when the snow did come there was a measure of enjoyment in it which I did not anticipate; and I have no doubt if I had had time to lay myself out for the mere enjoyment of the thing, I should have entered into it with quite Canadian zest. But to be groping about from two to six o'clock in the morning in strange places, and always in a great hurry, was—it will be readily understood—not the best set of conditions under which to drink in the poetry of the thing.

Poetry, I must confess, there is in it. Everyone seems to look forward to the snow and the exciting enjoyments which it affords. The little cutters are out scudding along with great speed. The cutter is a small one-horse sleigh, seated for two and so low that though there is a 'spill' it does not matter. You have only a short distance to fall and you come down on the downy, beautiful, white snow—soft as feathers and the very pink of purity. Not only so, but it is dry. You are not afraid that the patches of snow which adhere to clothes or shoes will melt and wet you.

I had only one fall of the kind. The Rev Mr MacDonald, Cambray, kindly yoked his horse and cutter and drove me to Glenarm. Along a part of the roadside was a ditch. Coming too near the bank, the cutter upset us both into the ditch. But we simply rolled over each other like two sheep which had their feet tied. We got up, shook ourselves, set the vehicle on its beams, mounted it and away again as if nothing had happened.

I meant to have said that this cutter has the shafts attached to the body as if there should be another pair to be attached for another horse. The effect of this is that when the horse runs along the single-horse path, the slides are out of the ruts. But the rule is for the horse to be out of the central path; and the intention of this side-yoking is to facilitate the passing of the vehicles. The slides are not so sure to respond to the pull of the horse to one side as wheels and the horse is placed so as to give him a double purchase when he meets another horse and has to go over entirely from the left side to the right.

The sleighs are of various forms and styles. Some are very ornamental and all, like every other yoke or 'rig', as the Canadians call them, are very light to suit the light, lively and quick, yet wonderfully tractable, horses. Sleighing is one of the winter enjoyments into which ladies particularly enter with great zest. The body of the car is furnished with cloaks and wraps and 'buffalos', which are great rugs of buffalo skins with the hair outside and woollen linings inside, while buffalo overcoats are put on by the pleasure-goers. The horses are harnessed in some cases with great elegance and at considerable cost— so great sometimes as to bring on a crisis in the small affairs of the families concerned.

Quite an excitement takes possession of the inhabitants when sleighing sets in and the horses themselves seem to participate in the exhilarating effect of the fine, free, pure air which man and beast inhale. How much the sheer cold of the season has to do with producing the activity which mingles with this excitement it is not easy to say. But if there has been a spell of wet, the roads and streets have been in such a state with mud and slush that all locomotion is unpleasant and is eschewed as much as possible. This adds to the pleasure with which sleighing is resorted to. But however this may be, real excitement is there—men, women, horses and dogs being all possessed with the spirit of motion.

In addition to this activity, there is the pleasant mingling of the sounds of bells. Among them is an undertone produced by an arrangement of small cups or thimbles—I do not know what they are called—attached to back bands of leather and keeping up a constant though subdued ringing. But there is no driving, no whipping, no shouting. The horses enter into the thing so heartily that all they want is the least motion of the rein one way or the other to guide them.

All this goes on in towns, the streets of which are lined with trees, mostly maple. When the sun shines brightly, as it often does, the sparkling of the crystals of frozen water is very beautiful. And in the evening, the gas lights along the lines of trees produce quite a strangely pleasurable feeling which I cannot well describe.

There are family expeditions thus on the snow—and party expeditions. In the evening, for example, one or two of the young ladies of a house come from the suburbs with the sleigh to bring home the breadwinners after their toil—another maiden having remained at home, perhaps, to have supper crisp and fragrant and nice for them when they return. The sleighers trip down and into the store or warehouse to see if father or brothers are ready to go home, bringing quite a delightfully fresh current of cool air into the heated interior; bringing, at the same time, into the arena of business the fine, bright, earnest faces and straight, graceful, easy carriages of Canadian young women.

I say 'women' here in preference to 'ladies' because I wish to pay all the compliment I can to the ladies of Canada for their fine, womanly character and their equally fine, womanly figures. And when I have said all I can of them in general, I feel there is still more due to those of Toronto. How is it that the Canadian women are at once such good women and such handsome ladies? Is it that they live such active, useful, earnest lives and that they have not the eaves-drops of an aristocracy falling upon them?

Leaving this question, I return to the store where I left my fair sleighers. But they are off. They have gone to do some business while the males are closing up. Back, however, they come. And the three or four, as the case may be, are soon off again. And, having tinkled and twinkled and scudded their way along the streets and through the avenues of town and suburbs, they go into a fine, large hall heated by a stove, take off their wraps, go in and wash their hands, and in a few minutes they are all, excepting the one who has been detailed for the attendance, sitting at one of the most cheerful meals you ever saw—a real Canadian supper which deserves a chapter to itself.

I have now travelled a good deal of this country—some of it by rail, some by steamer, a good deal in buggies and sleighs and a lot on foot. I have stayed in hotels, in taverns and in the houses of the farmers, large and small; and I consider that I am in a position to pronounce an opinion on the situation in some of its aspects. The climate and soil, for growing crops, cows, sheep and horses, are very fine. The country is here for occupation. And the people—the larger proportion of whom were poor—have made a wonderful job of it. This province of Ontario is now the settled, occupied country while our old country at home is lying waste.

I shall naturally now be asked my opinion of the country as a place to which the people of Scotland, and of the Highlands in particular, should emigrate. The first part of my answer to that question is that, although the first settlers had a terrible job of it, there will be no more of that. The hardships incident to entering the forest, axe in hand, and cutting out a field and a home, are matters of the past.

It is quite a romance the account of how men who are now on the brink of the grave came here, without a shilling in their pockets most of them, after being 10 weeks and more on the way between crossing the Atlantic and travelling from Quebec to Toronto. They first sought employment—road-making, chopping wood, lumbering or whatever offered. Having earned a little money, they made out towards the north where the land was cheap. And there they set to to clear a site for a 'shanty'—just a shed of logs. They cut down the trees and had the branches and the logs heaped up and set fire to as soon as the weather permitted. The ground thus partially cleared was sown with a small quantity of wheat—just among the stumps and without any ploughing. In a short time they had a crop of wheat and potatoes. But how was the wheat to be ground? There was no quern and no grist-mill within 20, 30 or sometimes 40 miles of them and no horse to go to mill with. The felling of the trees was hard work; the dragging of the beams and placing them in the pile for burning was worse; but to travel the above distances with a bag of wheat on one's back was worse still. And numbers of the veterans with whom I have conversed had journeys like this to perform. But when they got the length of a span of oxen they were up the hill and 'would not call the king their brother'!

Well, the land has been wonderfully occupied and right, left and middle the occupiers are provided with houses, cattle, horses, sheep, pigs, convey-ances and crops. When you get inside the houses you find plenty of food and raiment, good plain furniture and a good hospitable disposition therewith. And where the farmers keep to this order of things they are alright. But when they ambition fine houses, costly furniture, fine harness and stylish 'teams', the money-lender gets his hand over them and woe betide them.

The produce of the land is not so great as many have imagined. Wheat is the principal article depended on; and that has not averaged more than 20 bushels an acre for the last few years. This last year, fall wheat did very well. But from the shortness and precariousness of that kind during a long series of previous years, farmers have gone in for spring wheat; and that has not averaged more than 10 bushels, bringing the overall average down to what I have said. Then, when we take into account the small price the farmer gets for his produce, there is nothing with which to keep up a style of life such as our big farmers at home lead. And the result is that great numbers who have ambitioned this style have got into debt; and they are selling, or being sold out, to meet the mortgages.

I must dwell upon this business a little longer as it is the centre of a system which is the real canker of this country. There is a fully recognised system of mortgaging and few farmers miss getting under it. The interest is so heavy that it is exceedingly difficult to get clear once the yoke has been put on. And to me the thing looks all the more galling in that the money which ought to be promoting enterprise in commerce and agriculture in Great Britain is lent out all over this country and is proving a snare to the people. We have piers to build, roads to make, drains to open, houses to repair, lands to reclaim and a whole host of other things to do. But we cannot get the money to do them with. And our moneyed men send their fruits over here to make double interest—one return to them and another to the loan societies of this country.

I should be sorry to say a word which would go to discourage the brave men who have conquered the forest. But I hold that the money is really wanted in the old country and that, if we had our laws at home as good as they are here, we could make a good return for the cash advanced. It is the admirable land system which exists here that enables men to pay what they do pay; and if we had as good a system we would do better than they can do here. A 25-acre arable farm in Easter Ross, or near Inverness, Perth or Aberdeen, is as good for a family to have as a 100-acre farm here—provided we had as easy access to the land as they have. The 25-acre farmer with us, who works as he ought, handles more money than the 100-acre man does here. But the former pays so much more for his land, and has to work it under so many unfavourable conditions, that he is thrown behind the Canadian.

It is not the soil, the climate or situation which pushes our farmers so far behind, but the man-made conditions under which they work. If the difference were caused by climate, soil and situation, we might give up the cause of Britain and say: 'Leave the country and take up your abode under more favourable sky and on more fertile soil!' But seeing that the great difference is of man's making, we deliberately, and after much consideration, say: 'The duty of Britons is to turn round and clear away the feudal impediments which lie about to impede our progress!' If Britons do this, they will prove themselves worthy of the name they bear and benefit their posterity more than all that has been done by all the warriors, philosophers and scientific men who have gone before.

All this time I was thinking of home, for I was always anxious. Of course, I had sent home so much money that there ought not to have been any shortcoming. But I was getting no regular account of what was doing although I had left a very intelligent man, John Whyte, in charge. So home I was ready to go in the early days of 1880. But just then I received a telegram from Dr Carroll telling me that Charles Stewart Parnell and John Dillon would be in Philadelphia on January 10. Would I come? So I made by the most direct lines once more for Philadelphia.[7]

When I reached that city, the walls were posted with the names of Parnell and Dillon and, to my surprise, my name was along with them. This I did not expect. But I was not dismayed at finding myself committed to so formidable an undertaking. I knew well that Dr Carroll and his friends— Professor Robert E Thompson, a most accomplished and extraordinarily well-informed north of Ireland man, and Dr Shelton MacKenzie, son of an Inverness-shire bard—had thought the matter over ere committing me to this engagement.

When the time came for the great meeting in the Academy of Music, however, I was truly struck with amazement at the magnificent spectacle which presented itself. Every tier of seats and boxes and galleries was filled— well-dressed people figuring largely in the better parts and the elite of the city, and some from Washington, gracing the well-fitted platform. One after another of us was cheered: Mr Parnell, Mr Dillon, myself and the chairman, Colonel MacLure, editor of *The Philadelphia Times*. I could not tell who they all were who sat around me. I know that my friend Dr Shelton MacKenzie was there in good spirits. I think Dr Carroll and Professor Thompson were busy looking after affairs below.

In due time Colonel MacLure rose and opened the proceedings with so eloquent and noble a speech that it caused me some despairing thought on having to follow him in course of a short time. The speech was not long; but it was weighty with thought and elegant in the language in which it is the custom of American speakers to express themselves. And the noble utterance was received with great applause.

Soon Mr Parnell made his appearance and in his own cool and resolute manner told us his story of the bad harvest in Ireland, of the famine among the people and of the attitude of the British government in the matter— refusing relief or even inquiry. The speech was a plain statement by a man who was deeply impressed by the sense which he felt of what would befall his fellow countrymen unless the people of America came to their rescue. He spoke as if he had no thought of pleasing anyone; just aiming at telling the sad tale and relieving himself by the delivery of the melancholy message. The speech fell somewhat flatly on the meeting although it was delivered by a tall, handsome man in the prime of life and full of the courage of his opinions. I think I was somewhat disappointed.

Mr Dillon is a tall, dark, melancholy-looking man with every appearance of delicate health; and his speech was much in keeping with his own appearance. He, too, felt the suffering of his people and was, one would say, bowed down under the weight of his mission to do what he could to keep them from perishing. His also was a disappointing speech to people who are accustomed to real eloquence on every platform and who expected much from representatives of the race which gave Burke and Grattan and O'Connell and a host of other great orators to the bar, the platform and the Houses of Parliament. But Dillon's speech was more effective than his chief's; and, although as specimens of oratory both were disappointing, I was convinced that they made a deep impression.

When Mr Parnell had done, he was called out and I had not the honour of his presence when my turn came. Colonel MacLure also had to go and, as was well for me, my countryman Dr Shelton MacKenzie was put in the chair; and the son of the Castle Heather bard of Inverness did not restrain his gifts in introducing me. This, no doubt accompanied by the influence of the tartan, obtained for me the most hearty reception. I am the more full with this part external to myself as I do not remember the details of what I said. However, I know that while thanking the committee for affording me the honour of appearing before such an audience, I apologised for availing myself of the opportunity of speaking on the same platform as representatives of a race who were such masters of the English tongue that they were more eloquent than the English themselves.

But the story of Ireland and of the Highland people was eloquent in itself and spoke strongly in the simplest language to all rightly constituted minds. Already the American heart had been opened and liberal donations would be forwarded for the relief of the sufferers from English landlord iniquity. And when sending them contributions, I begged them to send also hurricanes of opinion which would have the effect of shattering the obsolete opinions which produced the periodic famines. 'The wiseacres there talked of sending you over our people,' I said. 'To this we objected. But we were willing to make you a present of the whole band of landlords and factors.' At this, they shouted: 'But we won't have them!' I continued: 'Then you will help us to take their destructive power out of their hands and let our people make the best use of the land which the Lord their God gave them.'

I will only further quote what appeared in the American papers. The *Irish World* of New York said: 'Dr MacKenzie, as chairman, introduced Mr John Murdoch, owner and editor of *The Highlander*, Inverness, Scotland, who clad in the manly and graceful costume of his race and clan, which he always wears, stepped to the front amidst cheer after cheer from tier after tier of Irishmen and delivered an arraignment of the English landlords for their treatment of the Irish and the Highland people which, for intensity and effect, has never been surpassed and which, from its opening to its closing sentence, swept all before it like a whirlwind.

'He said he knew the case of Ireland, having been in the country for 11 years. He added his testimony to the truth of all that had been said of the sufferings of the Irish people and added that the half had not, and indeed could not, be told of the horrors of the English land system. And darker yet was the history of it in his native Highlands. He described scenes that had never been attempted even in Ireland—the burning of the people's cottages, some of the occupiers being too weak to make their way from under the burning roofs. To the quack remedy of emigration, so loudly urged as a remedy for the ills of the Irish and Highland people, he replied that neither here nor in Canada had he heard anyone ask for the landlords to emigrate; and he asked, in all fairness, if rich and prosperous Americans and Canadians would not receive them and live under them, why should the poor Highlanders and Irish be obliged to submit to their impoverishing yoke?

'He spoke in telling terms of the libels of the English and pro-landlord press on the Highland people and of the exclusion of Highland wrongs from the press until, in 1873, he started up *The Highlander* as an organ for the opinions and aspirations of the Highland people. He spoke of the hand England had in keeping Irishmen and Highlanders divided. He declared how fitting it was that their union should be begun there that night under the chairmanship of Dr Shelton MacKenzie whose father was a famous Highland bard and whose mother was Irish. And he proceeded to predict that—marching, as they would, like men shoulder to shoulder—they would be irresistable.

'No words can adequately describe the effects of this telling speech, almost every sentence of which was cheered to the echo. Repeatedly he tried to conclude. But the audience would not have it. Cries of 'Go on, go on' still kept him before them until in sheer modesty, and apologising for presuming so much on their kindness, he closed one of the most spirited, timely and telling addresses ever heard by a great and popular assembly.'

1 For Murdoch's links with Carroll and other Irish-American nationalists, see Introduction.
2 Breslin was one of the trustees of the Clan na Gael 'skirmishing fund'. See Introduction.
3 For O'Donovan Rossa and the implications of the gift to Murdoch, see Introduction.
4 *Napier Commission*, 3093.
5 Miller was a Cromarty stonemason and pioneering geologist who became, in the 1840s, a prominent Free Church publicist. Like Murdoch, he was a vociferous critic of Highland landlords.
6 Cheap food imports from overseas were seriously undermining British agriculture in the 1870s and 1880s.
7 Parnell and Dillon were emerging as the leading Irish nationalist politicians of the time. See Introduction.

The Crofter Revolt
1881-1886

This final chapter is a much
abbreviated version of a series of
articles which Murdoch contributed
in 1886 to the *Paisley and
Renfrewshire Gazette* and which were
afterwards reproduced in pamphlet
form. Murdoch's aim was to expose
the activities of a number of
prominent Highland landowners and
to recount his own part in the
protest movement which preceded the
passing of the Crofters Act.

In the following pages I have made use of proprietors and managers of land who have long had possession of the public ear as good, wise and able administrators. I have not hunted about for notorious sinners. I have taken those who offered themselves and who have been accepted by secretaries of state and lords advocate as so good and so wise that their opinions and their examples were worthy of being taken as lights for the guidance of the legislature and of the government of the country. Their opinions, at any rate, have helped in moulding the Crofters Act and to limit any good which it was at all likely to accomplish.

I confess it was not a grateful task for me to combat the opinions which had been formed by the public in regard to these personages. But it was all the better that, in showing the character of the system, I should not make use of reprobates of whom no one would expect any good. I have accepted the specimen landholders and managers who have come to the front; and they are all the more valuable for my purpose in that they have secured the commendation and the willing service of the great body of the Scottish press.

The Duke of Argyll, a landlord by birth, possesses all the natural talents to fit him for business and for a leading place as a statesman. He is a man possessing ability, means, leisure and the disposition to inculcate mental independence and to enlarge the range of human thought and action.[1] But the main force of those gifts and attainments has been devoted to defending the privileges of a class which has been the disgrace and the ruin of the Scottish nation and to thwarting the efforts of those who have been doing something to raise the mass of the people from under the feet and the rod of those whose cause it is his pride to champion.

A brave and brilliant defence, even of a bad cause threatened with over-throw, appeals to that feeling within us which espouses the cause of the weak. But, unfortunately for our own feelings and for this champion of the landlords, he has not confined himself to the fair use of means; and when the day of reckoning, which is now dawning, is full upon us, the Duke of Argyll's defences will furnish the advocates of the popular cause with some of the sharpest weapons for the warfare which the landlords have provoked.

The Duke has been sorely provoked by the royal commission of 1883.[2] He has resented the interference with the privileges of his class, as much as to say, with another class already extinct, in America at least, 'Shall I not wallop my own nigger!'[3] It is intolerable that commission, agitator or land court should come between the landlord and the men who till the soil. The landlord holds by the privilege of drawing rent from land which he has not made and which he never ploughed, sowed nor improved; and he claims that this privilege carries with it the right to guide the actions of practical farmers, to thwart them, to toss them about, and to take from them and add to them as it pleases him to do. For any one to move in the direction of even obtaining a hearing for those who had been held as in a leash by the landlord was and is regarded as an attempt to deprive him of the management of his own affairs.

The Duke tells us, in his recent speech in the Lords, that he has suspended some draining operations in Tiree in view of the provisions of the Crofters Bill; and another landlord told us that he would rather have no estate at all than have it cut up before his eyes and the rent regulated by a court. The government of the nation must submit to have its exactions, in the shape of taxes, regulated to the farthing in the pound by Act of Parliament. But the landlord is superior to that. He must have the taxing of his subjects all in his own hands, no court or commission daring to interfere.

So largely have these ideas bulked in the utterances of the Duke, and of some others, that they deserve more than a passing notice. The Duke is in the forefront of those who complain of the royal commission and who have kept up a cry against agitators. On the other hand, I had the privilege of going in advance of the commission in some places, of coming after it in others and of hearing the evidence in others; so that I am more than ordinarily qualified to speak on these very points on which the Duke has been ringing the changes so persistently. I can speak specifically of the great advantages which the landlords and the factors possessed in going before the commission and of the corresponding disadvantages with which the crofters and their friends laboured.

Granting the fitness of the gentlemen of the commission for the work which they were sped to perform, individuals among them were, from their very interests and life associations, predisposed in favour of the landlords; and they must have felt that the complaints of the crofters were against their own class. Apart altogether from bias, they were liable to be prejudiced against individuals and against classes by oft-repeated false accusations indulged in by the men of power and standing in the country. They were sent to inquire into the relations between a powerful class on the one side and an impoverished, depressed and disorganised people on the other side. The ruling class possessed books, statistics, factors, clerks and officers of different grades to serve their purposes before the commision. Landlords were further advantaged in that they had no timidity and no bashfulness to overcome. Everything was in their favour; and the commission, in being equipped with their steamer and having only to land here and there where it suited best to hold court, did not make that acquaintance with the country which they might have made on foot, or even in carriages, and which would have been of use in helping them to estimate the quality of some of the evidence offered them.

For example, had they traversed the country they would have seen something of the general fact which the Crofters Act ignores—that they had to deal with a state of things which resulted from the arable and other better lands having been taken from the great mass of the native people and laid out in large farms for the few. They would have realised the enormity of the fraud which has been committed upon a large proportion of the people in exacting road rates where there are no roads. They would have seen how systematically main drainage and fencing have been neglected, excepting where tacksmen and sportsmen were to be benefited; and they would have seen the aggrieved trudging their weary way over bogs and rocks to the places of meeting while the lairds and their advocates drove defiantly over the roads made for them to a large extent by the roadless poor. They would have had a far better opportunity of understanding how 'congestion' had been produced in the poorer parts and how the better parts are becoming worthless in the hands of men who live, not by tilling the ground, but largely by reaping the fruits of what the evicted tillers left in it.[4] So that, with all the fairness in the world, our yachting commission was in no position to gather personal knowledge; and it was, from its very composition, particularly liable to be prejudiced in favour of the dominant party.[5]

The crofters, on the other hand, had no statistics, no functionaries to act with them or for them. It was impossible for them to draw up comprehensive papers showing the nature, causes and consequences of the evils of which they complained; and nothing short of a miracle would have served to emancipate them from the fear which had become a constituent part of the second nature which generations of landlord and factorial misrule had begotten within them. I am quite confident in saying that had the government which sped the commission been as solicitous to ascertain and to redress grievances as it was to stop complaints, it would have seen to the crofters being provided with assistance to make sure that their poverty and remoteness, their want of statistics, and of practice in speaking in the language of the court, should not militate against the bringing out of the whole state of matters. Even on the principal on which an advocate is appointed for the defence of the prisoner at the bar, who is too poor to obtain one, something should have been done to place the crofters on a level with those against whom they preferred complaints. There are numerous cases in which the commission was defeated in its objects from want of adequate preparation on the part of the complainants and from the perfection of the arrangements which had been made on the side of the landlords. But perhaps in no case were the objects of the inquiry more palpably defeated than on the estates of the Duke of Argyll.

The Duke himself very pointedly, though with a very different object, directs attention to the unprepared state in which the people of Tiree and of the Ross of Mull were for the commission. In the passage between himself and Lord Napier, chairman of the royal commission, in the House of Lords in June 1885, the Duke is reported to have said: 'The Commission had visited one of the most curious and interesting parts of his estate. They went to the place in a steamer and, taking two or three gigs, scampered off to a church some distance away without seeing a single croft. No notice had been sent to him of the intention of the commissioners; but notice had been sent to the people and a meeting was held in the parish church. A great deal of evidence was given at that meeting, a number of agitators having gone before the commission and instructed the poorer crofters throughout the Highlands as to what they were to say . . . and it was of immense importance that a number of the falsehoods that had been given currency should be contradicted.'

There is nothing plainer than that all inquiry was an offence to him; and the idea of not giving him notice while information was sent to those whose grievances were to be inquired into seems to have been quite beyond toleration. How dare the commission call the aggrieved together without letting him know the day, the hour and the place! The gentlemen did not see many crofts, they will admit, on their way to the parish church. That was not altogether because they 'scampered', but because the Duke had left but two along the roadside to be seen. These, however, are only indications of ducal impatience to convey a false impression that the crofts were not seen because of the hurry—and not because of the work of consolidation.

The Duke and others in the same camp have unhesitatingly and persistently spoken and written as if it were an undoubted fact that the crofters had been instructed what to say. Now, in the first place, this statement is no more definite than that the instruction was given by 'agitators'. It is noteworthy that, for all their boldness, the lairds and the factors have, so far as I know, been careful not to specify a single sentence of the actual instructions said to have been given. They convey the false thought in that form in which it is most difficult for outsiders to detect it; and the accused are not furnished with fact, time or place on which they can lay hold.

Some of the accusers have found it unsafe to be specific. One of them, in 1882, disposed of the whole uneasiness among the people with whom he had to deal by saying it was the result of the circulation of Irish Land League literature. I took him at his word and interrogated him on the spot.[7] But so baseless was his assertion, and so utter was his incompetence to speak, that he had not the shadow of a fact on which to fall back. But this method had been adopted to excite anti–Irish prejudices against the men of Skye. And, this accomplished, no one, it was thought, would do anything else than frown down the agitators. Stale prejudices against the Irish were to be made use of against the crofters; and that end was so good that it justified the use of any means the landlords chose to employ.

The whole of the idea that the crofters were moved and instructed from without is not only without foundation but absurd. I have shown that something was needed to make the balance even between crofters and landlords. But no approach was made towards putting the poor, defenceless and impoverished people on such a footing. This could only have been done at great expense and by a large agency at work for a long time beforehand. And if the agents were out, it is not what the people were to say that they required to be told. No one could tell them that to any purpose. The first thing required was to inspire the people with something of the courage of their forefathers so that they would say what they knew. And this was a work which could not be done in a speech or two.

Fear of the laird and of the factor—yes, and of the ground officer, of the men with the large farms and of everyone who was in favour with the laird— was a matter of long habit and was not to be shaken off at a word. Even the bravest of the crofters were so possessed with this fear that when the commission first got among them, the first question was: 'Am I to have protection against the factor if I tell the truth?'[8] It was of no use opening their mouths, they thought, if they were not thus protected. All the previous agitation had failed to strike this yoke of fear from the people's souls. And when the delegates ventured to speak, it is remarkable how frequently they confined their complaints to what had been done by the predecessors of the men then in power. In only a few cases did the delegates dare to speak of the living lairds and factors.

The fact is that no agitator could have done what the Duke says was done. I even go to the length of saying that no writer of fiction, however ingenious and fertile, could have invented the things of which the Duke's tenants have to complain. And after three years of speaking and writing on the subject there is nothing more patent today than all the commission did was to skin the surface of things. The Duke is wroth with the commission of 1883. But if one were sped today he would go out of his mind over the exposure.

I went out in advance of the royal commission and ran in a very hurried manner over Lewis, Lochbroom, Assynt, part of the Reay country and Arisaig. I made the merest dip into Tobermory and Salen in Mull, Lochaline in Morvern and Bowmore, Port Ellen and Port Charlotte in Islay. I did what I could to assure the people that they were to benefit in the end by making their case and *their own views* known; and I encouraged them to act like men under the sanction and protection of the Great Father who had given the earth not to the landlords but to the children of men. I was impressed most deeply with the fact that there was nothing so good, nothing so telling, to be given to the public as the ideas, the experiences and the traditions of which the people themselves were the sole masters. And I may say, although only in passing, that the eliciting of these things was a main object aimed at by *The Highlander*.

For example, the idea prevailed among the crofters that the land belonged to the whole people although landlords had usurped power over them and it. The landlords have always desired to remove this idea. Thus the Marquis of Stafford, who married the Countess of Sutherland, carrying with him the ideas and pretensions of his class in England, could not brook the claims of the people to their clan lands. They had the traditional title and they had the nine points of the law on their side—they were in possession of their paternal farms. Against this constitution of society under him he must take action. The craze for sheep runs was ready to his hand; so also was the war frenzy which then possessed the nation. Before he could remove the people from their houses and lands he must get rid of as many as possible of the manhood of the country. And with the aid of ministers and other recruiting officers, numbers of the young and powerful enlisted and left—carrying with them, however, strong and valid assurances that their homesteads and lands were to continue in the possession of their fathers and their families. But when the strong arms which should have been defending the houses of the clansmen were desolating other lands at the bidding of an unprincipled government, the Marquis, with the assistance of that government, terrorised, burned and otherwise tossed the people about and removed them so completely—whether to the rocks and bogs or to Canada—that no one could say, when the work was done, that he was in possession of the inheritance of his fathers. So that the Leveson-Gowers made themselves masters of Sutherland by a course of fraud and violence which may be taken as typifying on a large scale what has been done on minor scales in many other parts of the country.[9]

The Tiree people and the Mull people, too, had the idea that the great use of the land was to support the tillers. But the 'great' folk introduced the doctrine and the practice of making the land yield a large rental for the support and gratification of some one family, perhaps at a distance, although the mass of the tillers and rent-payers were in poverty. These people cherished the memory of their fathers and the history of their own districts and islands. But it became necessary for the purpose of the wise gentlemen above them to cast contempt upon all such native lore and substitute English history. Along with this came the practice of making little of the very language the people spoke and with withering up within them every feeling of respect for what pertained to their own race. They must be taught to despise their language, their history and their social polity; and render up the inheritance of their fathers to usurpers, speculators and sportsmen, while they themselves must just sink to the condition of slaves and deem it a privilege to toil for behoof of idlers.

On a small scale we have here what has been bearing such disastrous fruit in Ireland on a large scale. The governing of the Celt by the Saxon, who does not take the trouble to know the language or to understand the views and characteristics of those with whom he takes to do, has been and ever will be a failure. This is being discovered in regard to Ireland after every possible failure and crime. Is it too much to expect that what has thus to be confessed to the Irish people, and paid for by the British, will have some effect on those who are taking such a stupid course in regard to the people of the Highlands?

Perhaps the most serious matter in all this connection is that, when amelioration is made or proposed, it comes not in deference to reason but because violence has supervened. How much better it would have been to listen; to make acquaintance with that bugbear, the Gaelic language, and find out what it contains! If the intruder did that, he might discover that the native people had ideas of government, of rural and political economy, and of education itself, which were worthy of his respectful consideration. By a process thus less violent than a surgical operation, peer and commoner might come to see what was needed in the Highlands was not the introduction of crude notions formed in the minds of even intelligent strangers but scope and encouragement for the carrying out of a whole native policy—the growth of ages.

Behind the Gaelic language there is a delicate, a beautiful and an elevated education. Just to look above and around, there is a great department, as we may call it, of practical observation in regard to the weather and the seasons founded upon long centuries of experience and classified into a science. This found form and melody in rhythmical and alliterative verses and saws—literal and allegorical—easily remembered and pleasant to repeat and to hear. These were entertainments and lessons for the young and guidance for those who tilled the ground, tended the stock or fished the rivers and the sea.

There was a wonderful acquaintance with plants and a skill in the use of their seeds and flowers, their stems and roots in healing diseases. And see how the skill in dealing with the ills to which flesh is heir merges into art! The tartans are in part the outcome of this skill in using the virtues of plants; and, in the other part, they are the outcome of an intuitive taste in the race which may be said to have been nurtured by the sun and the clouds producing the varied gorgeous combinations of colours which are nowhere to be witnessed to such perfection as in the cloud scenery of the Atlantic seaboard. In the primitive fabrics of the tartans we have the dyes obtained from the plants applied so as to produce a variety and an arrangement of colours so true in harmony and so just in proportion that, amid all the mutations of fashion, tartans hold their own among things useful and ornamental.

Then there is the taste of the Celt for natural beauty in scenery. He knows colours, knows how to combine them; and whether it be natural to him, or that he was educated centuries ago to do so, it is a fact that he knew and appreciated the effects of form and colour, of harmony and of contrast, and of the blending of all shades and forms in the landscape with which nature clothes herself in beauty. Johnson went over the Highlands as blind as a bat to a beauty now universally acknowledged; and until Scott produced *Waverley, Rob Roy* and *The Lady of the Lake*, the Saxon had no eyes to see what was everywhere spread around him.[10] On the other hand, the poetry and prose of the Highlander contains abundant evidence that in this respect his education had been attended to. Centuries before the Norman Conquest, when the Saxon was not able to put two lines together in metre or in rhyme, the Celtic Highlanders and Irish were weaving the forms and colours displayed in the varied scenery of their respective countries into the most beautiful products of poetic genius.

The joys and sorrows of the people found expression in verse; natural objects around threw their colours and shapes into these compositions; and in the course of time, hills and streams, woods and moors became, in a sense, vocal with the most intense experiences of the dead and of the living; and they were so dear to the people that to part with them was like submitting to have their heartstrings torn out by the roots.

There is no occasion to separate art in form and colour from the art of musical versification. The two come before us together; and while they point to far back antecedents and causes, we cannot be positive which had the start of the other. This is the most difficult part of my subject because while English speakers possess what they call poetic art, there is no more comparison between it and the musical and metrical expression of Gaelic poetic thought than there is between a barrowful of the raw material in a timber yard and a perfectly finished pianoforte. Yet even the unlearned in Gaelic listen to a piece of Gaelic poetry and notice the play of melodious and harmonious vowels which goes on—just as if the genius of the race had laid it down long ago that he who ventured to put his ideas together for others must do so in terms which cannot detract from, but which must add to, their effect on the ear and on the mind. It is not merely rhyme and metre which were required in Gaelic. There is cadence; there are assonances with frequent alliteration; rhymes within rhymes; contrasting and chording of sounds and merging of one sound into another by the delicate intervention of dipthongs.

In other words, Gaelic versification is a fine art which could not by any possibility have come to its present standard of excellence excepting in the use of highly cultured facilities in the singers and by means of a language upon which learning and skill and taste had been at work of set purpose in the course of long ages to make it a worthy vehicle of thought and a pleasing means of culture. The simple fact that merely English speakers find it so difficult to follow me here—the fact that I have to labour so to convey some notion of the cultivated skill and grace which are so well known to the most unlettered Gael—indicates how crude is the stage which the English language has reached as compared with the flexibility, the polish and the melody to which the Gaelic language attained centuries ago.

Gaelic, of course, is the great medium by which the old doctrine of the Land for the People comes down to us from antiquity. The Lowland people, having lost the Gaelic language, lost the tradition of ever having cherished the idea that they had any right to the land but what they might acquire by purchase or by contract with the landlord. This accounts for the deadness of southern and eastern Scots in regard to the land. And when the landlords look about them and notice that the most vital activity against landlordism is found where the Gaelic language has full possession of the minds and hearts of the people, it is no great wonder to find them setting about pulling down the whole fabric of the language and all it contains. The landlords have taken forcible possession of the people's land and, instead of confessing their sin and making restitution, they use all their influence and their cunning in destroying the people's titles and in extinguishing the spirit which would uphold them in pressing their rights. So that there is a motive for, and a method in, the antagonism to Gaelic for which individuals among them have been so long distinguished. It is something like the case of a burglar who, to destroy all trace of the robbery, sets fire to the house.

But the fine old education of the clans has nurtured, even in poverty, the spirit of brotherhood. And so the crofters, few in number and scant of means, have compelled attention to their cause in the front of which stands the right of the clansmen to the clan lands—the principal that the land of the nation belongs to the people of the nation. And this education is telling in the immediate efforts now making to regain possession of that land in obedience to the command of God—whether landlords will have it or not.

The case of South Uist will serve as a fair sample of the whole Highlands. Along the west side are the best lands. Here from one end to the other, with very slight exceptions, the arable land was taken from the people and the fine farms of Kilbride, Askernish, Bornish, Milton, Ormacleit, Dremisdale, Geirinish and Nunton made up to what they are. These lands were put in order by the peasantry; and then the poor people were sent to their own outruns towards the foot of the mountains and their arable land given to tacksmen.[11] When they were trying to make new homesteads for themselves there and hoping that, with the help of the cattle on the hill, they might scrape through, the tacksmen on the west got even the hills on the east. One of these farms, Ormacleit, is in the hands of Mr Ranald MacDonald, head factor to the landlord, Lady Gordon Cathcart; and not long ago some of the crofters of Stoneybridge and cottars of Locheynort were prosecuted for setting about, some of them, to repossess themselves of land taken from their fathers to make up that choice farm.

In the summer of 1875, as editor of *The Highlander*, I made a tour of the Long Island and found the state of matters such that I made bold to call the attention of Mr Gordon, the then proprietor, to them, urging him, for the sake of the people and of his own good name, to come down and see for himself.[12] I gave him a slight sketch, as he had not been there for 10 or 12 years, I was told; and then I begged of him to come and put the questions which arose beyond every doubt by his personal knowledge.

Mr Gordon and his lady, having taken the hint, came down the following year and made a survey of the islands. And so far were my statements borne out by what they found that in 1877 they came again with a scheme of improvements embracing redistribution of land. In keeping with this, schedules were issued to the people that they might fill them up with such particulars as the extent of the land each desired, the stock and capital he possessed, etc. The *bona-fides* of this again was borne out by the islands being surveyed and the boundaries of the new holdings marked off. Redistribution of land was clearly before the people and a new era was dawning on them.

As editor of *The Highlander* I was taken with the contemplated improvements and entered into the beneficient enterprise so far as to use my influence with the people to urge them to commence a course of improved husbandry themselves—and thus help on the good work begun by Mr Gordon. I began a series of suggestions as to what they should do and printed them in Gaelic in the paper. And at the outset, so as to carry laird, factor and people with me, I sent samples of these 'hints' to Mr Macdonald that he might lay them in English before Mr Gordon with a view to his co-operation. Note two points: first, that my complaints of the state of things I found were not contradicted by the authorities but rather they were confirmed by their entering at once on a course of amelioration; and, second, that I entered *with* the proprietor and his managers into their scheme, not against them, taking it for granted that good was contemplated and that arrangements adopted would be the result of careful consideration on the part of persons both able and willing to promote that good.

By and bye, the farm of Ormaclete fell out of lease, just as providence would have it, in the right time for being divided to enlarge the crofts in accordance with the intentions indicated. But what was the surprise of simple trustful people to find that the fine large farm, to which they looked so hopefully for relief, was actually taken as a whole by the factor—the very man who was entrusted with the carrying out of the beneficent scheme of redistribution. It was clear at once that the right-hand man, on whom Mr Gordon depended for carrying out his scheme, was opposed to it. Since then most of the six other farms which were in the hands of tacksmen have been out of lease, besides two large farms which have all along been in the hands of the proprietors; yet not one of them has been broken up for the augmentation of the crofts.

So the scheme of redistribution has not been carried out. But the people have been kept in a state of uncertainty and their agriculture paralysed by the prospect of being shifted any year or any month. True, some piers were built; yes and hotels and even some show cottages. Roads were made to places where there were no crofters; and outlets from lochs were opened; and the mansion house was overhauled. The sensation connected with these changes was kept up by a confusing succession of changes among the sub-managers on the islands. Almost any change was possible but the one of restoring the land to the people—although all the large farms mentioned were made up of lands taken from the people who were all this time sick of heart from hope deferred.

As a consequence, I found the people in a worse condition in 1882 than they were in 1875—and again still worse in 1885. And naturally enough, when the farms were not given back to those from whom they were taken and when they were let to other persons by favour of the factor, there was some disturbance.[13] And what else can be expected? The only experience these people have of the law of the nation is as an engine of oppression in the hands of the landlords and their agents. Commonsense dictated that when gross injustice, fraught with poverty and ruin, was being done to them, they should resort to the only course open to them—that of entering again into possession of what had been taken from them. Repossessing the land, the Stoneybridge men, and those on Locheynort, were sent to prison.

By the time I reached Bunessan in Mull in 1883 the royal commission had been there and in Tiree; and I could only go a-gleaning after them. But if I was of any service in going before the commission, I was of the most positive service in coming after them because I was able to gather the most conclusive evidence of the success which attended the efforts of the local functionaries, with the Duke of Argyll's chamberlain from Inveraray at their head, in defeating the objects which brought the commission there. The first thing I did was to call a meeting in the Bunessan school of the surrounding population. Finding the people much disappointed with the meagre statements made to the commission, I placed myself at their disposal to lay what had been omitted there before the commission in Glasgow or in Edinburgh. I listened to what the people had to say and I questioned them rigorously in the presence of many witnesses so that any slip might be corrected. I then visited the townships and inquired from house to house—seeing the crofts, the gardens, the habitations and the personal appearance of the subjects of inquiry. I went back again and had another winnowing at a public meeting in Bunessan, after having one at Creich. I was to have had a third meeting. But alarm was taken and somehow the key was not forthcoming. That evening I devoted to reading my notes along with some of the more intelligent and experienced of my informants so that I should be sure that their story, and not mine, was being carried away.

Next day I proceeded westward, making for Iona; but passing Creich I found the people desired a second meeting. I acquiesced; but here they were confronted with a letter from the clerk of the school board prohibiting the teacher from letting 'Mr Murdoch have the use of the school for any purpose'. I said: 'That letter is an impertinence and a piece of folly. I do not want the school. I have no personal purpose to serve and I will not go inside it excepting on your invitation.'

I followed up with the statement that the place was their's and they should act accordingly. With that I went away. But by and bye I had an invitation to meet the people in the school. I think the impertinent letter must be credited with the fact that before dispersing that evening the people organised an association which, with its secretary, Mr John MacCormick, takes charge of crofter affairs in the Ross of Mull to this day.

At Iona I was confronted with an equally peremptory prohibition of the use of the school from the same school board clerk. In addition to what I had said at Creich I said I could carry nothing out of Iona that would tell more of the reign of terror under which the population of the Sacred Isle lived than that, so far had they sunk under the feet of the servants of their servants, they dare not meet in the house which their own money was upholding. I left them not knowing what they would do. However, in the evening I was requested to attend a meeting in the prohibited place. I did not inquire, and I do not know now, what steps they had taken to gain admittance. But, before I was called in, they showed their independence by passing a vote of censure on the school board for sending such a letter.

How the clerk of the board got authority to issue these letters I do not know. With the Duke and his officials playing into his hands, there is no doubt he might exercise a good deal of freedom when he thought he was checking inquiry into the combined actions of the parochial and estate functionaries. These persons had been very successful in defeating the objects of the royal commission a few days previously; and they were not going to have their doings laid bare by a volunteer commission on foot such as I was.

This co-operation between the proprietor's servants and what ought to be the servants of the ratepayers is an important factor in most parts of the Highlands. I hardly know an estate of any magnitude on which the policy is not pursued of bringing the parochial officers, the schoolmasters and the ministers under factorial influence and keeping them sweet. This policy has been so far successful that in the vast majority of cases the men who are paid by the proprietor, and those who are supported by the rates and out of the voluntary contributions of the people, constitute a reactionary and repressive power against which the humble classes have to contend as if it were an openly alien institution established by an enemy in the land.

Some of us know these things. But nothing yet has been done at all in keeping with the necessity to cope with the great powers—in money and position—which are now a strong fortification around the landlords. We are handicapped in more ways than one. The landlord papers are bold in stating what is untrue and newspaper proprietors who run with the crofters are so much afraid of the landlords that they will not publish what may involve them in a prosecution for libel. And so the truth, the cause of the crofters and the interests of the nation at large are sacrificed to what is regarded to be the interest of newspaper men.

But this sort of improvising will not long be tolerated. The Bonar Bridge conference of the Highland Land League has registered a growth of strength of which some of the movers there have but a faint notion; and the men who are to give expression in the press to that strength will have to be of a different stamp.[14] The meeting at Bonar may be said to have inscribed the following objects on the banner which the Land League nailed to the mast on September 22 and 23, 1886: the restoration to the people of the land and of the right to distribute, to value and to regulate the same; the prevention of eviction and depopulation; the doing away with all game, forest and fishing monopolies and class privileges; the free and fair administration of justice in the Highlands by men fully versed in the language of the country; the free and full representation of the manhood of each nation in its own proper parliament and in all county and parish boards; the cherishing of the spirit of the people so that, casting off all fear of man, they will work shoulder to shoulder so as to have their opinions embodied in the laws of their country and their right made good to all that was meant to be their's on the land which the Lord their God gave them. Thus is the true expression of the measure of manhood registered. And the ring of utterances from all parts of the Highlands left no doubt that, whatever timid editors and others may do or say, the people of the Highlands mean to take action.

The progress of events since I began to lay these materials before the public adds to their value. The sending of the government physical force to support the Duke of Argyll in Tiree has created a sensation. And what I have not had space to do is being done by Lord Macdonald, Sheriff Ivory and Colonel Fraser.[15] They are showing the spirit which pervades landlordism; and when we see what these men dare in the face of the public we need not doubt what is said of their underlings who work for them far beyond the light of public opinion.

There have been, and there will be, blunders committed by the poor people. What else could be expected! Are not the claims of the landlords pressed as if the tenants were not deserving of any consideration? And are not the instruments which the law officers are now using in every way calculated to irritate the people and provoke them to violence? Not only so, but the misdirection of the jury in the case of the Tiree men, the consequent verdict, and the sentence which followed, go to convince the defenders of the croft homes that they may as well resort to violence as not. The Tiree men did not mob, riot or deforce and they never meant to do anything of the kind. And now it is seen that what his lordship meant as a death blow to agitation has given it fresh force. Innocent men are condemned and awarded cruel punishments. What more can be done to those who do mob, riot and deforce?

The Duke of Argyll, Colonel Fraser, Lord Macdonald and Sheriff Ivory have been the chief agitators; and while they think they are crushing the spirit of the crofter, they are in reality wakening him up and putting plainly before him that he has as bitter, if not a more bitter, fight before him than in any foreign campaign in which his Highland forefathers ever engaged. These well-paid agitators are doing more. They have stirred up thousands who, a few months ago, did not care to know what a crofter was. No sooner were the Tiree men in jail than meetings were held in different connections to give practical expression to sympathy for the sufferers; and, by the next steamer, meal and flour and other necessaries were off for the support of the families of the martyrs.

One of the things which came out in the Tiree case is the willingness of the men to suffer in a good cause. They have gone into the enterprise with their eyes open and with their highest convictions fully alive to the quality of their actions. They have given the true and practical application of the doctrine of sacrifice. No good comes without sacrifice; and honour be to those who offer themselves up. These men chose, like the Covenanters and the early Christians, to obey God rather than men. And just as they had the moral courage to trample the law of man under foot in obeying God, they carried out the divine command again in not resisting evil when the minions of the landlords and the law came to do them evil. They did not raise hand or foot to injure the invaders. These are the moral lessons of the Tiree agitation and the doctrines will spread—even by the help of those who try to suppress them.

One of the things largely required now, in furtherance of the cause of the Land for the People, is that the prisons be filled with well-doers. The people can now see that they can get into prison without breaking the law; and that one of the surest ways of gaining this distinction is obeying God rather than obeying men. They are thus producing the required sensation and drawing public attention to the movement. It comes out clearly thus that the crofters, the cottars, and all who are interested along with them, are to avoid all moral offences, are to obey the commandments—and leave the sensation caused by crime to be produced by the landlord forces.

There is just one thing more which is coming out. Scotland, as a whole, has been slow to spend in support of a cause. The recent doings of landlords and law lords have done something to remedy this defect in the Scottish character. Sympathy is being awakened in the Lowlands and men in the cities are learning rapidly that the cause of the crofters is only a part of the great cause which embraces revival of trade, increase of wages to the artisan, greater profits from honest trade and relief from the pauperism, the crime and the other burdens imposed by landlord lawmakers. The Irish cause was not felt to be irresistible until it was seen that the people were ready to suffer to any extent in person and in pocket. This is taking hold of the Scottish mind, mixed and all as it has become with that of the Saxon; and what with good feeling for those who suffer and a keen sense of the bearing of the proper solution of the land question on every other interest, it will, it is to be hoped, lead to a more liberal application of the resources of the country to the purpose of forming that public opinion which ought to be the object of all agitation. If Scotland is to rise from under the heel of Anglo-Norman landlordism, her people as a whole must prove themselves like the poor crofters.

Books, pamphlets, tracts, public meetings and all the other means and agencies of a great and enlightened movement are required. The land movement is greater in its objects and in its effects than were the anti-slavery and anti-corn law movements in the past. It is the complement of them and of the temperance movement of our day. All true men, then, to the front! Just remember that the system of iniquity and lies which I have traced in the isles is rampant all over the country; and the duty of being up and at it is irresistible.

1   This was the eighth Duke of Argyll who held government office under Gladstone, who resigned from the cabinet in protest at the Irish Land Act of 1881 and who afterwards became principal spokesman for British landowners in their struggles with the many land reformers of the period. The Duke owned extensive estates, including those in Mull and Tiree to which Murdoch refers below.

2   The Napier Commission, See Introduction.

3   The reference is to American slaveowners' attitude to the campaign to abolish slavery in the United States.

4   This was the general pattern produced by the clearances: overcrowded crofting townships on poorer land; large sheep farms on better land.

5   A majority of the commission's members, including its chairman, Lord Napier, were themselves landowners.

6   Murdoch was quoting a press report. The Duke's speech, as reproduced in *Hansard* for June 23, 1885, is worded slightly differently—but its import is much the same.

7   This was Donald MacDonald, factor on the Glendale estate.

8   See, for example, the evidence of the commission's first witness. *Napier Commission*, 1. Driving out the crofting population's 'fear' of landlords was one of Murdoch's constant preoccupations during his *Highlander* period. See Introduction.

9   George Granville Leveson-Gower, second Marquis of Stafford, first Duke of Sutherland, was responsible for the clearances in Sutherland in the early nineteenth century. These occurred when many young men from Sutherland were serving in the British army—then engaged in the Napoleonic Wars. For a detailed account of Murdoch's views on traditional land tenures, see Introduction.

10 Samuel Johnson's *Journey to the Western Isles of Scotland* was published in 1775. Sir Walter Scott's novels helped initiate a romantic cult of the Highlands.

11 Tacksmen, tenant farmers. For an account of these proceedings in early nineteenth century South Uist, see Hunter, *Crofting Community*, 39–40.

12 See Chapter 7, notes 9, 11.

13 There were a number of illegal occupations of land in South Uist in the 1880s.

14 This was the meeting at which the Highland Land Law Reform Association was renamed the Highland Land League.

15 The military intervened to restore order in Tiree in the summer of 1886. Several Tiree crofters were subsequently jailed. MacDonald and Fraser were Skye landlords, the latter having initiated the libel action described in Chapter 7. William Ivory was Sheriff of Inverness-shire in the 1880s. He led a series of expeditions against Skye crofters.

Index

Printed by HMSO, Edinburgh Press
Dd 0762173 C2 5/86 (230777)